Reading

Policy, Politics, and Processes

Reading

Policy, Politics, and Processes

by

Mengli Song
American Institutes for Research

and

Tamara V. Young
North Carolina State University

Information Age Publishing, Inc.
Charlotte, North Carolina • www.infoagepub.com

Library of Congress Cataloging-in-Publication Data

Song, Mengli.
  Reading : policy, politics, and processes / by Mengli Song and Tamara V. Young.
      p. cm.
  Includes bibliographical references.
  ISBN 978-1-59311-853-2 (pbk.) -- ISBN 978-1-59311-854-9 (hardcover) 1. Reading--United
States. 2. Reading--Research--United States. 3. Education--Political aspects--United States. 4.
Education and state--United States. I. Young, Tamara V. II. Title.
  LB1050.S587 2007
  428.4071073--dc22

                                                                        2007037775

ISBN 13: 978-1-59311-853-2 (pbk.)
           978-1-59311-854-9 (hardcover)

Printed in the United States of America

CONTENTS

Preface   *vii*

1. **Introduction**   *1*
   The Evolving Great Debate   *1*
   State Reading Policy Environment   *4*
   Organization of the Book   *15*

2. **Policy Actors and State Reading Policy Networks**   *17*
   Composition of the State Reading Policy Domain   *17*
   State Reading Policy Networks   *23*

3. **Policy Actor Influence on State Reading Policy**   *43*
   Influence from the Social Network Perspective   *43*
   Centrality, Prestige, and Perceived Influence of
   Reading Policy Actors in Texas   *45*
   Patterns of Policy Actor Influence on
   Reading Policy Across States   *51*

4. **Policy Beliefs About Level and Trend of**
   Reading Achievement, Reading Pedagogy,
   State Standards, and State Tests   *71*
   Measurement of Policy Beliefs   *72*
   Level of Reading Achievement   *73*
   Trend of Reading Achievement   *77*
   Reading Pedagogy   *79*
   State Reading Standards   *86*
   State Reading Tests   *90*
   Discussion   *96*

5.	**Causal Stories and Proposed Solutions**	*99*
	Stone's Framework of Causal Theories	*100*
	Perceived Causes of the Reading Achievement Problem	*101*
	Problem Solutions: State Reading Policies	*125*
	Congruence Between Causal Stories and Proposed Solutions	*137*
6.	**Interest Groups' Lobbying Tactics in the State Reading Policy Domain**	*141*
	Lobbying Tactics	*141*
	Interest Groups' Use of Lobbying Tactics in the State Reading Policy Domain	*144*
	Interest Groups' Use of Lobbying Tactics and Their Influence on State Reading Policy	*154*
	Discussion	*164*
7.	**Recap and Concluding Observations**	*167*
	Recap of the State Reading Policy Processes	*167*
	Implications for Policy Research in Education	*172*
	Empowerment of Educational Professionals and Practitioners	*176*
	Closing Remarks	*180*
Appendices		*183*
References		*217*

PREFACE

This book would not have been possible without the assistance of many people. We extend our foremost gratitude to Cecil Miskel who has served as our teacher, adviser, mentor, advocate, colleague, and now good friend. In 1998, Cecil launched The University of Michigan's Reading Policy Project (RPP), which was designed to examine the development of reading policy at both national and state levels. As graduate research assistants on the project, we had the opportunity to participate in the design, data collection, and analysis of the RPP data from which this book stems. Many of the ideas presented in this book reflect Cecil's influence. We are deeply indebted to Cecil for his careful review of the manuscript at various stages and his constructive feedback and insights—his commitment to academic rigor and excellence is unparalleled. We are truly grateful for Cecil's wise counsel, patient guidance, and much-needed encouragement; we are equally appreciative of his forthright critique of our work on occasion. Simply, without Cecil, there would have been no book.

This book would not have come into being either without the exceptional work of several fellow graduate research assistants who participated in various aspects of the RPP. We extend our gratitude to (in alphabetical order): Jane G. Cogshall, David E. DeYoung, Ruth Isaia, Julie McDaniels, Celia H. Sims, Rich Osguthorpe, and Thomas V. Shepley. It was truly a privilege to be part of such a fine research team. We were indeed fortunate to have had the opportunity to learn not only from Cecil but also from each and everyone on the team. We were also fortunate to have received strong institutional support for both our project work and our doctoral studies from The School of Education and the Center for

Improvement of Early Reading Achievement at The University of Michigan.

We owe a special thanks to the hundreds of study participants and consultants, who graciously offered their time to talk to us about reading policy in their respective states. Their observations and insights were invaluable, and they made what was otherwise opaque—the minutiae of politics—transparent. Indeed, it was our participants' collective stories that shaped our understanding of the state reading policy domain. We hope that we have accurately represented their voices in this book.

Additionally, a project on such a large scale would not have been possible without generous financial support. We sincerely thank the two granting agencies that sponsored this research. The Field Initiated Studies Program, PR/Award R305T990369, Office of Educational Research and Improvement (currently The Institute of Education Sciences), U.S. Department of Education supported the research in five states—California, Connecticut, Michigan, North Carolina, and Texas. The Spencer Foundation Major Grants Program, Grant No. 200000269, funded parallel efforts in Alabama, Indiana, Maine, and Utah. Of course, the contents of the book do not necessarily reflect the views or policies of the Department of Education or the Spencer Foundation, and readers should not assume their endorsement.

We would also like to express our deep appreciation for Information Age Publishing, Inc. We want to particularly thank our publisher, George Johnson, for believing in the value of our work. We also thank the production editor, Benjamin Gonzalez, for making the technical aspects of the publication seem effortless.

Finally, we wish to express our profound gratitude to our parents for their unwavering love, encouragement, and support. This book is dedicated to them.

CHAPTER 1

INTRODUCTION

THE EVOLVING GREAT DEBATE

Debates about how reading should be taught, or the so-called "reading wars," have been going on for over a century (Chall, 1996; Ravitch, 2000). They have occurred in waves and have often been characterized as "pendulum swings" as support for effective reading instructional methods has been shifting between meaning-emphasis and code-emphasis. While earlier waves of debates were similar except for the direction of the pendulum swing, debates in the 1980s and early 1990s assumed two distinct features. First, as Chall (1996) notes in the third edition of *Learning to Read: The Great Debate*, the body of knowledge and practices under debate during this time period was the first to claim validity on scientific grounds. Second, debates during this period were no longer confined to the circle of professional educators and reading specialists, but took place with the prevalence of "outsiders" (e.g., interested laymen, linguistic scholars, and psychologists). These features continued to characterize, in strengthened forms, debates from the mid-1990s to early 2000s—the time period covered in this book.

To a large extent, the increased emphasis on scientifically based research by all sides of the recent wave of debates was attributable to two prominent reports: *Preventing Reading Difficulties in Young Children* pro-

Reading: Policy, Politics, and Processes, pp. 1–16
Copyright © 2008 by Information Age Publishing
All rights of reproduction in any form reserved.

duced by the National Research Council (Snow, Burns, & Griffin, 1998) and the congressionally mandated *Teaching Children to Read* released by the National Reading Panel (2000). Both reports were based on a comprehensive synthesis of research literature on early reading, and stirred considerable interest in as well as contest about what counts as scientifically based research (Eisenhart & Towne, 2003).

The emphasis on scientifically based research among the reading research community was further fueled by recent federal education legislations that mandate federally funded education programs be grounded in scientifically based research. These legislations, the Reading Excellence Act of 1998 and the No Child Left Behind Act of 2001 in particular, spurred numerous research efforts that claim to provide scientific evidence supporting certain reading instructional methods and discrediting rival methods. The legislations also generated concerns about what qualifies as scientifically based research. In short, during 1990s, particularly the latter half of the 1990s, the Great Debate about reading pedagogy evolved from a debate rooted primarily in ideology to a debate grounded in research that was claimed to be scientifically based.

The Great Debate also grew more politically charged. The late 1990s saw a continued expansion in both the number and the types of participants in the Great Debate. Partly triggered by the 1994 National Assessment of Educational Progress (NAEP) results, low reading achievement roused widespread concerns among both policymakers and the general public across the states. As reading became recognized as a grave problem and attained heightened agenda status, a plethora of individuals and groups were galvanized into action and drawn to the Great Debate. They brought with them diverse backgrounds and perspectives, varying values and beliefs, and often conflicting, personal, political, and professional agendas. They vied for influence and strove to sway reading policy in their desired directions. As such, the reading policy community was substantially expanded, with more actors embedded in more complex relationships and engaged in increased activities.

In addition to more of the same, the recent wave of debates assumed new features that set it apart from previous waves. Most notably, the recent debates occurred within an era of standards-based accountability. Although standards-based educational reforms are often traced back to the *A Nation at Risk* report (National Commission on Excellence in Education, 1983) and the 1989 Charlottesville Education Summit convened by former President Bush and the nation's governors, they did not exert appreciable impact on curriculum, instruction, and assessment until the latter half of the 1990s. As a case in point, in the area of reading and English language arts, the number of states that had developed standards jumped from 20 to 49 between 1995 and 2000 (Council of Chief State

School Officers, 2000). During this time period, states were also actively creating new statewide assessments or modifying existing assessments to align assessments with standards. Reading, as a fundamental skill and an essential area of schooling, was always at the forefront of states' efforts to build standards-based accountability systems. Debates about reading instructional methods inevitably became part of a larger dialogue about the development of standards and assessments.

Against the backdrop of state accountability systems, the Great Debate in the late 1990s became much broader in scope. It was no longer confined to pedagogy per se, but extended to standards and curriculum framework, assessments, teacher education and professional development, and instructional materials, among others. Over time, the Great Debate shifted from a largely ideological debate among reading researchers and educators to an evidence-based (or it so claims) and politically-charged debate among a wide array of policy actors with far-reaching impact on reading-related policies in state accountability systems.

Research in the field of reading, however, has not kept up with the evolution of the Great Debate. Despite the tremendous impact of the Great Debate on the larger policy system, most existing reading research has been focusing primarily on the effectiveness of specific instructional methods or programs. We know relatively little about how the reading policy system works, or about how a plethora of actors with diverse beliefs and agendas compete for policy influence and collectively shape reading policy development. The two recent large-scale reading policy studies— the National Reading Policy Study and the State Reading Policy Study— conducted between 1999 and 2003 by a group of researchers (including the authors) led by Cecil G. Miskel at the University of Michigan represent an important step toward filling in the gap in policy research in reading.[1]

This book presents findings from the State Reading Policy Study, which was an extension from our earlier study at the national level (see McDaniel, 2001; McDaniel, Sims, & Miskel, 2001; Miskel & Song, 2002; and Song & Miskel, 2002 for findings from the national study). Drawing upon interviews with 366 policy actors from nine states and relevant archival documents, our research team conducted a comprehensive investigation of the state reading policy domain employing multiple theoretical frameworks and analytic methods (see Appendix A for details about study design). Both findings unique to individual states and findings revealing general patterns across states shed light on the multifaceted nature of the policy processes in the field of reading. Findings from this study also bear important implications for both policy actors and education professionals. Moreover, this study contributes to policy research in education by demonstrating how theoretical frameworks and analytic methods that have not yet been fully utilized in education could serve as powerful tools for exploring educational policy processes. Before we present our findings, an overview of the reading policy environment in each of the nine states under study is in order.

STATE READING POLICY ENVIRONMENT

As mentioned earlier, the 1994 NAEP results served as a prominent problem indicator that incited widespread concerns about low reading achievement and attracted political attention to the reading problem across the states. In addition to the dissatisfaction with student test scores, two other conditions may also help to explain why reading became a hot policy issue in the 1990s. First, under a recent national mood that has placed strong emphasis on education in general and reading in particular, politicians on both sides of the political fence have identified themselves as supporters of education reform and considered reading a politically advantageous issue that is likely to bring about political accomplishment with minimum political risk. As a member of a teacher union in Michigan aptly put it, "Being against ... sound reading policy is like being against motherhood or democracy." Second, many states saw improved fiscal conditions in the late 1990s and were able to afford new education programs. From 1991 to 2001, for instance, state education expenditures grew from $106 billion to $201 billion (Snell, Eckl, & Williams, 2003). Major federal grants, such as the Reading Excellence Act and Reading First, have also provided additional resources to fund state reading programs.

The combination of the above conditions led to the opening of a "window" for policy change in many states in the late 1990s (Kingdon, 1995), and galvanized a diverse array of reading policy actors into action. Just within a few years, a profusion of reading legislations and initiatives had been generated across the states. By the year 2002, 35 states had created or were developing major reading initiatives (Manzo, 2002), including the nine states that we studied (i.e., Alabama, California, Connecticut, Indiana, Maine, Michigan, North Carolina, Texas, and Utah). In the remainder of this section, we provide a synopsis of the reading policy context in each of the nine states, with a particular focus on the unique features of each state.

Alabama: The Power of the Reading Czar

Reading policy development in the Camellia State has been spearheaded by the Alabama Department of Education (ADE). What earned the department most credits within the state and even a national reputation was the Alabama Reading Initiative (ARI) launched in 1998 under the leadership of Katherine Mitchell.[2] At the behest of the Alabama State Board of Education, Mitchell convened the Alabama Reading Panel in 1996 as a precursor to a statewide reading initiative. Although the panel included members from opposite sides of the "reading wars," it was able to reach the consensus that the teaching of beginning reading must follow a balanced approach. The panel's recommendations formed the basis of the teacher professional development program that was at the center of the ARI. The initiative was first implemented in only 16 pilot schools with private funds in 1998. With strong fiscal support from both the governor and the state legislature as well as broad political support from diverse interest groups, the initiative was eventually expanded to all elementary schools in the state by summer 2006. The state gained further momentum toward reaching the goal of 100% literacy when it was, as one of the first three states, awarded the Reading First grant in 2002.

The accomplishments of the ADE have been attributed in a large part to the entrepreneurship of Mitchell. For many Alabamians, the ADE was synonymous with the name of Katherine Mitchell. A reading association representative opined, "Katherine Mitchell is a goddess [laughs], a reading goddess." Her influence, according to an administration official, stemmed partly from the support from the governor: "The governor really considers Katherine Mitchell the reading czar." Although the power of the "reading czar" could be a little overwhelming for some (Song, forthcoming), for many, Mitchell's leadership was instrumental and her accomplishments were amazing, particularly "given the historical reading wars," as observed by a university professor. At the 2005 Alabama Governor's Reading Summit, the U.S. Secretary of Education Margaret Spellings remarked that the improvement in reading achievement among Alabama's students was impressive, and lauded the ARI as a model for states across the nation (Alabama Association of School Boards, 2005). She particularly acknowledged Mitchell's contribution to the success of the ARI. Currently serving as the director of the Alabama Reading First Initiative and the state's first assistant superintendent of education for reading, the reading czar continues holding the reins on reading policy in the Camellia State.

California: Shift of Direction and Tension at the Top

California students' declining scores on the NAEP reading test in the 1990s, particularly their abysmal performance on the 1998 NAEP, thrust reading into the spotlight. Defying the common view about the weak policy influence of state boards of education (e.g., Mazzoni, 1993; Marshall, Mitchell, & Wirt, 1989), the California State Board of Education (CSBE), spearheaded by policy entrepreneur Marion Joseph, took a strong leadership role in revamping the state's reading policy. Its most significant impact on state reading policy came from its adoption of the *English-Language Arts Content Standards for California Public Schools: Kindergarten Through Grade Twelve* in 1997, and the subsequent adoption of the *Reading/Language Arts Framework for California Public Schools* in 1999. With a strong phonics emphasis, the 1997 standards and curriculum framework marked a significant shift from past direction as represented in the literature-based 1987 *English-Language Arts Framework*, which was often associated with whole language and blamed for the widespread reading failure among the state's children.

Sharing the pro-phonics view with the CSBE, the California office of the governor and the state legislature were also actively involved in reading policy development. In 1996 alone, eight pieces of legislation dealing with a variety of reading-related issues were signed into law by Governor Pete Wilson. This set of legislation, together with two bills passed in 1995, has been collectively referred to as the 1996 California Reading Initiative. The two bills from 1995, Assembly Bills 170 and 1504, nicknamed the "ABC bills" for their sponsors (Alpert, Burton, and Conroy), were of particular importance, as they marked the beginning of tight legislative control over reading curriculum and instruction in California. The bills mandated that reading instructional materials in Grades K-8 must include "systematic, explicit phonics." Similar prescriptions also appear in legislation concerning teaching credentialing and professional development.

While the CSBE, office of the governor, and state assembly all showed a strong preference for phonics, the California Department of Education (CDE) was trying to keep to the middle ground. In 1995, the Reading Task Force convened by the department attributed students' low reading achievement directly to the 1987 English-Language Arts Framework, and declared that the 1987 framework "did not present a comprehensive and balanced reading program and gave insufficient attention to a systematic skill instruction program" (CDE, 1995, p. 2). The CDE recommended that reading instruction should follow a balanced and comprehensive approach, and incorporated the recommendation to its reading program advisory (CDE, 1996).

Clearly, the CDE's stance on reading pedagogy was not completely in line with the other government actors; and a constant tension between them was noted by quite a few of participants in our study. In fact, this tension could probably be traced back to the 1993 lawsuit filed by the CSBE against the state superintendent of public instruction, which established the CSBE as the foremost education policymaking authority in California (Young, 2002). The primary role of the CDE has since then been relegated to administering and implementing policies established by the CSBE instead of creating policies. The political feuds and the ideological disagreements between the CSBE and CDE, combined with the alliance between the CSBE and the office of the governor by virtue of the political structure of the state (i.e., the governor appoints the CSBE), made California the only state among the nine states we studied where the state department of education was overshadowed by the state board of education in terms of influence on state reading policy.

Connecticut: The Blueprint for the Two Connecticuts

While taking great pride in being the highest-ranking state on the 1998 NAEP fourth-grade reading test and being named a "shining star" in early reading achievement (National Education Goals Panel, 1999), educators and policymakers in Connecticut were deeply troubled by the persistent achievement gap between children from high-poverty districts and their peers from affluent suburban areas. An official from the Connecticut State Department of Education (CSDE), for example, observed during an interview, "The whole concept of the two Connecticuts is becoming more and more apparent in the Mastery Test Scores." Similarly, a reading professor described Connecticut as "a two-tier state with a population at the top and a population at the very bottom." Largely driven by the enduring achievement gap, and fueled by the 1989 *Sheff vs. O'Neil* lawsuit over educational inequities in the Hartford public schools, preventing reading failures for all children, especially low-achieving and at-risk children, became a top educational priority for Connecticut.

Starting with Public Act 97-256: The School Readiness Act, the Connecticut General Assembly passed a slew of reading legislation. The single most significant reading legislation in the state's history is PA 99-227: An Act Concerning a Statewide Early Reading Success Institute. As required by the act, the CSDE convened an early reading success panel in 2000 to review research on how people learn to read and what knowledge and skills teachers need to teach reading effectively. The panel's conclusions and recommendations were documented in *Connecticut's Blueprint for Reading Achievement: A Report by the Early Reading Success Panel* (CSDE, 2000). Promoting a comprehensive approach to reading instruction, the blueprint became the most influential guidance for reading instruction in classrooms across the state. It also provided the basis for designing statewide professional development and for establishing state literacy standards for teacher certification. Moreover, the blueprint set the stage for the use of Connecticut's 2001 Reading Excellent Act grant and the more recent Reading First grant.

In addition to the panel report, the CSDE, under the entrepreneurial leadership of Commissioner Ted Sergi, released *The Connecticut Framework: K–12 Curricular Goals and Standards* and adopted the *Standards of Reading Competency for Students in Grades K–3* in 1998. It also updated the statewide assessments, Connecticut Mastery Tests, in 2000 (third generation) and 2006 (fourth generation) to align the tests with state standards and curriculum framework. The CSDE's policy activism has continued after our study ended. It released the *Connecticut's Preschool Curriculum Framework* in 2004, and more recently approved the *2006 Connecticut English Language Arts Curriculum Framework* and published *Beyond the Blueprint: Literacy Instruction and Literacy Across the Content Areas, 4–12,* in 2006. Despite the state's sustained commitment to reading improvement, however, bridging the gap between the two Connecticuts has remained a challenge. As the 2005 NAEP results revealed, Connecticut still had the largest achievement gap in the nation between rich and poor students in both fourth-grade reading and eight-grade reading, which has overshadowed the high overall achievement level of the shining star (The Connecticut Alliance for Great Schools, n.d.).

Indiana: Phonics Tools for Better Teachers

Like many other states, it was largely disappointing test scores on both NAEP and the state test (Indiana Statewide Testing for Educational Progress-Plus) that caught people's attention to the reading problem in Indiana. Assuming primary leadership for state reading policy, the Indiana Department of Education (IDOE) launched the state's first reading initiative, Reading and Literacy for a Better Indiana, in 1997. A key component of the initiative, the Early Literacy Intervention Grant Program, provided funding for a variety of early reading intervention programs, among which Reading Recovery, a program often associated with whole language, received significant amounts of funding, particularly during the early years of the program.

A growing emphasis on phonics, however, characterized the IDOE's later efforts in the area of state reading policy. Viewing existing standards as lacking focus and rigor, State Superintendent for Public Instruction, Dr. Suellen Reed, established the Phonics Task Force in 2000 to incorporate phonics and phonemic awareness into existing Grades K–3 standards. The focus on phonics, according to IDOE officials that we interviewed, was a move away from the state's whole language tradition to a balanced reading instructional approach that begins with a heavy emphasis on phonics. To help teachers to align instruction with the new standards, the Phonics Task Force developed the *Phonics Tool Kit*, which provided teachers with current information about the importance of phonics knowledge and was made available to all K–3 teachers in the state in 2000. With the assistance of Indiana University, the IDOE also developed an online staff development course, *Phonics Online*, to help teachers better utilize the *Phonics Tool Kit*.

The IDOE's policy activism was backed by strong support from the office of the governor and the state legislature. Governor O'Bannon established Indiana's Education Roundtable as a policy advisory body in 1998, and cochaired the roundtable with Superintendent Reed. The governor also launched his Ready to Read initiative in 1999. The Indiana General Assembly was far from being quiet either. It was a strong advocate for strengthening accountability by means of statewide standards and mandatory tests. It was also a firm supporter for the IDOE's emphasis on phonics. In 2000, Senator Clark sponsored an amendment, as part of Senate Bill 352, to the state's teacher licensure law, requiring all elementary teacher certification candidates to demonstrate proficiency in comprehensive reading instruction skills, including phonemic awareness and phonics instruction. More recently, House Bill 1488 passed in 2005 added a definition for "phonological weakness" to Indiana Code concerning education. It required the IDOE to develop a plan for training reading teachers about phonologic weakness and determining effective instruments for detecting phonologic weakness and assessing student reading development. Given the concerted efforts among policy actors to sharpen the focus on phonics in reading curriculum and instruction through a variety of means, it seems likely that what teachers do behind the closed doors may actually be changing in the Hoosier State.

Maine: Solid Foundation for Learning Results

With the state's long-standing tradition of local control, the Maine State Legislature was not as active as that in some other states in mandating education policy. Nevertheless, Maine's Education Reform Act of 1984 and the more recent concerns about students' reading performance on NAEP and the Maine Education Assessment prompted a number of highly visible legislative activities related to reading. In 1993, the Maine State Legislature formed the Learning Results Task Force to develop long-range education goals and standards for school and student performance. Based on the recommendations of the task force, the Maine Department of Education (MEDE), along with Maine State Board of Education, developed *Learning Results Standards* in eight subject areas, which was approved by the state legislature in 1997. Partly out of consideration for local independence, the 1997 standards were couched in fairly broad terms, and notably missing from the English language arts standards were the terms "phonics" or "phonemic awareness."

As mandated by the state legislature, the MEDE reviewed and revised the 1997 standards, and submitted the revised standards to the state legislature for approval in January 2007. Compared to the 1997 standards, the revised English language arts standards are more concrete, and feature phonemic awareness and phonics much more prominently among "a variety of strategies" that students need to master. The new emphasis on "a variety of strategies" could be largely attributed to the work of the Early Literacy Workgroup, which was convened by the MEDE in 1998 to examine effective early literacy practices occurring in Maine schools. The report from the workgroup, *A Solid Foundation: Supportive Contexts for Early Literacy in Maine*, identifies the common characteristics of the contexts that support high literacy achievement (MEDE, 2000). The conclusion from the report is clear: No single program will work for all students; teachers should adopt a "balanced" approach to reading instruction and use "a variety of instructional methods" grounded in assessments of students' needs (p. 44). The *Solid Foundation* report was widely disseminated throughout the state, and provided an important practical framework for schools to support literacy development.

It is important to note that reading policy development in Maine was a collaborative process and reflected concerted efforts from diverse actors. Other than the state legislature and the MEDE, the office of the governor, and particularly First Lady Mary Herman, were also strong supporters of reading initiatives. The first lady served as the honorary chair of the Maine Family Literacy Task Force and was credited with being instrumental in bringing reading to the top of the state's education policy agenda. Institutions of higher education were also important participants in the state's reading policy development. Faculty members at the University of Maine and the University of Southern Maine, for instance, served on the Early Literacy Workgroup, informed policymakers with their professional knowledge and expertise, and contributed significantly to the building of a solid foundation for improved reading achievement among the state's schoolchildren.

Michigan: The Evolving Definition of Reading

In Michigan, reading became a hot policy issue in the 1990s, as students' poor performance on both NAEP and state reading tests attracted a great deal of attention, and as Governor John Engler set "reading by the fourth grade" as a state goal and launched his multipronged Reading Plan for Michigan in 1998 to attain the goal. Reading policy development, however, started long before that in Michigan. The state introduced the Michigan Educational Assessment Program (MEAP) as early as 1969, and was among the first in the nation to establish statewide standards in 1973. Reading, in the 1973 standards, was simply defined as the ability to identify words and read fluently. In 1984, however, a group of reading professionals, led by Elaine Weber of the Michigan Department of Education (MIDE) and Karen Wixson from the University of Michigan, started an effort to redefine reading as "constructive, interactive, and dynamic, [with] a real focus on literature as well as comprehension strategies" (quote from a respondent). The group garnered significant support for the new definition, and an updated version of MEAP based on the constructivist definition of reading was subsequently implemented in 1989.

In 1993, Karen Wixson and Sheila Potter were requested by the Michigan State Board of Education to develop language arts standards and curriculum framework for the state. Their constructivist perspective on reading, however, met with strong resistance from the pro-phonics newly-elected president of the state board. Despite the lengthy and widely publicized battles, Wixson and Potter managed to hold their ground. In 1995, the state board of education approved 12 English language arts content standards with benchmarks, which were included in the *Michigan Curriculum Framework* released in 1996. The language arts standards were general in concept and broad in scope, and set up under a "balanced literacy framework" with a focus on meaning and communication.

An increased emphasis on phonics, however, recently emerged from the MIDE. In response to the testing requirement of the No Child Left Behind Act of 2001, the department developed *K–8 Grade Level Content Expectations* in 2004, and updated it in 2005. While the terms "phonics" and "phonemic awareness" were nowhere to be seen in the original set of expectations, they were prominently listed as two essential skills in reading in the updated version. A recent emphasis on phonics also occurred to the Michigan Literacy Progress Profile (MLPP), an early literacy assessment program developed by the MIDE as a key component of Governor Engler's Reading Plan for Michigan. Lacking explicit sections on phonics and vocabulary, MLPP was deemed by the U.S. Department of Education as an unacceptable assessment tool for the Reading First grant it awarded to Michigan in 2002. As a result, the MIDE began to add additional tools to the MIPP toolkits, especially in the areas of phonics, phonemic awareness, and vocabulary (Stevens, n.d.). Indeed, as Putnam (2002) puts it, "the hook of dangling dollars in front of state officials is steering Michigan towards phonics or what's being called scientific-based reading research" (para. 6). The bulk of the Reading First grant would be used to purchase phonics-oriented textbooks, hire reading coaches to work with school teachers, and train teachers statewide in phonemic awareness, phonics, fluency, vocabulary, and text comprehension. Moreover, teacher training programs at 32 colleges in the state were to be reviewed to make sure that they include phonics in the curricula for future reading teachers. Given Michigan's tradition in the constructivist perspective on reading that is often associated with whole language, the recent push toward phonics might actually make its "balanced literacy framework" a little closer to a true balance.

North Carolina: Return to Basics

Soon after the release of the 1992 NAEP results showing 44% of the state's fourth-graders read "below basic," North Carolina's *English Language Arts Standard Course of Study* became a target of criticism. It was blamed for lack of attention to basic reading skills and likened to California's whole language curriculum in the 1980s. Responding to the concerns, the North Carolina General Assembly passed two bills aimed to strengthen accountability and improve reading curriculum and instruction. The 1995 Senate Bill 16 required the North Carolina State Board of Education (NCSBE) to reorganize the North Carolina Department of Public Instruction (NCDPI) and develop a statewide accountability plan. The resulting plan, ABCs of Public Education, established the state's first accountability system, which focused on *accountability* with high standards, teaching the *basics*, and local *control*. It also included a plan for revising the *Standard Course of Study*. The general assembly approved the accountability plan, and further required, in its 1996 Senate Bill 1139, that the board of education develop a comprehensive reading plan and revise *Standard Course of Study* as part of the plan so as to "provide school units with guidance in the implementation of balanced, integrated, and effective programs of reading instruction" (Section 8.2).

Despite its purported endorsement for "balanced" reading instruction, Senate Bill 1139 explicitly mandated that the revised *Standard Course of Study* should include early and systematic phonics instruction. Referred to as the "phonics legislation" by some, the bill was viewed by many as reflective of the legislature's desire to promote phonics in the state, which might partly be attributed to the lobbying efforts of conservative groups, particularly the National Right to Read Foundation. In 1997, the NCSBE adopted the Comprehensive Reading Plan for North Carolina. Under the plan, the NCDPI revised the *K–12 English Language Arts Standard Course of*

Study to include more emphasis on early and systematic phonics instruction within a balanced reading program. The revised *English Language Arts Standard Course of Study* was approved by the NCSBE in 1999, and was updated again with minor clarifications in 2004.[3] The revised standards provided a guiding curriculum framework for classroom instruction, laid the foundation for the state's assessment programs, and also served as the ultimate guide for textbook selection.

Texas: Governor's Agenda and the Little Red Book

For several decades, many of the most profound education policies in Texas have been initiated by the office of the governor. George W. Bush continued that tradition by vowing to be an "education governor." Governor Bush announced the Texas Reading Initiative (TRI) as the centerpiece of his education agenda in 1996, and proposed to supplement TRI with accountability measures in 1998. At Bush's request, the Governor's Business Council established the Governor's Focus on Reading Task Force and organized a series of reading summits to examine scientifically-based reading research. Echoing the opinions of experts attending the summits, Bush stated his position on reading pedagogy most openly and tersely in the October 17, 2000 presidential debate with Al Gore: "Phonics works, by the way, it needs to be part of our curriculum" (PBS, 2000, para. 41).

Although supportive of the governor's reading initiative, the Texas Education Agency (TEA) took a more moderate stance on reading pedagogy. In 1996, Commissioner Moses convened a group of top reading educators for the purpose of generating a consensus on reading pedagogy. The consensus reached was that reading instruction should follow a "balanced and comprehensive" approach (TEA, 1997a, p. 1). This consensus was also incorporated into the revised state standards—*Texas Essential Knowledge and Skills*, which was adopted by the Texas State Board of Education in 1997 and became a key component of the new accountability system proposed by Bush and codified in Senate Bill 4 in 1999.

The most visible accomplishment of the TEA in the area of reading was probably the publication of the famous "Red Book": *Beginning Reading Instruction: Components and Features of a Research-Based Reading Program* (TEA, 1997b). As the official statement of the principles underlying TRI, the little red booklet was widely distributed across the state and "served as a basis for professional development, the development of curriculum standards and instructional materials, as well as the establishment of research-based reading programs in schools" (TEA, 2002, p. 3). The TEA released a revised edition of the red book in 2002 and also developed companion documents to the red book.

In addition to disseminating the "Red Book Series," the TEA also created teacher reading academies in 1999 to provide professional development to all K–2 language arts teachers in the state. The state legislature authorized additional funding in 2001 for expanding the program to Grades 3–4. Although the extent of improvement in reading achievement since the mid-1990s and the credibility of the so-called "Texas miracle" have been open to debate, some of our respondents did note that the statewide professional development had indeed produced "a lot of changes" in Texas' classrooms.

Utah: Rebound From the Downward Trend

Although Utah's students have consistently performed above the national average on NAEP reading, their scores took a downward turn during the 1990s, making Utah one of the two states in the nation (the other being Wyoming) with continuously declining NAEP scores between 1992 and 1998. Deeply disturbed by the declining reading scores, Governor Michael Leavitt placed reading at the top of his education agenda and also at the center of the Utah's Promise program launched in 1999. Building upon Utah's Promise, Lt. Governor Olene Walker established the Utah Reads project,[4] which emphasized teacher professional development, tutoring programs, and community partnerships, and featured prominently the Read to Me campaign led by Utah's First Lady Mrs. Leavitt.

On the legislative side, a particular important legislation, House Bill 67: Children's Reading Skills, was passed in 1997. It mandated that a reading assessment be administered in Grades 1–6, and that reading instruction shall include early and explicit teaching of phonetic decoding skills, exposure to quality literature, writing, and time to read across the curriculum. Two years later, the state legislature passed House Bill 312, which provided an unprecedented $8 million to ensure that all Utah students read at grade level by the end of third grade. In an effort to tighten state control over assessments as mandated by House Bill 67, the state legislature enacted House Bill 177 in 2000, which stripped local school boards of their control over testing, and transferred their performance assessment duties entirely to the state board of education. The bill further established the Utah Performance Assessment System for Students as the new statewide testing program.

For the Utah State Office of Education (USOE), reading has always been on the front burner. However, it had been unable to secure much legislative support until the governor declared reading as his top educational priority. Under Utah Reads, the USOE developed the all-inclusive *Utah Reads K–3 Literacy Model,* which defined a balanced reading pedagogy for Utah and was instituted to guide reading instruction throughout the state. The model also laid the foundation for the state's future work on curriculum and instruction. In 2003, the Utah State Board of Education adopted the *Utah Elementary Language Arts Core Curriculum: Kindergarten–Sixth Grade*, which became the central component of the *Utah Literacy Model* that replaced the original *Utah Reads K-3 Literacy Model*. Although Utah's literacy model changed its label, its essence remained. The coherence and consensus that characterized the state's reading policy seemed to have paid off, as evidenced by Utah fourth-graders' strong rebound on the 2002 NAEP reading test from earlier downward trend.

ORGANIZATION OF THE BOOK

Having provided an overview of the reading policy context in general and a description of the unique reading policy environment in individual states, we will present findings from our study on key aspects of the state reading policy systems in the next five chapters, highlighting both features unique to individual states and general patterns based on cross-state comparisons. Specifically, in chapter 2, we examine the composition of the state reading policy domain and identify the structural properties and relational patterns of the state reading policy networks using social network analysis. These structural properties and relational patterns have important implications for both individual actors and the overall networks. In particular, they affect the influence distribution among actors within the state reading policy networks, which is the topic of chapter 3.

The next two chapters deal primarily with the belief systems of the state reading policy actors. In chapter 4, we explore policy actors' beliefs on five key reading-related issues: levels of reading achievement, trends of reading achievement, reading pedagogy, state reading standards, and state reading tests. We then move on to a special type of policy belief—beliefs about the causes of the reading achievement problem—in the next chapter. Guided by Stone's (2002) framework of causal stories, we analyze the causal stories told by the state reading policy actors. In addition, drawing upon McDonnell and Elmore's (1987) framework of policy instruments, we review the policy solutions adopted by reading policymakers in each state and explore the connections between the causal stories told and the policy solutions proposed.

Finally, in chapter 6, we look at the behavioral aspect of the state reading policy domain, focusing specifically on interest groups' lobbying activities. We examine both the types of lobbying tactics that interest groups employed to influence state reading policy and the intensity with which interest groups used various lobbying tactics. Further, we assess the relationships between the use of lobbying tactics and interest groups' policy influence.

We conclude this book in chapter 7 by recapitulating major findings from our investigation, reflecting on relevant policy theories and research methodology, and discussing implications of the study for educational researchers, professionals, and practitioners. At the end of the book are five appendices that provide further information about study design and additional findings.

NOTES

1. The National Reading Policy Study was conducted as part of CIERA, the Center for the Improvement of Early Reading Achievement, and supported under the Educational Research and Development Centers Program, PR/Award Number R305R70004, as administered by the Office of Educational Research and Improvement (currently The Institute of Education Sciences), U.S. Department of Education.

   The State Reading Policy Study was conducted under the auspices of the U.S. Department of Education and the Spencer Foundation. The Field Initiated Studies Program, PR/Award R305T990369, Office of Educational Research and Improvement (currently The Institute of Education Sciences), U.S. Department of Education supported the research in five states-California, Connecticut, Michigan, North Carolina, and Texas. The Major Grants Program, Grant No. 200000269, Spencer Foundation funded our parallel efforts in Alabama, Indiana, Maine, and Utah. The program officers at both institutions provided us with highly useful and flexible assistance at critical times during the project. We wish to acknowledge their munificent contributions to our work.

2. The ARI was awarded the 2002 Education Commission of the States Innovation Award, which recognizes a state for excellence in the policy area of literacy. Its potential for transforming reading instruction has also prompted other states (e.g., Massachusetts and Florida) to establish pilot initiatives modeled after the ARI.

3. The North Carolina has maintained a standard course of study since 1898, which has been updated every 5 to 7 years. The most recent version was revised and approved in 2004.

4. Utah Reads is no longer supported by the Utah State Office of Education and has been replaced by the STAR (Student Tutoring Achievement for Reading) program. See http://www.schools.utah.gov/curr/STAR/ for details about the STAR program.

CHAPTER 2

POLICY ACTORS AND STATE READING POLICY NETWORKS

COMPOSITION OF THE STATE READING POLICY DOMAIN

With intensified attention to reading and reading policy across the states, the state reading policy domain has become the battlefield of constellations of actors striving to sway reading policy in directions favoring their respective interests. Across the nine states, we identified 433 individuals as having a substantive interest in shaping state reading policy, of whom 366 representing 243 policy actors[1] participated in our study, with an overall response rate of 85% (see Appendix A for detailed information about sampling).[2]

Similar to the national reading policy domain and other national policy domains where over two thirds of the key policy actors were outside of the government (Laumann & Knoke, 1987; McDaniel, Sims, & Miskel, 2001), the state reading policy domain was dominated—in number—by a diverse array of nongovernment actors without formal policymaking authority. Of the 243 policy actors that participated in our study, 181 were interest groups, 51 were government agencies, and 11 were individual policy actors acting on their own. The heavy presence of interest groups in the state reading policy domain suggests that, like government actors, interest groups are also important participants in the

Reading: Policy, Politics, and Processes, pp. 17–42
Copyright © 2008 by Information Age Publishing
All rights of reproduction in any form reserved.

policymaking processes, and that the "study of groups is central to an understanding of American politics" (Petracca, 1992, p. 7).

Interests, Interest Groups, and Advocacy Explosion

Before examining interest groups in the state reading policy domain, an explication of the concept of interests is in order. Most contemporary scholars agree that private values or wants and public policy are the two central components of the definition of interests. Salisbury (1991) observes, "It is the conjunction of private wants and public action that constitutes the interest of an interest group" (pp. 375-376). It follows that interests are not necessarily givens as are usually assumed, but something that emerges from the interactions of private values and public actions. Similar to Salisbury's notion of emergent interests, Heinz, Laumann, Nelson, and Salisbury (1993) claim that interests are revealed as public policy intersects with the wants and values of private actors. Interests hence are created when private values are affected or likely to be affected by government action, and the same values may not be interests if they bear no relationship with government action (Baumgartner & Leech, 1998). Early reading achievement, for example, is not in itself an interest, but becomes so only when those sharing the value make demands on government in order to promote the value by means of public policy.

The definitions for interest groups are closely related to the definitions for interests, Salisbury (1991), for example, states, "An organization's status as an interest group depends on whether or not its values are entangled with public policy" (p. 376). Thomas and Hrebenar (1992) likewise define an interest group as "any association of individuals, whether formally organized or not, that attempts to influence public policy" (p. 153). In a study of education interest groups, Sipple, Miskel, Matheney, and Kearney (1997) stress the importance of adopting a broad definition so that few assumptions are made about interest groups, their memberships, or their ideologies. For the purpose of this study, ideas from a number of scholars (e.g., Baumgartner & Leech, 1998; Hrebenar, 1997; Kollman, 1998; Thomas & Hrebenar, 1992) are combined to form the following broad definition: interest groups refer to membership organizations, advocacy organizations not accepting members, businesses, and other organizations or institutions, whether formally organized or not, that try to influence public policy. In the state reading policy domain, interest groups span a wide spectrum, covering teacher organizations, K-12 and higher education associations, parent and citizens groups, think tanks or policy institutes, media, business groups, and foundations. Examples include California Teachers Association,

Connecticut Reading Association, Indiana Parent Teacher Association, Maine Public Radio, Texas Business and Education Coalition, and Michigan Foundation for Educational leadership, to name just a few.

From the definitions for interest groups, it is clear that interest groups are truly part and parcel of policymaking and politics. With the government expansion in the 1960s and the decentralization and fragmentation of the federal government in the 1970s and 1980s, interest groups have become particularly visible players in the political arena during the past few decades, as those governmental changes have provided many more points of access through which interest groups may enter and attempt to influence the policymaking process (Schlozman & Tierney, 1986). Petracca (1992) characterizes the recent changes in the landscape of American interest groups in terms of "a significantly larger number of groups of greater diversity, located throughout the political system and interacting in new configurations with each other and with the government" (p. 13).

The proliferation of the interest group system and the escalation of group activities have been referred to by many as "advocacy explosion" (e.g., Berry, 1997; Knoke, 1986, 1990a), which has occurred at both the national and the state levels. As one of the most basic political institutions, public schools have understandably became the target of increasing numbers of advocacy groups as the reform movement of the 1980s plunged education even more into the political mainstream (Mazzoni, 1995). Although just a few decades ago, American education policymaking was dominated by policymakers together with a handful of professional associations, it is now shaped by a growing number of interest groups of diverse natures that have been mobilized to have their interests represented in education policies (Marshall, Mitchell, & Wirt, 1989; Salisbury, 1990; Thomas & Hrebenar, 1991). According to Baumgartner and Leech (1998), the number of education associations increased from 563 in 1959 to 1,312 in 1995. In our previous research on national reading policy, our colleagues and we found that over 100 interest groups and government agencies were actively vying for influence in this policy arena (McDaniel, 2001; McDaniel, Sims, & Miskel, 2001; Song & Miskel, 2002; Song, Miskel, Young, & McDaniel, 2000; Song, Miskel, Young, Osguthorpe, & Shepley, 2001).

The proliferation of education interest groups at the state level closely mirrors that at the national level. As Mazzoni (1995) commented,

> By the mid-1980s, state education policy systems had become congested with individuals and groups trying to set agendas and shape decisions. The mainline K-12 groups representing teachers, administrators, and boards had been joined over the decades by a myriad of other organized interests

in education. In addition, noneducation groups other than business—for example, parent, civic, urban, labor, farm and foundation groups—wanted to have a crack at changing schools. (p. 64)

As an essential area of schooling, reading has inevitably became a target of intense interest group activity. In the nine states that we examined in the study reported here, the number of reading policy actors in a given state ranged from 18 to 40, with a total of 243 actors across the nine states. If the 33 nonrespondents were taken into account, the total number of actors would reach 276 across the nine states. It is to note, however, that despite the expanded interest group system in the field of education, interest groups in education have received less attention than they warrant, and the empirical base on educational interest groups remains "fragile and fragmented" (Malen, 2001, p. 168), which clearly speaks to the need for the present study.

It is also to note that other than the proliferation and diversity that were common among the states, the state reading interest group systems also demonstrated state-specific features. Being a rural state lacking large urban centers, Alabama, for example, does not have a state affiliate of the American Federation of Teachers (AFT); the state affiliate of the National Education Association (NEA), the Alabama Education Association, is the only teacher organization in the state. In Maine, although a state affiliate of the AFT (Maine Federation of Teachers) does exit, it seemed to be rather inert, for no information was available for the group in publicly accessible data sources, and none of our respondents in the state ever mentioned the group during the interviews. In contrast, Texas not only has both a state affiliate of the AFT (Texas Federation of Teachers) and a state affiliate of the NEA (Texas State Teacher's Association), but also has another two teacher organizations—the Association of Texas Professional Educators and the Texas Classroom Teachers Association, which makes Texas unique in this regard.

Government Agencies in the State Reading Policy Domain

The political activism in the field of reading has manifested itself not only outside of government, but also inside government, which reflects the "new context of governance" of education policy with the states cast in the leadership role (Fuhrman, 1987). Particularly since the release of the *A Nation at Risk* report (National Commission on Excellence in Education, 1983), states have been obligated to address the perceived education crisis by overhauling the education system with various reform initiatives. Once concerned primarily with school finance, state government officials have assumed an unprecedented proactive role in education policymaking, adopting standards and assessment, instituting programs for teacher training and certification, and proposing policy alternatives to improve student achievement.

At the forefront of education policymaking have been state legislatures, which have emerged as the supreme policymakers in American Education (Fuhrman, 1994; James, 1991). Rosenthal and Fuhrman (1983) observe that the power over education policy has shifted from professional educators and traditional interest groups to state legislatures since the 1970s. They thus wrote:

> [State] legislatures have been able to assert themselves in education, as in other policy domains, because they have come of age as political institutions. They developed institutional capacity and the ability to lead policy making by improving their staffs, facilities, and support services. Legislatures and their members have become more professional, meeting more frequently and spending more time on the job, and acquiring the knowledge to challenge professional experts. (p. 22)

State governors, who traditionally have had little interest in education policy beyond fiscal concerns, have also begun to pay serious attention to education policy and commit themselves to education reform agendas since the early 1980s (Lewis & Maruna, 1999). Sensing a prevailing national mood focusing heavily on education and particularly on reading, many state governors have seized upon education policy as an effective vehicle for advancing their political careers, claiming themselves to be "education governors" or even "reading governors," and granting reading a prominent position on their policy agendas.

Another major type of government actors in the state reading policy domain is state education agencies—state departments of education and state boards of education, which are obviously players with a high level of legitimacy where education policy is concerned. With substantial federal aid since the 1960s, state departments of education have expanded considerably both in size and in function (Lewis & Maruna, 1999; Murphy, 1980). Nowadays, these departments not only carry the traditional function of implementing and administering state policies, but also are actively involved in establishing standards and assessments, selecting texts, and appropriating funding for schools. In close relationships with state departments of education are state boards of education, although the latter does not seem to be as actively involved in shaping education policy as the former (Campbell & Mazzoni, 1976; Marshall, Mitchell, & Wirt, 1989; Sroufe, 1970).

In the state reading policy domain, the major types of government actors discussed above—offices of the governor, state legislatures, and state education agencies—were all active participants in the nine states that we studied. Other than those common actors, many states also had government actors unique to the states. Texas, for example, is the only state in our sample where office of the lieutenant governor, in addition to office of the governor, was an important member of the reading policy community. Maine is the only state in our study where office of the first lady was a consequential actor for its reading policy. What distinguishes Connecticut from the other states is that its state board of education was not part of the reading policy community, for it had virtually no involvement in the state's reading policy, and no one even mentioned the board during our interviews. Moreover, the reading policy domain in Connecticut included two agencies in addition to the education committee within the general assembly, the Commission on Children and the Office of Fiscal Analysis, which were unique to the state. In the case of Utah, it had a special governing board overseeing the state's higher education system— the Utah State Board of Regents, which was not found in the reading policy domain in the other states. The Michigan reading policy community also had a special government agency that did not exist in the other states: the Reading Plan for Michigan Advisory Council appointed by the governor. This council was the only government agency dealing specifically with reading among all reading policy actors in the nine states.

Aside from the above-mentioned state-specific government agencies dealing with reading policy, there were also types of government agencies common in some states, but not in others. Both Maine and Connecticut, for instance, have a joint education committee in the state legislature, while the other seven states have separate house education committees and senate education committees. Another type of government agency that was part of the reading policy community in some states but not others was agencies whose primary responsibility is governing teacher licensing. This type of agency existed in four of the nine states that we studied: the California Commission on Teacher Credentialing, the Indiana Professional Standards Board, the North Carolina Professional Teaching Standards Commission, and the Texas State Board for Educator Certification.

Individual Policy Actors in the State Reading Policy Domain

Finally, in terms of the composition of the state reading policy domain, four of the nine states in our sample included individual policy actors not representing any government agencies or interest groups. Being the largest in size among the nine states, the California reading policy domain had as many as six individual policy actors, five of which were academics and one was a lobbyist. Connecticut also had three individual reading policy actors, two of which were legislators and one was an academic. North Carolina had only one individual reading policy actor, who was a conservative policy activist; and Utah had one as well (a legislator). Reading policy actors in the other five states were either government agencies or interest groups.

STATE READING POLICY NETWORKS

The reading policy domains in different states were similar not only in general composition, but also in structural properties. Concerned with a common issue of interest, the diverse array of reading policy actors were not acting alone, but were engaged in interactions with one another, and operated in what Heclo (1978) calls "issue networks."

Issue Networks

One of the consequences of the proliferation of interest group system and the escalation of group activities has been the emergence of increasingly complex relationships among interest groups, who are no longer working in isolation, but engaging in policy endeavors in "shifting, almost kaleidoscopic configurations" (Salisbury, 1990, p. 212). Heclo (1978) observes that such interactions among policy actors are not just confined within the interest group community, but occur in a larger context—at the level of issue networks, which, as McFarland (1992) defines, are communication networks of people knowledgeable in a particular policy area, including government authorities, legislators, business people, lobbyists, and even academicians and journalists. Increasingly, it is through such webs of people that public policies tend to be refined, evidence debated, and alternative options worked out—though rarely in any controlled, well-organized fashion (Heclo, 1978). The same idea is also captured by Kingdon's (1995) notion of policy community in his multiple streams model of policymaking.

Indeed, as Heclo (1978) forcefully asserts, with heightened government activities and interest group proliferation, policymaking is no longer contained in the traditional closed *iron triangles* or *subgovernments*, wherein a small number of legislative committees, executive agencies, and established interest groups form all-powerful alliances and operate in symbiotic dependence. Instead, policymaking now takes place in fairly open issue networks, which provide a major source of countervailing power, generating new forces, creating strains, and causing changes in public policies. The transformation that has been underway in American politics has also taken place in the politics of education, which, according to Cibulka (2001), has changed in recent decades from one approximating professionally dominated subgovernments to issue networks characterized by more ideational, macropolitical interest groups as well as shifting and unstable coalitions.

As members of issue networks, both government and nongovernment actors are important participants of the policy processes. These two types of actors are not working in vacuum, but are interacting both among themselves and with one another. As Kingdon (1995) notes:

> The line between inside and outside government is exceedingly difficult to draw.... The communication channels between those inside and those outside of government are extraordinarily open, and ideas and information float about through these channels in the whole issue network of involved people. (p. 45)

Laumann and Knoke (1987) concur, "the boundaries between public and private sectors are blurred, and irrelevant, even in noncorporatist societies" (p. 381). They further states that policy actors are embedded in networks of relationships; and that public policies are the product of complex interactions among both government and nongovernment actors, each seeking to influence collectively binding decisions that affect their respective interests. Granovetter (1985) also emphasizes the embedded nature of social systems, asserting that one must conceive of the relational context to understand social actors' attitudes and behaviors. Hence, one needs to acknowledge the importance of relational or structural factors in shaping a distinctive policy domain in order to derive an accurate account of how government and nongovernment actors jointly govern the policy domain.

The Social Network Perspective

Focusing on the interweaving relations through which social actions are organized, the social network perspective provides a useful lens for our investigation of the state reading policy domain. (Galaskiewicz & Wasserman, 1994; Laumann & Knoke, 1987). As both a theoretical perspective and a methodological tool grounded in structural sociology, the social network perspective is ideally suited for examining the relational system in which social actors dwell and for exploring how the nature of relationship structures impacts actor attitudes, behaviors, and well-being. Wasserman and Faust (1994) propose five central principles that distinguish the social network perspective from other research approaches. First, social network perspective focuses on the relationships among social units, which is "the hallmark of a network analysis" (Laumann, 1979, p. 394). Second, actors and their actions are viewed as interdependent rather than independent and autonomous. Third, the relationships among actors are channels for the transmission of either material or nonmaterial resources. Fourth, the network structural environment affects individual behavior by providing opportunities for or imposing constraints on individual actions. Finally, the structure of the network is composed of lasting patterns of relations among actors.

As an emergent mode of inquiry, the social network perspective has attracted growing attention from and proven useful in multiple social and behavioral science disciplines. Although social network analysis has also been applied to educational research for several decades, its application has been very limited and overwhelmingly focused on affective relationships (e.g., Coleman, 1961; Cohen, 1977; Hallinan, 1979; Shrum, Heek, & Hunter, 1988). Policy research in education employing social network analysis have been virtually nonexistent except for a recent dissertation study on national reading policy by McDaniel (2001) and the dissertations of both authors based on the state reading policy study presented in this book (Song, 2003; Young, 2005). Guided by the social network perspective, our study of the state reading policy domain demonstrates how network analytic methods can be fruitfully applied to educational policy research. In the remainder of this chapter and the next chapter, we report some of the insights that we have gathered about the state reading policy domain from the structural perspective as well as their implications for network actors and the overall policy networks.

Relational Patterns of the State Reading Policy Networks

Rooted in a structural understanding of social systems, the social network perspective has developed over the past half century a unique set of methods and measures for exploring the relational aspects of social systems. Unlike traditional social science research that relies on quantified individual attributes as the primary data source, social network analysis uses relational data that describes the relationships between social actors, and uses pairwise relationships as the unit of analysis.

Relational Data and Sociomatrices

The relationship of interest for our study was the collaboration or interaction between pairs of actors regarding state reading policy. All the interview transcripts and archival documents that we had collected were coded in ATLAS for such relationships (Scientific Software Development, 2001), based on which, an *N*-by-*N* asymmetrical data matrix was constructed for each state in UCINET 5.0 (Borgatti, Everett, & Freeman, 1999), a network analysis software program, with *N* being the number of policy actors in the specific state. In the matrix, each actor occupies one row and the corresponding column; and each cell records the relationship between a pair of actors. The value of the cell at the cross-section of the ith row and the jth column, denoted as x_{ij}, for example, indicates whether there was a relationship from actor *i* to actor *j*. If such a relationship existed, the value of the cell would be 1; otherwise, it would be 0. The sociomatrices thus created served as the data sets for network analyses.

Given certain deficiencies in the relational data from North Carolina, the state was dropped from network analyses. We further refined the initial sample by applying the criterion of consequentiality—a basic criterion for delimiting network boundaries, which not only simplifies network analyses, but also makes the analyses more theoretically useful (Knoke & Kuklinski, 1982; Knoke & Laumann, 1982; Laumann & Knoke, 1987). Based on this criterion, 11 interest groups were identified as inconsequential actors and removed from the initial sample.[3] The resulting final sample of 208 actors for network analyses consisted of 46 government agencies, 152 interest groups, and 10 individual policy actors across eight states (see Table 2.1).

Network Visualization: Sociograms

There have been two basic approaches to network analysis: visualization and measurement (Freeman, 2000). Network visualization explores the relationship patterns embedded in social networks through the use of visual images, whereas network measurement refers to the assessment of

Table 2.1.   Number of Policy Actors by Type and State for Social Network Analyses

State	Government Agencies	Interest Groups	Individual Policy Actors	Total
Alabama	5 (5)	13 (21)	0 (0)	18 (26)
California	6 (13)	26 (31)	6 (6)	38 (50)
Connecticut	5 (15)	18 (22)	3 (3)	26 (40)
Indiana	6 (14)	22 (25)	0 (0)	28 (39)
Maine	5 (16)	14 (19)	0 (0)	19 (35)
Michigan	6 (26)	23 (27)	0 (0)	29 (53)
Texas	7 (15)	22 (29)	0 (0)	29 (44)
Utah	6 (14)	14 (18)	1 (1)	21 (33)
Total	46 (118)	152 (192)	10 (10)	208 (320)

Note: Number of interviewees is shown in parentheses.

structural properties of social networks by using algebraic formulations. In the remainder of this chapter, we present the relational patterns of the state reading policy networks revealed by means of network visualization techniques. We will discuss network measurement findings in the chapter to follow.

The function of network visualization, as Brandes, Kenis, Raab, Schneider, and Wagner (1999) contends, goes far beyond illustration. Network visualization enables researchers to explore specific properties of social networks that cannot be easily identified through quantitative analysis of the data. It also facilitates the discovery of structural similarities and differences across different networks. From a practical point of view, graphic presentations of social networks are often a more effective means to communicate research findings to technically less sophisticated audiences (e.g., policymakers) than are numbers. In the field of research on policy networks, at least four types of visualization methods are currently in use: sociograms, multidimensional scaling (MDS) scattergrams, dendrograms, and Venn diagrams, of which sociograms and MDS scattergrams have been the most commonly used ones.

Sociograms, the network visualization tool with the longest history (Moreno, 1932, 1934), are the most intuitive way of presenting the structural configurations of social networks. A sociogram depicts a network with a set of nodes and a set of lines between the nodes in a two-dimensional space, with nodes representing actors and lines representing relationships between actors. Actors with a high degree of centrality—that is, actors who are directly connected with many other actors—are generally placed toward the center of the sociogram. In network analysis, actor centrality is an indicator of policy influence, because the greater number of network ties empowers central actors by giving them direct access to timely information and other types of valuable resources (Knoke, 1990b). The positions of actors relative to one another, therefore, reflect the distribution of policy influence among actors in a given network.[4]

Figure 2.1 presents the sociogram of the Alabama reading policy network created in NetDraw (Borgatti, 2002), a recently-developed network visualization software program. The sociogram shows in a straightforward way not only who interacted with whom, but also the directions of the relationships (see Appendix C for the full names of policy actors in each of the eight states). The large number of crisscrossing lines suggests that this was a well-connected network, with every actor involved in multiple relationships and some involved in particularly dense network ties. Moreover, most of the relationships were reciprocal rather than unilateral as shown by the arrowheads at both ends of most of the lines in the sociogram.

The sociogram also depicts the relative network positions of the Alabama reading policy actors: those well-connected actors, such as the

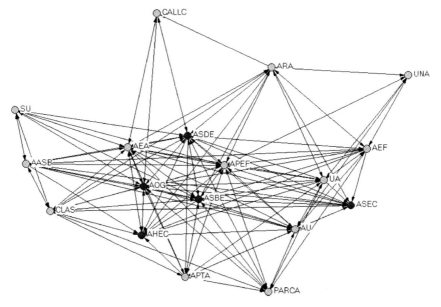

Figure 2.1.   Sociogram of the Alabama reading policy network (N =18).

A+ Education Foundation (APEF) and the Alabama State Board of Education (ASBE), were located in the central region of the space, which vividly demonstrates Freeman's (1979) idea that central actors are "in the thick of things" (p. 219). Sparsely-connected actors, such as the Central Alabama Laubach Literacy Center (CALLC) and the University of North Alabama (UNA), in contrast, were relegated to peripheral positions of the network.

Figure 2.1 further reveals that government actors, represented by dark-colored nodes, generally occupied more central positions than non-government actors. Government actors, however, were not always the most central actors. The APEF, a citizens group, for example, secured the most central spot in the network, exerting strong influence on Alabama's reading policy. The Alabama Senate Education Committee (ASEC), a government agency with formal policymaking authority, on the other hand, only occupied a periphery network position with limited influence over the state's reading policy.

The more central positions of government actors compared with nongovernment actors were also apparent in the other seven state reading policy networks (see Figure 2.2a-g). Another common feature of the state reading policy networks was a high degree of cohesion among the actors. The sociograms show clearly that a fairly large

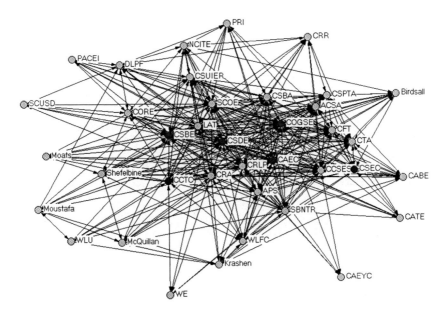

Figure 2.2a.   Sociogram of the California reading policy network (*N* =38).

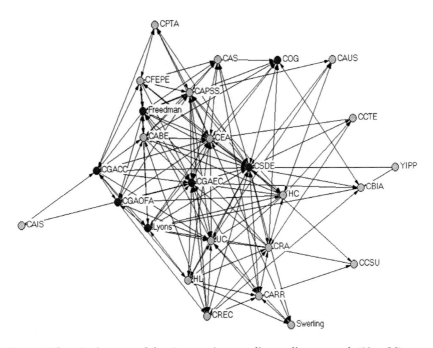

Figure 2.2b.   Sociogram of the Connecticut reading policy network (*N* = 26).

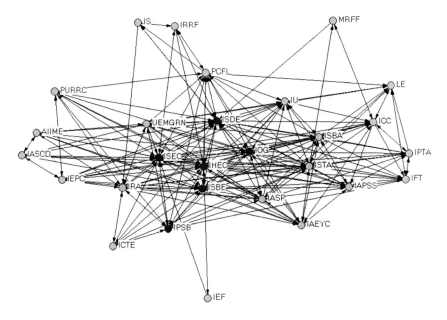

Figure 2.2c. Sociogram of the Indiana reading policy network ($N = 28$).

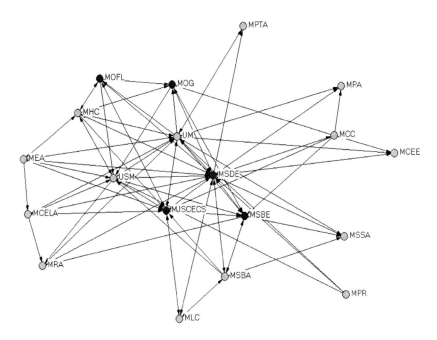

Figure 2.2d. Sociogram of the Maine reading policy network ($N = 19$).

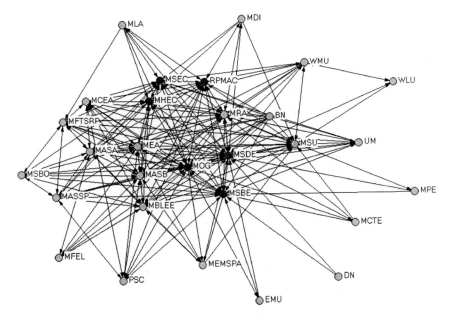

Figure 2.2e.   Sociogram of the Michigan reading policy network ($N = 29$).

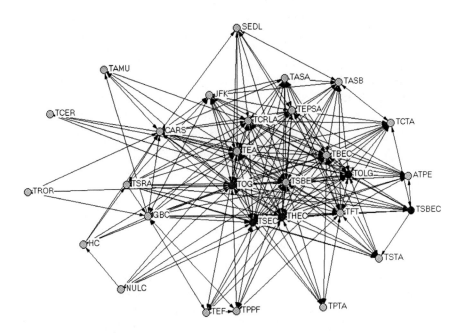

Figure 2.2f.   Sociogram of the Texas reading policy network ($N = 29$).

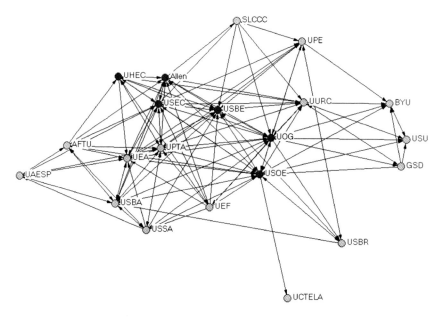

Figure 2.2g.   Sociogram of the Utah reading policy network (*N* = 21).

proportion of potential ties were present in the reading policy networks in all the eight states. An assessment of network density—the ratio of the number of ties present to the number of potential ties in a given network—confirmed that all the eight state reading policy networks were well connected. Table 2.2 presents the network density values based on both directed relationships and undirected relationships for each state. Overall, the state reading policy networks were well connected, with almost half of all the potential ties present across the states. Even in the network with the lowest density (i.e., Maine), about one third of all possible relationships were established.

The high levels of density shown in the Table 2.2 indicate that the state reading policy networks were highly dynamic arenas of policy activities. The large numbers of open communication channels in those networks enabled timely and unobstructed exchange of information, ideas, and resources among actors concerned with state reading policy. It is worth noting that the densities of the state reading policy networks stood in sharp contrast with the density of the national reading policy network. The national reading policy network, according to McDaniel (2001), was fragmented and sparsely connected, with a density of only .08 for the overall network of 134 actors, and a density of .21 for the elite network of 41 actors based on directed relationships. The much higher levels of

Table 2.2. Densities of the State Reading Policy Networks

State	Density Based on Directed Relationships	Density Based on Undirected Relationships
Alabama	.58	.71
California	.43	.51
Texas	.43	.49
Indiana	.43	.49
Utah	.41	.49
Michigan	.39	.46
Connecticut	.35	.40
Maine	.32	.39
Average	.42	.49

density of the state reading policy networks relative to the national network may be attributed to factors such as easier access to one another because of geographic proximity and more interactional opportunities arising from a larger amount of common issues of interest for the state actors than for the national actors.

Network Visualization: Multidimensional Scaling

Sociograms provide an intuitively appealing way to visually represent social networks. They become unwieldy, however, for networks containing large numbers of actors. For large networks, MDS scattergrams serve as a useful alternative, which depict the overall network structure by mapping actors onto a two- or three-dimensional social space based on some measure of proximity (similarities or dissimilarities) between pairs of actors without actually drawing the lines connecting the actors (Kruskal & Wish, 1978; Scott, 2000). One commonly used proximity measure is geodesic distance, which, in network terminology, refers to the shortest path distance, or the smallest number of links, between pairs of actors. In an MDS scattergram based on geodesic distances, actors with a shorter geodesic distance between them are placed closer to each other, whereas actors with a longer geodesic distance are placed further apart. Moreover, actors with higher centralities tend to occupy more central positions in the scattergram than do actors with lower centralities.

Figure 2.3 is an MDS scattergram for the largest network examined in this study, the California reading policy network. Before creating the scattergram, we first converted the undirected binary data matrix for the network into a matrix of geodesic distances, which served as the input to MDS in the UCINET 5.0 program. Although simple in appearance

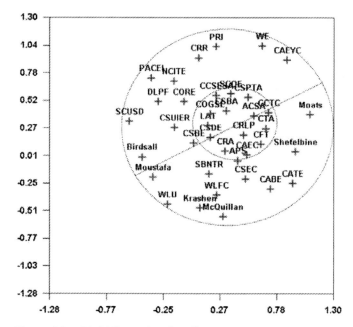

Figure 2.3.   Multidimensional scaling scattergram of the
California reading policy network (N = 38).

without all those crisscrossing lines as in sociograms, the MDS
scattergram shown in Figure 2.3 contains rich information about the
structure of the California reading policy network.

A number of features of the MDS scattergram for the California reading
policy network were particularly noteworthy. First, the 38 actors spread all
over the space, suggesting a differentiation in terms of actor centrality. If
the network had been undifferentiated in actor centrality, then all the
actors would have appeared along a circle at the same distance from the
center of the network. Indeed, the overall network manifested a core/
periphery structure as revealed by the two imaginary concentric circles
imposed on the graph.[5] Fourteen actors constituted a tight core, sur-
rounded by 24 actors loosely scattered in the periphery of the network. It
clearly differed from some national policy domains, which were found to
be of a hollow core structure—with most actors occupying the periphery of
the network but few or none at the center (Heinz et al., 1993).

Such a core/periphery structure implies a differentiation in network
involvement among the 38 California reading policy actors. Occupying
central positions in the network, core actors were generally engaged in
extensive networking activities, had ready access to alternative resources,

and possessed control over the communication between many other actors. Such positional benefits made the core actors highly prominent within the network; the core was where policy influence concentrated. Peripheral actors, on the other hand, had lower levels of network involvement, and were less visible players in the state reading policy arena.

A second feature of the California network as depicted by the MDS scattergram was that both the core and the peripheral regions of the network contained a mix of government and nongovernment actors. The core of the network, for instance, included not only government agencies (e.g., California State Department of Education (CSDE), and California Office of the Governor/Secretary for Education (COGSE)), but also interest groups (e.g. California Teachers Association (CTA) and California Reading Association (CRA)). Similarly, the periphery of the network was also populated by both government agencies (e.g., California State Board of Education (CSBE) and California Senate Education Committee (CSEC)) and nongovernment actors (e.g., Consortium of Reading Excellence (CORE) and Individual Policy Actor–Louisa Moats (Moats)). This mix of government and nongovernment actors throughout the network indicates that policymakers were not necessarily the most central actors; interest groups could also be central players highly influential in the policy domain. The structure of the California reading policy network suggests that both government and nongovernment actors were important participants in the policy processes.

Although a mix of government and nongovernment actors was found at both the center and the periphery of the California network, such a mix was by no means thorough or random. In fact, a differentiation in network positions can be detected between government actors and nongovernment actors. As shown in Figure 2.3, the six government actors were located close to one another, with four within the core (i.e., California Assembly Education Committee (CAEC), California Commission on Teacher Credentialing (CCTC), California Office of the Governor/ Secretary for Education (COGSE), and CSDE) and the other two near the core (i.e., CSBE and CSEC). Nongovernment actors, on the other hand, spread over the whole policy sphere.

Within nongovernment actors, an important positional differentiation existed as well. As revealed by the imaginary line drawn through the center of the network, all the single-issue nongovernment actors—that is, actors focusing specifically on reading and literacy—except the California Reading Roundtable (CRR) were located in the region below the line. Those actors included five of the six single-issue groups (i.e., California Association of Bilingual Educators (CABE), California Association of Teachers of English (CATE), California Reading Association (CRA), California Reading and Literature Project (CRLP), and Whole Language

Umbrella (WLU)), and all the five reading academics (i.e., Krashen, McQuillan, Moats, Moustafa, and Shefelbine). The only exception, the California Reads Roundtable (CRR), differed from the other single-issue groups in that its membership consisted of organizations instead of individuals, which might account for its remote position from the other single-issue groups. The majority (16 out of 21) of the general nongovernment actors—that is, actors dealing more broadly with educational issues, in contrast, were located in the half sphere above the line.

In light of the spatial arrangement of the actors in the California reading policy network, two inferences could be drawn about the interactions among the actors. First, given that the distance between a pair of actors in an MDS scattergram represents the shortest path distance between them, proximity in the scattergram implies fewer intermediaries and more direct contact. Hence the aforementioned positional differentiations indicate that the three types of actors—government actors, single-issue nongovernment actors, and general nongovernment—were more likely to interact directly with actors of a similar type than with actors of a different type.

The second inference was drawn based on "the principle of integrative centrality" (Laumann & Pappi, 1973, p. 219). The principle states that actors playing key integrative or coordinating roles in a given structure will tend to be located in the central region of the structure, which will, on average, minimize their distances from, or access to, other actors in the space. According to this principle, the core actors in the California reading policy network, mostly government actors, played important coordinating or bridging roles for actors in the periphery. The bridging role of the core actors also implies a highly diversified array of policy contacts for those actors: they were not only interacting with actors similar to themselves, but also with actors of different types, which contributed to the visibility and prominence of the core actors within the California reading policy network.

Figures 2.4a-g presents the MDS scattergrams of the other seven state reading policy networks.[6] A comparison of the eight MDS scattergrams reveals very similar overall network structures across the eight states: all the networks could be delineated into a core and a periphery, with half of the networks (i.e., Alabama, Connecticut, Indiana, and Utah networks) also containing one or two outliers beyond the periphery. The differentiation in coreness or peripherality of the reading policy actors reflects the differentiation in network involvement of those actors. In general, core actors were active participants of the policy processes, who were involved in extensive relationships with other actors, assumed important integrative and coordinating roles, and were highly visible and prominent within the policy arena. Peripheral actors, on the other hand,

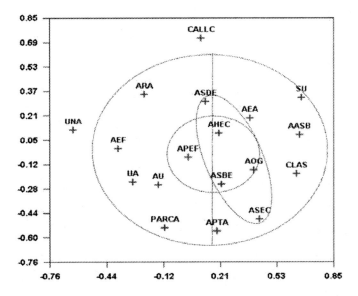

Figure 2.4a.   MDS scattergram of the Alabama reading policy network *(N = 18).*

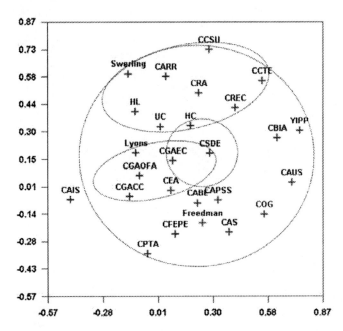

Figure 2.4b.   MDS scattergram of the Connecticut reading policy network *(N = 26).*

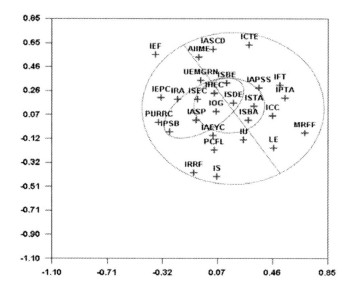

Figure 2.4c.   MDS scattergram of the Indiana reading policy network (*N* = 28).

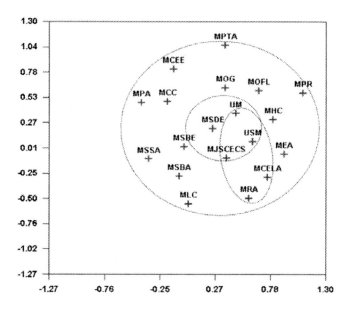

Figure 2.4d.   MDS scattergram of the Maine reading policy network (*N* = 19).

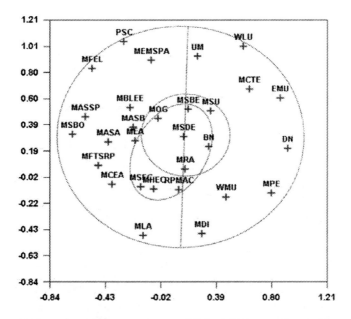

Figure 2.4e.   MDS scattergram of the Michigan reading policy network (*N* = 29).

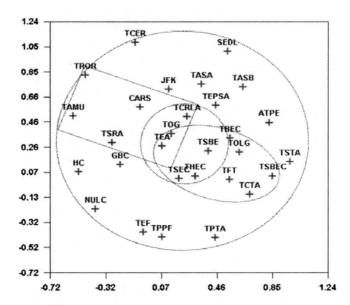

Figure 2.4f.   MDS scattergram of the Texas reading policy network (*N* = 29).

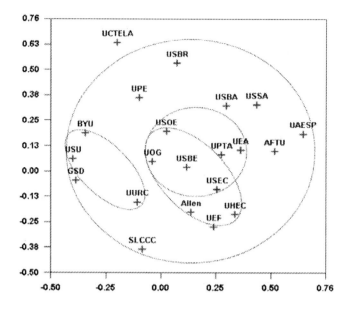

Figure 2.3g.   MDS scattergram of the Utah reading policy network ($N = 21$).

had limited network involvement, often depended on core actors for communication with others, and were less visible policy players.

The MDS scattergrams further reveal that in all the eight states, both the core and the periphery of the network consisted of a mix of government and nongovernment actors. It suggests that although overall government actors were significantly more central than nongovernment actors (Song & Miskel, 2005), certain nongovernment actors (e.g., A+ Education Foundation (APEF) and LA Times (LAT)) could be highly central and influential as well. Like government actors, nongovernment actors are also integral members of the policy networks; actors both within and without the government have been collectively shaping reading policy in the states.

In addition to the core/periphery structure, another commonality among the state reading policy networks was the positional differentiation between different types of actors. As the MDS scattergrams show, in all the eight states, government actors tended to concentrate in particular regions of the reading policy networks, so did single-issue nongovernment actors (see Table 2.3). Such positional differentiations imply that government actors tended to interact directly with other government actors, and single-issue nongovernment actors likewise tended to interact directly with other single-issue nongovernment actors. In other words, there was a higher level of cohesion within both types of actors than between actors of different types.

The interactional pattern, though, was not as consistent for general nongovernment actors. In California, Connecticut, Indiana, and Michigan, general nongovernment actors tended to be in direct contact with other general nongovernment actors, as reflected in the positional concentration of those actors. In Alabama, Maine, Texas, and Utah, however, general nongovernment actors scattered over the entire network space without concentrating in any particular regions, which suggests that general nongovernment actors in these four states were only loosely connected at best, without displaying any particular preference for the types of policy contacts. An alternative explanation is that the number of general nongovernment actors in some of the networks might be too small to reveal any appreciable interactional pattern. In support, we found that networks with positional concentrations of general nongovernment actors tended to be networks with a relatively large number of such actors (see Table 2.3). The average number of general nongovernment actors was 24.5 in networks with positional concentration of those actors, whereas the number was only 16 for networks with scattered general nongovernment actors.

The structural properties and relational patterns of the state reading policy networks that we have examined in this chapter have important implications for both network participants and the overall networks. One important implication pertains to the influence distribution among actors within the policy networks, which is the topic that we will turn to in the chapter to follow.

Table 2.3. Positional Concentration of Different Types of Actors in the State Reading Policy Networks

State	Government Actors	Single-Issue Nongovernment Actors	General Nongovernment Actors	Number of General Nongovernment Actors
Alabama	Concentrated	Concentrated	Scattered	13
California	Concentrated	Concentrated	Concentrated	32
Connecticut	Concentrated	Concentrated	Concentrated	21
Indiana	Concentrated	Concentrated	Concentrated	22
Maine	Concentrated	Concentrated	Scattered	14
Michigan	Concentrated	Concentrated	Concentrated	23
Texas	Concentrated	Concentrated	Scattered	22
Utah	Concentrated	Concentrated	Scattered	15

NOTES

1. Following Laumann and Knoke (1987), we defined policy actors as organizations rather than natural persons in a given policy domain. Specifically, for the purpose of this study, policy actors refer to government agencies, interest groups, and individuals not representing any organizations or groups that had a substantive interest in shaping state reading policy. Individual policy actors could be either government or nongovernment actors.

2. Those response rates were particularly high compared with those of previous studies on state interest groups (Gray & Lowery, 1998; Nownes & Freeman, 1998).

3. To identify inconsequential actors, we adopted a decision rule, which defines an organization as inconsequential if the following two conditions are both met: (1) At least one interviewee from the organization perceived the organization as having little to do with shaping reading policy in the state; (2) At least one interviewee from another organization perceived the organization as playing only a peripheral role at best in shaping reading policy in the state, or, nobody from other organizations ever mentioned the organization as being a player in the state reading policy domain during the interviews.

4. The concept of centrality and its relationship with policy influence will be discussed more fully in the next chapter.

5. We also formally assessed the structure of the state reading policy networks by means of the core/periphery function in UCINET 5.0, which indicated that all the eight state reading policy networks could be split into a core and a periphery, with a model fit ranging between .62 and .95. The results were robust and did not depend on the direction of the relationships.

6. The circles, ellipses, and lines in the MDS scattergrams were added to the graphs in order to make the positional differentiations of the actors more easily discernable to the readers.

CHAPTER 3

POLICY ACTOR INFLUENCE ON STATE READING POLICY

As Mawhinney (2001) notes, underlying policymaking and politics are two fundamental issues: who wields power and influence and whose views are represented in a democracy. It can be expected that influential policy actors are more likely to see their values, beliefs, and preferred mechanisms and approaches receiving serious attention than less influential actors (Marshall, Mitchell, & Wirt, 1986). The importance of a given system's influence structure also lies in that it provides the environing and orienting framework within which individual actors organize their own strategic efforts to affect one another's actions (Laumann & Knoke, 1987). Laumann and Knoke further observe that influence distribution in a social system is of central significance for conflict resolution and collective decision making. Policy actor influence, therefore, was an important aspect of our investigation of the state reading policy systems.

INFLUENCE FROM THE SOCIAL NETWORK PERSPECTIVE

Traditional organizational research on power and influence has followed two major strands: the sources and bases of power and influence (e.g., Etzioni, 1964; French & Raven, 1959; Laumann & Knoke, 1987; Molm, 1990; Rosenthal, 1998), and influence means and tactics (e.g., Berry,

Reading: Policy, Politics, and Processes, pp. 43–69
Copyright © 2008 by Information Age Publishing
All rights of reproduction in any form reserved.

1977; Heinz, Laumann, Nelson, & Salisbury, 1993; Kollman, 1998; Schlozman & Tierney, 1986; Walker, 1991). Both strands essentially assume an atomistic point of view, focusing primarily on the characteristics and behaviors of individual actors while ignoring the relational context in which the actors reside. Granovetter (1985) argues, however, social actors are embedded in relational systems, and one must conceive of the relational context to understand their attitudes and behaviors. Pfeffer (1981) more explicitly asserts that power is first and foremost a structural phenomenon.

Indeed, as Browne (1998) aptly puts it, "Key people make things happen in politics ... and they don't do it alone" (p. 238). Embedded in issue networks, the potential power and influence of policy actors are contingent on how they link to and interact with each other and how they connect to and intersect with policy elites, political parties, the mass media, and the broad public (Malen, 2001). Therefore, knowledge of the alignments and allegiance, linkages and interactions among policy actors becomes critical in understanding how power is distributed among policy actors as well as its implications for policymaking processes and policy outcomes. Emphasizing the relational aspects of social systems, the social network perspective provides a useful lens to examine social phenomena and offers a structural understanding about power and influence, as embodied in the notions of actor centrality and prestige.

Actor Centrality

As briefly mentioned in the previous chapter, from the network perspective, a central actor is one involved in many relationships (Freeman, 1979; Wasserman & Faust, 1994). The most commonly used measure of centrality, degree centrality, is defined as the number of direct ties that an actor has with other actors in a given network.[1] Knoke (1990b) claims that network centrality is synonymous with influence, for the greater number of network ties empowers central actors by giving them access to and control over valuable information on conditions, opportunities, and constraints. Similarly, Rowley (1997) defines centrality as power obtained through network structure, and asserts that organizations occupying peripheral network positions are "at a power disadvantage" because they do not have easy access to information flows (p. 903). In support, numerous empirical studies have demonstrated a strong association between centrality and influence (Boje & Whetten, 1981; Brass, 1984, 1985; Burkhardt & Brass, 1990; Galaskiewicz, 1979; Krackhardt, 1990; Laumann & Pappi, 1976; Marsden & Laumann, 1977).

Actor Prestige

The notion of actor prestige, which has been variously called *status, rank, deference, popularity,* and even *power,* is intended to capture the importance of network actors from a different angle than actor centrality. While actor centrality focuses only on the volume of relationships between actors, actor prestige takes into account the direction of the relationships. Degree prestige, or *indegree* in network terminology, is the simplest and most commonly used actor prestige index, which measures the relationships received rather than initiated by a focal actor. It is based on the assumption that relations are often asymmetric and that powerful and prestigious actors tend to be the objects rather than the sources of communication (Knoke & Burt, 1983). The asymmetry of relations reflects authority and deference produced by inequalities in control over valued resources, and reflects the distinction between leaders and followers. It is also consistent with Porter, Allen, and Angle's (1981) argument that most political activities are directed upward. Actor prestige thus captures power and influence derived from formal hierarchical positions, and has been shown to be associated with power and influence (Brass & Burkhardt, 1993; Burkhardt & Brass, 1990; Knoke & Burt, 1983).

CENTRALITY, PRESTIGE, AND PERCEIVED INFLUENCE OF READING POLICY ACTORS IN TEXAS

Employing network measures of centrality and prestige, we assessed policy actors' influence on state reading policy in eight states. To triangulate the results from network analyses, we also assessed policy actors' influence using the traditional reputational approach. Specifically, we asked each respondent during the interview to name the most influential actors on state reading policy, and measured perceived influence, or influence reputation, of each actor as the number of nominations the actor received from other actors within the state. Given space limitation, we will only discuss in detail in this section our findings on the centrality, prestige, and perceived influence of reading policy actors in one state, Texas, which was chosen in light of the strong publicity of reading policy development in this state and its impact on federal reading legislation, Reading First in particular (Miskel & Athan, 2001; Miskel & Song, 2004). In the section to follow, we will summarize our findings about policy actor influence on state reading policy across the eight states that we investigated.

Table 3.1 lists the values of degree centrality, degree prestige, and perceived influence of actors in the Texas reading policy network.[2] Given

Table 3.1.   Values and Correlations of Centrality, Prestige, and Perceived Influence of Actors in the Texas Reading Policy Network (*N* = 29)

Policy Actor	Centrality (Rank)	Prestige (Rank)	Perceived Influence (Rank)
TX Office of the Governor (TOG)	.96 (1)	.75 (4)	.75 (1)
TX Education Agency (TEA)	.89 (2)	.89 (1)	.57 (2)
TX State Board of Education (TSBE)	.86 (3)	.82 (2)	.07 (10)
TX House Education Committee (THEC)	.82 (4)	.79 (3)	.39 (5)
TX Senate Education Committee (TSEC)	.79 (5)	.71 (5)	.39 (5)
TX Business and Education Coalition (TBEC)	.68 (6)	.64 (6)	.46 (3)
Center for Academic & Reading Skills at University of TX-Houston (CARS)	.68 (6)	.64 (6)	.36 (7)
TX Center for Reading & Language Arts at University of TX-Austin (TCRLA)	.68 (6)	.64 (6)	.25 (8)
TX Office of the Lieutenant Governor (TOLG)	.64 (9)	.57 (9)	.07 (10)
TX Federation of Teachers (TFT)	.64 (9)	.54 (10)	.00 (15)
TX Elementary Principals and Supervisors Association (TEPSA)	.61 (11)	.50 (11)	.11 (9)
Governor's Business Council (GBC)	.57 (12)	.46 (13)	.46 (3)
Just For Kids (JFK)	.50 (13)	.50 (11)	.00 (15)
TX Association of School Boards (TASB)	.46 (14)	.43 (14)	.04 (14)
TX State Reading Association (TSRA)	.46 (14)	.43 (14)	.07 (10)
TX Association of School Administrators (TASA)	.46 (14)	.39 (17)	.07 (10)
TX Classroom Teachers Association (TCTA)	.43 (17)	.43 (14)	.00 (15)
Association of TX Professional Educators (ATPE)	.43 (17)	.39 (17)	.00 (15)
TX State Board for Educator Certification (TSBEC)	.43 (17)	.25 (20)	.00 (15)
TX State Teachers Association (TSTA)	.39 (20)	.36 (19)	.00 (15)
SW Education Development Laboratories (SEDL)	.29 (21)	.18 (23)	.00 (15)
TX Public Policy Foundation (TPPF)	.25 (22)	.25 (20)	.00 (15)
TX Parent Teacher Association (TPTA)	.25 (22)	.21 (22)	.00 (15)
TX Eagle Forum (TEF)	.25 (22)	.18 (23)	.00 (15)
Houston Chronicle (HC)	.21 (25)	.11 (26)	.00 (15)
National Urban Literacy Coalition– Houston READ Commission (NULC)	.21 (25)	.00 (29)	.00 (15)
TX A & M University (TAMU)	.18 (27)	.18 (23)	.00 (15)
TX Center for Education Research (TCER)	.14 (28)	.07 (27)	.00 (15)
TX Reach Out and Read (TROR)	.11 (29)	.07 (27)	.00 (15)

Spearman Rho Correlations

	Centrality	Prestige	Perceived Influence
Centrality	1.00		
Prestige	.98**	1.00	
Perceived Influence	.84**	.80**	1.00

Note: Centrality, prestige, and perceived influence are all standardized indices.
** $p < .01$ (2-tailed)

that all the three measures depend on network size, they were standardized by being divided by their maximum value $N - 1$, with N being network size, which enables comparisons across networks of different sizes. The standardized centrality and prestige indices range from zero to one, indicating the proportion of other actors who were directly connected with or who initiated a contact with the focal actor respectively. Also ranging from zero to one, the standardized perceived influence index represents the proportion of other actors in the network who nominated the focal actor as being most influential on state reading policy.

Table 3.1 shows that both network measures of policy actor influence and perceived influence varied widely. Standardized degree centrality values, for instance, ranged from .11 at the lowest to .96 at the highest. With a standardized degree centrality of .96, Texas Office Of The Governor (TOG) was directly connected to all but one (96%) of the other 28 actors in the Texas reading policy network, occupying the most central position in the network. In contrast, Texas Reach Out and Read (TROR), a single-issue interest group, had direct contact with only 3 (11%) of the other 28 actors, and was positioned at the bottom of the centrality hierarchy.

A wide range of values was also evident in the actor prestige results for the Texas reading policy network. As shown in Table 3.1, standardized degree prestige for Texas reading policy actors varied from zero to .89. Being the target of contact for 25 of the other 28 actors, the Texas Education Agency (TEA) was the most prestigious actor within the network. Again, the least prestigious actor turned out to be a single-issue interest group, the National Urban Literacy Coalition—Houston READ Commission (NULC), which received no contact at all from the others regarding the state's reading policy.

Like the network measures of influence, the reputational measure of influence also varied substantially. About half (15 out of 29) of the actors were not perceived as being influential by any other actors in the Texas reading policy network. Among those who were nominated as being most influential, the TOG clearly sat atop, with nominations from 75% of the other 28 actors in the state. The three alternative measures of influence were highly correlated, with rank correlations ranging between .80 and .98 ($p < .01$).

The wide range of the three influence indicators suggests that the Texas reading policy network was highly differentiated in terms of actor influence. A particular noticeable manifestation of such differentiation is that government actors generally ranked higher than nongovernment actors based on all the three influence indicators. The top five most influential actors in the network, for example, were all government agencies based on both the centrality and the prestige measures; and all the government actors except the Texas State Board for Educator Certification were among the top 10 most influential actors in the Texas reading policy network based on all the three measures of policy influence. It appeared that policy influence was not equally distributed between government and nongovernment actors.

Comparisons of means reveal that government actors were indeed more central and prestigious, and had a higher level of perceived influence than nongovernment actors in the Texas reading policy network (see Table 3.2). Specifically, each government actor on average was directly connected to about 22 (77%) of the other 28 actors, whereas each nongovernment actor was only in direct contact with about 11 (40%) other actors in the Texas network. Overall, government actors also occupied more prestigious network positions than nongovernment actors, and were almost twice as likely to be contacted by others than were nongovernment actors (68% vs. 35%). Moreover, government actors in the Texas network were perceived as being more influential than nongovernment actors. On average, each government actor was nominated as being most influential by nine (32%) other actors, whereas each nongovernment actor only received about two (8%) influence nominations. Independent-samples t tests indicate that the differences between government and nongovernment actors were statistically significant for both the centrality ($p < .001$) and the prestige ($p < .01$) measures, and marginally significant for perceived influence ($p < .10$). The lack of significance for the perceived influence measure might be attributed to the small sample size, particularly the small number of government actors ($N = 7$) in the Texas sample. Related to small sample size, the assumption of homogeneity of variance across groups did not

Table 3.2.   Results of Independent-Samples _t_ Tests Comparing Government and Nongovernment Actors on Centrality, Prestige, and Perceived Influence in the Texas Reading Policy Network (_N_ = 29)

	Mean (Standard Deviation)			
	Government Actors (N = 7)	Nongovernment Actors (N = 22)	t	p - value
Centrality	.77 (.18)	.40 (.19)	4.54	.000***
Prestige	.68 (.22)	.35 (.20)	3.85	.001**
Perceived influence	.32 (.28)	.08 (.15)	2.22	.070~

Note: Centrality, prestige, and perceived influence are all standardized indices.
~ $p < .10$, ** $p < .01$, *** $p < .001$ (2-tailed).

hold for the *t* test on perceived influence, which further reduced the statistical power of the test.

Regarding the level of influence of various actors in the Texas reading policy network, the comments from some of our respondents are particularly illuminating. In explaining the strong influence of the TOG, for example, a business group representative observed that the office served as a "bully pulpit" and a vehicle for the governor to get funding and advocate his policy ideas. Hence, issues that the governor was willing to promote were likely to become salient issues that were given serious consideration by the policy community.

Governor Bush's interest in and influence on reading policy could also be partly traced to his family background. Close members of the governor's family had been and still are involved in literacy issues. His mother, former first lady Barbara Bush, had made literacy a personal crusade during the time her husband was president and continued her work though the Barbara Bush Foundation for Family Literacy. The governor's wife, then first lady of Texas, Laura Bush, had been a librarian and schoolteacher with a strong interest in reading. As one former member of the governor's administration said, "[Governor Bush] was living [reading] every day, and obviously his family has had a long-term interest in literacy and reading. It is just part of his gene pool, I guess." Given such a family history, the governor was almost destined to become an important player in reading policy.

A policy researcher, however, offered a less sanguine view of the reasons behind Bush's active involvement in reading policy: "I think that Bush thought that, and still thinks, as does just about every politician, that education is a good political issue. That was the niche that he carved out." No matter what were the reasons behind, there was little disagreement about the governor's heavy influence on Texas' reading policy. A former TEA official thus commented: "There wasn't the push for literacy until George Bush was in office." An interest group representative concurred:

> If I could name four individuals who had the most to do with [Texas' reading policy], it would start with Governor Bush and Mike Moses [former commissioner of education], and then closely followed by Margaret LaMontagne and Robin Gilchrist as their chief staff people involved in this area.

Other than the TOG, the TEA was also seen as highly influential as suggested by the respondent quoted above. An officer of an education association thus explained the power of the TEA: "There is no doubt that the three commissioners … have a very … powerful role in this state because they're ceded a lot of direct authority from the legislature." Many respondents particularly acknowledged Mike Moses' impact on Texas' reading policy, as shown by the following statement from a member of a school administrator's association:

> [Mike Moses] really helped to frame that position for the governor and pro-vided the leadership to gain support [for the Texas Reading Initiative] in the education community ... Mike Moses was really the one that was able to bring people together around the initiative and gain broad, statewide sup-port. Now the governor and the legislators may have been more critical in terms of gaining legislative support for the initiative, but I'd have to give credit to Mike for building that support among educators statewide.

Compared with government actors, nongovernment actors were clearly at a power disadvantage where reading policy was concerned. They had less network involvement and lower centrality and prestige, and received much fewer influence nominations from other actors (see Table 3.1). A policymaker's education advisor attributed the lack of influence of most Texas education associations to their lack of interest in education policy per se:

> They're employee groups. I mean, they are here to lobby legislature about health insurance, retirement benefits and things that relate to number one. And not really interested in educational policy for kids, best I can tell.... Their main reason for existence is employee benefits.

A staffer for a state legislator similarly remarked, "The school groups, the teachers' groups, and the school boards ... they focus so much on their own issues. I think they lose some credibility when it comes to education policy."

With regard to the lack of influence of teacher organizations, some of our respondents believed that it also had to do with the fact that the state of Texas has four teacher organizations instead of two as most other states do. An interest group representative commented, "I do not believe that our legislators are controlled in any way by the teacher unions. We have too many here in Texas (laughs) ... they really don't [have much influence]." A state senator likewise observed, "The prob-lem is there are four [teacher organizations]. When they ever do get together on an issue, they're unbeatable. But they do have a tendency to stratify sometimes."

Although nongovernment actors as a whole were not as influential as government actors on reading policy in Texas, certain nongovernment actors possessed considerable influence. Texas Business and Education Coalition (TBEC), for example, ranked just below the TOG and TEA in terms of perceived influence and ranked sixth in terms of centrality and prestige among the 28 actors in the Texas reading policy network. The other business group in the Texas network, the Governor's Business Council (GBC), tied with TBEC for the third place in perceived influence; although it ranked somewhat lower in terms of centrality and prestige.

Our study participants repeatedly mentioned the strong impact that business groups had exerted on Texas' reading policy during the interviews. For instance, when asked whether the two business groups were influential on state reading policy, a senator claimed, "Extremely! We couldn't have had an accountability system without them.... I really think probably anywhere, any state, you need the business community's support to get anything done." A representative of a business group also stated with pride:

> I think we're particularly influential ... because we represent the business and education communities. I think we've had a real influence on education policy in the state because of that ongoing dialogue. And then the relationships we've developed for the policymakers.... They know that our recommendations are thoughtful, researched, and constructive, and represent a consensus between business and education. They can write legislation knowing they've got support in both camps.

The executive director of a research organization opined that the influence of business groups also came from their close association with the governor's reading initiative. He stated:

> The groups that are the most influential ... have been those that have attached themselves around the governor's reading initiative. And it is primarily the governor, the Governor's Business Council, and TBEC ... [Those] would, in my opinion, be the ones that have had the major impact, because so many of the other people that you listed here are under those three.

PATTERNS OF POLICY ACTOR INFLUENCE ON READING POLICY ACROSS STATES

In the previous section, we presented our findings about the influence of various actors in the Texas reading policy network based on both network and reputational measures. In this section, we examine the findings across the nine states investigated in this study, focusing on both the similarities and differences in policy actor influence among the states. We begin the section with an explication of the general patterns of influence on reading policy across the states, and then discuss the influence of three types of actors—government actors, nongovernment actors, and policy entrepreneurs—respectively.

General Patterns Across States

An examination of the findings about reading policy actors' influence in the nine states reveals that like the national reading policy domain (Song & Miskel, 2002; Song, Miskel, Young, & McDaniel, 2000), the state reading policy domain was also heterogeneous in terms of actor influence. In all the nine states, the three influence indicators—centrality, prestige, and perceived influence—varied widely among the actors.[3] Take actor centrality for example, the highest standardized degree centrality values ranged from 89% to 100%, whereas the lowest standardized degree centrality values ranged from 5% to 29% across the eight states. Even in Alabama, the state with the smallest variation in actor centrality, the disparity was still substantial: the most central actors (Alabama House Education Committee and A+ Education Foundation) had direct access to 94% of the other actors in the network, whereas the least central actors (Central Alabama Laubach Literacy Center and University of North Alabama) had direct assess to only 29% of the other actors in the network. Such large disparities were found for all the three influence indicators across the nine states, which suggests that the state reading policy networks were not homogeneous, but highly differentiated in terms of actor influence.

Our analyses also reveal that the three indicators of policy actor influence were highly correlated, with rank correlation (i.e., Spearman's Rho correlation) ranged from .46 to .98 (see Table 3.3). The correlations between centrality and prestige were particularly high, which is consistent with findings from prior research (Knoke & Burt, 1983) and attests to the validity of these alternative measures of policy influence. Nevertheless, those correlations were less than perfect, for after all, centrality, prestige, and perceived influence are intended to capture different aspects of the multifaceted construct of influence. It is therefore advisable to use multiple indicators to assess policy influence so that a richer understanding about the relative influence of actors in a specific policy domain could be obtained.

Another recurrent finding about policy actors' influence on state reading policy was that government actors were more influential than nongovernment actors. Table 3.4 summarizes the results of independent-samples *t* tests comparing government and nongovernment actors on the three influence indicators in the nine states. The table shows a highly consistent picture. Despite the relatively small sample sizes, government actors were significantly more influential than nongovernment actors based on both centrality and prestige in all the eight states where network data were available. The difference in perceived influence between government and nongovernment actors was also significant in six of the

Table 3.3. Rank Correlations Between Centrality, Prestige, and Perceived Influence of Reading Policy Actors in Eight States

	Rank Correlation (Spearman's Rho)		
State	Centrality–Prestige	Centrality–Perceived Influence	Prestige–Perceived Influence
Alabama	.85**	.65**	.46~
California	.93**	.66**	.73**
Connecticut	.93**	.67**	.67**
Indiana	.93**	.67**	.62**
Maine	.91**	.64**	.77**
Michigan	.93**	.91**	.88**
Texas	.98**	.84**	.80**
Utah	.92**	.82**	.71**

Note: ~ $p < .01$; ** $p < .01$.

Table 3.4. Results of Independent-Samples *t* Tests Comparing the Centrality, Prestige, and Perceived Influence of Government and Nongovernment Actors on State Reading Policy

State	Centrality	Prestige	Perceived Influence	Number of Policy Actors
Alabama	*	**	*	18
California	***	**	*	38
Connecticut	*	**	~	26
Indiana	***	***	NS	28
Maine	*	*	**	19
Michigan	**	***	**	29
North Carolina	NA	NA	*	24
Texas	***	**	~	29
Utah	*	*	**	21

Note: NA: not available, NS: not significant; ~ $p < .10$; * $p < .05$; ** $p < .01$; *** $p < .001$.

nine states, marginally significant in two states, and not significant only in Connecticut. These results are consistent with the findings from Laumann and Knoke's (1987) study of the national energy and health domains, Marshall, Mitchell, and Wirt's (1989) study of the state education policy domain, and Mazzoni's (1993) longitudinal study of education policymaking in Minnesota, among others.

With regard to the relatively weaker influence of nongovernment actors on state reading policy, our study participants offered insightful observations. A member of an education association in Connecticut, for example, made the following comment regarding interest groups' lack of influence on reading policy and the importance of communication and involvement for acquiring policy influence:

> I think the educational organizations ... they have to speak up. I think we did only because we kept communicating and other organizations did not.... These people, they were very quiet ... their voice gets lost, and they should be influential, I guess, is what I'm saying, and they weren't.

A university professor in Texas likewise noted the lack of involvement from the educational organizations, and attributed it to their unwillingness to take any risks that might be incurred by adopting a particular stance on reading policy:

> What's true about most of these [educational] organizations, including the university, is that they've been ... remarkably acquiescent and silent on most of the initiatives related to reading. And most often they are covering their own butt.... So there was a lot of that kind of silencing going on, not just in universities, but in all these organizations. There's constant trade-offs going on.... "We're looking for teacher raises next year." "We're looking for these benefits." ... Well, get in line, folks! ... You find organizations here where the memberships are clearly opposed to what's going on and yet there is acquiescence, if not silence, if not even endorsement by these groups of what's going on because of the trade-offs that are being involved.

Further, interest groups' lack of influence was also believed to result from their focus on the implementation rather than the development of reading policy, as indicated by the following observation from a teacher organization representative in California:

> Many of [the interest groups] are more in terms of implementation level. They take whatever the state does and then translates it for teachers.... The Literature Projects do that. I don't think they really go up there and fight ... or influence policy that way. I mean I don't know for sure that they in the networks lobby.... Just like Reading Recovery. I don't know that they go up there and lobby.

The Influence of Government Actors

Having discussed the general patterns of actor influence across the states, we now turn to a detailed examination of policy actor influence within and without the government respectively. Table 3.5 lists government actors' ranks among all actors on centrality, prestige, and perceived influence in each of the nine state reading policy networks in the order of

Table 3.5.   Government Actors' Ranks in the State Reading Policy Networks

Alabama	Centrality	Prestige	Perceived Influence	Michigan	Centrality	Prestige	Perceived Influence
AHEC	1	6	7	MSDE	1	1	3
AOG	3	1	4	MIOG	2	2	1
ASDE	3	4	1	MSBE	3	3	8
ASBE	3	6	3	MSEC	7	6	4
ASEC	9	6	7	RPMAC	9	6	12
				MHEC	9	10	7
California				*North Carolina*			
CSDE	1	1	3	NSBE	NA	NA	1
CSBE	2	1	1	NSDPI	NA	NA	2
COGSE	6	6	2	NGA	NA	NA	5
CAEC	6	5	4	NOG	NA	NA	7
CCTC	10	13	15	NPTSC	NA	NA	14
CSEC	14	11	6				
Connecticut				*Texas*			
CSDE	1	1	1	TOG	1	4	1
CGAEC	2	2	2	TEA	2	1	2
Lyons	5	6	9	TSBE	3	2	10
CGACC	8	7	3	THEC	4	3	5
CGAOFA	12	9	19	TSEC	5	5	5
Freeman	8	10	7	TOLG	9	9	10
COG	18	14	5	TSBEC	17	20	5
Indiana				*Utah*			
IHEC	1	1	5	USDE	1	1	1
ISDE	1	1	1	UOG	2	2	3
ISEC	3	3	13	USEC	3	4	4
ISBE	4	5	13	USBE	3	4	4
IOG	4	4	2	Allen	7	7	12
IPSB	16	12	13	UHEC	10	10	2
				USBR	18	17	10
Maine							
MSDE	1	1	1				
MJSCECS	4	3	2				
MSBE	5	5	8				
MEOG	6	6	4				
MOFL	8	7	4				

descending centrality. The most noticeable feature of the table is the prominence of state departments of education. In eight of the nine states—with the exception of Alabama—the state department of education ranked among the top three in terms of influence on state reading policy based on both network and reputational measures. In four states (Connecticut, Indiana, Maine, and Utah), the state department of education ranked highest on all the three influence indicators.

These results seem somewhat different from those obtained by Marshall et al. (1989) over a decade ago. Marshall and her colleagues found that in all the six states that they investigated, state legislatures were perceived as being the "insiders" (i.e., the most influential) in terms of influence on state education policy, and state departments of education were seen as being in the "near circle" of the influence sphere, next to the insiders. Our study, however, suggests that overall state departments of education were more influential than state legislatures on reading policy, with the former perceived as being more influential than the latter across the nine states in our study (see Table 3.5). Such a difference might be attributed to the increasing power of state departments of education during the past decade (Lewis & Maruna, 1999; Lusi, 1994). It might also has to do with the fact that Marshall et al.'s study looked at influence on state education policy in general, whereas our study examined state reading policy in particular. Nevertheless, both studies demonstrate that state departments of education were highly influential in the state education policy domain. A high level of prominence of state departments of education was also reported by Thomas and Hrebenar (1991, 1999) in their study of the influence of various types of interests across the 50 states using reputational data.

Where reading policy is concerned, our study reveals that state departments of education were particularly active. They not only kept close working relationships with other policymakers, but also actively reached out to various groups and worked with them on reading-related issues. An Indiana State Department of Education official told us:

> We've also worked with the various groups—the reading proponents and other entities to get legislation passed and to add support for reading.... One of the things in order to get things through the general assembly [is that] you have to work with all these people ... I think what we do is we tend to stick together and talk about what's important.

The Texas Education Agency also made conscious efforts to engage diverse constituencies in the policy process and to ensure that their voices were heard, as shown by the following statement from a representative of a Texas education administrators' group:

[The] associations are invited to the table early in the process, and we always appreciate that. The state agency sends notice out to all the associations when something is going to happen on curriculum or a requirement might be changed, the discussion is occurring about that.... [The] state agency invites all the associations ... to come and talk about ... what are the things we have not thought about. How is this going to come and be received in the districts? And we can prevent a lot of problems early on from that.

Further, with the exception of North Carolina and Utah, the state departments of education in seven out of the nine states convened some kind of panel or task force for the development of state reading policy: Alabama Reading Panel (1996), California Reading Task Force (1995), Connecticut Early Reading Success Panel (2000), Indiana Phonics Task Force (2000), Maine Early Literacy Workgroup (1998), Michigan Early Literacy Committee (1998), and Texas Commissioner's Advisory Council on Reading (1996). Those panels or task forces often represented a wide range of constituencies: reading researcher and experts, educators, legislators, and various civic and educational groups, which highlighted the leadership role of the state departments of education and enhanced their visibility and influence in the policy arena.

Another pattern that has emerged from the data regarding the influence of government agencies is that issue-specific government agencies had relatively lower levels of influence compared with government agencies dealing more broadly with various issues in education. There were six issue-specific government agencies in this study: Connecticut General Assembly's Office of Fiscal Analysis (CGAOFA), Reading Plan for Michigan Advisory Council (RPMAC), California Commission on Teacher Credentialing (CCTC), Indiana Professional Standards Board (IPSB), North Carolina Professional Teaching Standards Commission (NPTSC), and Texas State Board for Educator Certification (TSBEC). All the six agencies ranked lowest on at least one of the influence indicators among government actors in their respective states; and five of the six agencies (with the exception of TSBEC) were one of the two lowest-ranking government actors based on all the three influence indicators in their respective states (see Table 3.5).

The influence of government actors other than state departments of education and issue-specific agencies varied more widely across the states. Take office of the governor for example. The Texas Office of the Governor (TOG) ranked highest on both centrality and perceived influence and fourth on prestige among reading policy actors in Texas (see Table 3.5). The Michigan and Utah offices of the governor (MIOG and UOG) also fared well, ranking next in influence only to the state department of education on both centrality and prestige, and ranking highest and third respectively among all reading policy actors in the state on perceived influence. In contrast, the Connecticut Office of the Governor (COG) ranked lowest on both centrality and prestige among government actors in the Connecticut reading policy network, and ranked even below many actors without formal policymaking authority in terms of the two network measures of influence. Its rank on perceived influence, however, was much higher. Once again, the disparity in the results based on alternative measure of influence speaks to the importance of not relying on a single indicator in examining the multifaceted phenomenon of policy influence. Another relatively weak office of the governor was that in Maine (MEOG); which turned out to be the second least influential government actor based on both network and reputational measures of policy influence.

A similar wide between-state variation in influence rank also existed for legislative committees. The Indiana House Education Committee (IHEC), for instance, tied with the state department of education for the most influential position based on both centrality and prestige; and ranked fifth on perceived influence among Indiana's reading policy actors. The Connecticut General Assembly's Education Committee (CGAEC) was highly influential too, ranking next only to the state department of education on all the three influence indicators among reading policy actors in the state. The Alabama Senate Education Committee (ASEC), however, had much less influence, ranking the lowest among government actors based on all the three influence indicators.

The variation in government actors' influence across the states reflects different levels of political activism and policy involvement of actors holding similar formal positions in different states. In Texas, for example, then Governor George W. Bush had been extremely active in the field of reading policy. During his tenure, Governor Bush had concentrated much of his administration's energy on improving the reading achievement of Texas' schoolchildren. In January 1996, Governor Bush launched a major piece of reading legislation, the Texas Reading Initiative, which served as the foundation for the Reading First Initiative in the No Child Left Behind Act of 2001 enacted after Bush assumed presidency (Miskel & Athan, 2001). To garner support for his reading initiative, Governor Bush engaged in extensive politicking, reaching out to diverse reading policy actors in the state. The governor, for example, convened over 20 reading summits, which were attended by reading researchers and experts, educators, and other policy actors. Working closely with the Governor's Business Council, Governor Bush was also instrumental in the creation of the Governor's Focus on Reading Task Force, which included representatives from the business community, private foundations, reading research community, state and local educational agencies, as well as parents (Shepley, 2002b). Indeed, as one state senator observed, "The governor's office is extremely active. One of the things that the governor did was to, from the very start, hold meetings and pull people in who had a stake [in reading]." It is therefore no wonder that the Texas governor was perceived as being most influential by three quarters of the other actors in the state. A newspaper reporter, for instance, stated, "At the top of the [influence] list has to be George Bush at the moment."

Standing in sharp contrast with the Texas governor was the Connecticut governor. Although Governor John Rowland of Connecticut came into office with a strong educational platform and vowed to be remembered as "the reading governor," he did not take an active role in the development of Connecticut's reading policy, but rather left the issue with his education aide, Commissioner Ted Sergi. When asked whether the governor was active in reading policy, an official in the Connecticut House of Representatives replied:

> No, the answer is no.... The governor has complete faith in Commissioner Sergi. They have a very good relationship.... [The] governor, he truly has delegated educational policy to his commissioner. From every indication, he has complete trust and faith in Commissioner Sergi. So whatever Commissioner Sergi is doing, he's doing it on behalf of the governor, so the governor doesn't need to get personally involved in these issues. And there really is no gap between the two. There's no tension at all. So when Commissioner Sergi says something, it's as good as getting it from the governor.

A Connecticut senator made a similar comment: "The governor ... really was a follower on this and not a leader, until after the fact when [the Early Reading Success Act] was proven to be so successful, and then he did include additional dollars in his budget." Although Governor Rowland did not play a major role in the development of the Early Reading Success Act (PA 98-243)—the most prominent piece of reading legislation in Connecticut during the past decade—he did launched the Governor's Summer Reading Challenge program, encouraging kids to read during the summer months. However, even for this "governor's program," the governor did not receive much credit, as indicated by the following observation from a teacher organization member:

> I don't have a great view of the governor, but I think that the governor trusts Ted and allows him to do a lot of ... to take the lead. And in that he's wise. So I don't have much criticism of the governor. But ... I don't believe he has a real role when he has the governor's reading program. That's Sergi's program.

Given the passive role Governor Rowland took with regard to state reading policy, it came as no surprise that the Connecticut Office of the Governor was the least influential government actor on the state's reading policy. Meanwhile, the power and authority that the governor delegated to Commissioner Sergi also explains the most influential position of the Connecticut State Department of Education headed by Sergi in the Connecticut reading policy network.

The Influence of Nongovernment Actors

With regard to the influence of nongovernment actors, a major finding of this study is that in most of the states examined, teacher organizations were not the most influential nongovernment actors in the state reading policy arena. Of the nine states that we investigated, state affiliates of the National Education Association (NEA) were the highest-ranking nongovernment actors in only two states (Connecticut and Indiana) based on actor centrality, in three states (Alabama, Connecticut, and Indiana) based on actor prestige, and in three states (Indiana, Michigan, and North Carolina) based on perceived influence (see Table 3.1 and Appendix C). In none of the states, state affiliates of the American Federation of Teachers (AFT) were the most influential nongovernment actors.

Previous studies of education interest groups, however, indicate that teacher organizations are the most influential interest groups on education policy at the state level. Marshall et al.'s (1989) cross-state study of education policymaking, for example, reveals that teacher organizations were perceived to be in the "near circle" of education policy, next in influence only to the "insiders" (i.e., state legislature) (p. 18). Thomas and Hrebenar (1991, 1999) similarly found that teacher organizations ranked highest among the 16 most influential and active interests in the 50 states. Mazzoni (1993) and Karper and Boyd (1988) also reported that teacher organizations were particularly influential among education interest groups in Minnesota and Pennsylvania respectively.

One plausible explanation for the seemingly inconsistent findings from prior research and our research is that the aforementioned prior studies all focused on influence on state education policy in general, whereas we examined influence on state reading policy in particular. In support, many of our study participants attributed teacher organizations' lack of clout on state reading policy to their lack of focus on the specific content area of reading. As a university professor in Maine observed:

> I haven't seen the MEA [Maine Education Association] be a strong player as an organization with regard to reading while the Maine Reading Association has [been]. That hasn't been the case for MEA. And I think they are always focused on sort of larger issues. They are not getting necessarily down to the nuts and bolts.

Similarly, a representative from a private foundation in California noted teacher organizations' lack of attention to reading issues, remarking, "They are dealing with lots of other issues, and unfortunately [reading] hasn't made it to the top of their list." An official in the Connecticut State Department of Education concurred:

> What's interesting is ... the superintendents group and CEA [Connecticut Education Association] and CFT [Connecticut Federation of Teachers], but you know they each come to their legislative concerns with concerns, interestingly enough, other than content. And if you look at the legislative package, for example, of the superintendents' group ... quite frankly, it's hardly ever about reading. It's about other issues. So their focus tends to be on things other than content.

A member of a Texas teacher organization admitted that reading was not an important issue for them, stating, "Our primary issues have been more along the line of salary and benefits and retirement and class size." He went on to suggest that when they did get involved in reading policy, they "generally [were] not the ones to initiate [contacts] by any means." Our interviews reveal that other state teacher organizations had similar issues of interest. A citizens group representative in Utah, for example, made the following comment on the Utah Education Association's lack of interest in reading: "Their issues are money, supplies, and salaries. Those are the three things they really focus on. And our local teachers' association is very much the same way too. It's not concerned with academic achievement for kids necessarily."

Given teacher organizations' lack of focus on reading, the finding about their lack of influence on state reading policy is not hard to understand, nor does it represent a contradiction to the findings of prior research. It is likely that overall, teacher organizations are still the most influential interests in the state education policy domain, although they are not necessarily the most influential on education policy in a specific subject area. Indeed, policy actors' overall influence may not translate into specific instances of influence manifestation, especially in light of the dynamic, transitory, and context-specific nature of power and influence (Greenwald, 1977; Knoke, 1990a; Mitchell, Agle, & Wood, 1997).

An alternative explanation for teacher organizations' lack of influence on state reading policy lies in the advocacy explosion that has occurred in the state education policy domain. With the proliferation of the interest group system, state education policymaking is no longer confined to policymakers plus a handful of major traditional education interests such as teacher organizations, but rather takes place in open issue networks populated by actors of an expanding number and diversity (Heclo, 1978; Marshall et al., 1989; Thomas & Hrebenar, 1991). As Rosenthal (1993) observes, "Policy making in many places is more pluralistic than before, and any single interest is less likely to dominate" (p. 216). Mazzoni (1995) likewise remarks, "Crowded arenas and competitive politics constrained the influence of any particular group" (p. 64). In the state reading policy domain, with a growing number of interests competing for power and influence, the chances that teacher organizations, or any particular organizations, have in securing dominant positions are likely to diminish, which attests to Salisbury's (1990) assertion of "more groups, less clout."

Another recurrent pattern about the influence of teacher organizations is that state affiliates of NEA were generally more influential than state affiliates of AFT. Table 3.6 lists the influence ranks of teacher organizations in the nine state reading policy networks. In four of the six states where data on both AFT and NEA affiliates were available, the state affiliates of NEA ranked higher than the state affiliates of AFT on all the three influence indicators. In California, although CTA ranked somewhat lower than CFT in terms of perceived influence, it ranked higher than CFT on both centrality and prestige. Only in Texas, the NEA affiliate ranked below the AFT affiliate on all the three indicators.

The stronger influence of the state affiliates of NEA compared to those of AFT might be attributable to their longer history and larger membership. The Connecticut Education Association (CEA), for example, was founded in as early as 1848 and currently has 34,000 members. The longevity of the CEA and its enormous membership and hence monetary resources make it a well-established group with high visibility and strong influence in the Connecticut reading policy arena. Compared with the CEA, the CFEPE was established almost a century later in 1947, and has a much smaller membership (25,000). It thus seems quite natural that the CFEPE was much less influential than the CEA.

While it was common among most of the state reading policy networks that teacher organizations were not the most influential nongovernment actors, the specific ranks of teacher organizations varied across the states. ISTA, the NEA affiliate in Indiana, for example, ranked highest among nongovernment actors on all the three influence indicators. The NEA affiliate in Texas, TSTA, however, ranked much lower, and was in fact less influential than most of the other nongovernment actors in the Texas state reading policy network.

Such between-state variations also existed for other types of nongovernment actors. Citizens groups, for instance, were generally not influential on state reading policy, and were even inconsequential in some states (e.g., California Christian Coalition, Connecticut Christian Coalition, and Connecticut Eagle Forum). For those that were consequential actors in the state reading policy domain, their relative influence was usually weak. Indiana Eagle Forum, for example, was the least influential interest group in Indiana based on both network and reputation measures. An Indiana State Department of Education official succinctly explained why the group lacked influence: "Eagle Forum didn't do anything." In contrast, the A+ Education Foundation (APEF), a citizens group in Alabama, was highly influential. It was the most influential interest group based on both centrality and perceived

Table 3.6. Teacher Organizations' Influence Ranks in the State Reading Policy Networks

State (N)[a]	Teacher Organization	Centrality	Prestige	Perceived Influence
Alabama (18)	Alabama Education Association (AEA)	3	1	9
California (38)	California Teachers Association (CTA)	14	8	11
	California Federation of Teachers (CFT)	18	13	9
Connecticut (26)	Connecticut Education Association (CEA)	3	3	7
	Connecticut Federation of Education & Professional Employees (CFEPE)	13	16	12
Indiana (28)	Indiana State Teachers Association (ISTA)	4	6	3
	Indiana Federation of Teachers (IFT)	17	17	18
Maine (19)	Maine Education Association (MEA)	8	9	6
Michigan (29)	Michigan Education Association (MEA)	5	10	2
	Michigan Federation of Teachers (MFT)	13	13	10
North Carolina (24)	North Carolina Association of Educators (NAE)	NA	NA	2
Texas (29)	Texas Federation of Teachers (TFT)	9	10	15
	Texas Classroom Teachers Association (TCTA)	17	14	15
	Association of Texas Professional Educators (ATPE)	17	17	15
	Texas State Teachers Association (TSTA)	20	19	15
Utah (21)	Utah Education Association (UEA)	6	6	10
	AFU/UT (AFTU)	12	12	12

Note: [a]The number in parentheses is the total number of actors in each state reading policy network.

influence and the second most influential interest group based on prestige in the Alabama reading policy network.

The strong influence of APEF was built upon its active involvement in state reading policy. Under the leadership of its president, Caroline Novak, the APEF worked closely with the state department of education and the governor's office to promote the Alabama Reading Initiative, an ambitious statewide reading reform in Alabama, and became the primary fundraiser for the initiative. Other than its financial support for the Alabama Reading Initiative, the APEF's influence, according to a member of the Alabama State Board of Education, could also be attributed to their extensive connections to other actors, as indicated by the following dialogue:

Interviewer: Do you attribute part of their having success to their being able to bring these various groups of people together?

Respodent: Yes, I think so ... A+ will tap individuals that they think have ideas that are helpful. Ideas that will move you forward. They tap those individuals for their board. If not the board, for workshops or forums. They've had a number of forums that many of us have participated in, and they've brought individuals in to listen. A+ has some of ... the best folk around involved, ... You know that there is something that is going to result from the work.

The prominence of the APEF brought about by its extensive ties to other actors was also seen in the remark made by an official in the Alabama Governor's Office:

We really use A+ as the conduit to everybody else. We believe A+ represents business. They represent the Eagle Forum. They represent the School Board. And it's so difficult for myself or for ... or especially for the governor, to have contact with all of these folks, that we see A+ as that spokesperson ... A+ kind of spoke for everybody, and we used them ... one person at a table, rather than 50, but representing 50 different views.

The strong influence of the APEF and the lack of influence of teacher organizations serve as a good illustration for the view that having a large membership and various resources only provide an actor with the potential for policy influence; an actor's actual influence also depends on the strategic actions of the actor (Mintzberg, 1983; Molm, 1990). In other words, an actor must act in order to realize its influence potential. In fact, the strategic actions of policy actors may not only affect their influence, but may also be used to compensate for relatively weak resources or to make less valuable resources more potent, and hence lead to even greater influence (Brass & Burkhardt, 1993; Molm, 1990). That explains why some actors not on a par with teacher organizations in terms of membership size, money, or other types of resources turned out to be more influential than teacher organizations in the state reading policy domain.

The Influence of Policy Entrepreneurs

In addition to government agencies and interest groups, our study also sheds light on the influence of key individuals, or the so-called "policy entrepreneurs" (Cobb & Elder, 1983; Kingdon, 1995; Polsby, 1984) or "idea champions" (Daft & Becker, 1978), in the state reading policy arena. Policy entrepreneurs are the activists within the policy community, who are persistent and persuasive, and vigorously invest resources such as time and money in promoting their values and in advocating their favorite ideas. They play a pivotal role in bringing about policy change by raising issue consciousness, "softening up" the policy community, and by "hook[ing] solutions to problems, proposals to political momentum, political events to policy problems" (Kingdon, 1995, p. 191).

In this study, two types of policy entrepreneurs were distinguished—those working for government agencies or interest groups, and those not affiliated with a particular organization but mainly acting on their own. We found that in many influential organizations, one or a few policy entrepreneurs were particularly active and involved, which contributed to the strong influence of those organizations. The influence of the Connecticut State Department of Education (CSDE), for example, could to a large extent be attributed to the entrepreneurial leadership of the education commissioner, Ted Sergi, who was regarded as "a tremendous leader" and "a real pusher" on the state's reading policy. In addition to his role as the commissioner, Sergi also served as the secretary of the state board of education and the education aide to Governor Rowland. He worked closely with the governor advising him on education policy, and also maintained good relationships with the legislature, particularly the co-chairs of the education committee, Senator Thomas Gaffey and Representative Cameron Staples.

Commissioner Sergi's collaborative leadership style was not only reflected in his relationships with policymakers, but also in the rapport he had established with various interest groups in the state. The commissioner, for example, met monthly with the Connecticut Coalition for Public Education, a coalition of seven major educational organizations, bringing them up-to-date on what was going on at the department, working with the groups, and using the groups as a doorway to different constituencies. A member of a teacher organization in Connecticut thus described Sergi:

> We get extraordinary leadership from Ted Sergi ... I think that he not only has been around a long time, but he's well informed and he's got some great people skills, and he believes in inclusion, in bringing people to the table.

With Sergi's entrepreneurial leadership emphasizing collaboration and inclusion, the CSDE established an extensive network of policy contacts, which made it both the most central and the most prestigious actor in the Connecticut reading policy network. The commissioner's policy activism also helped to bring high visibility to the department and hence enhanced its influence in the perceptions of other actors.

Another notable policy entrepreneur is Margaret LaMontagne, the education policy adviser for the then Texas Governor Bush. In describing LaMontagne's relationship with the governor, one policymaker in the Texas Education Agency remarked, "[LaMontagne] answered the questions that [the governor] needed answered." LaMontagne was present at every major education policy meeting, advising Governor Bush on the best way to address his concerns about poor reading achievement. She was also involved in focusing the attention of school district superintendents on reading. She, along with the governor and the education commissioner, held small group meetings with almost 30 superintendents from the largest school districts in Texas to discuss progress in reading. As a matter of fact, LaMontagne was one of the most frequently mentioned names during our interviews. For instance, in response to our question who were the most influential reading actors in Texas, a state senator asserted, "I would say, behind the scenes, probably the most influential person in the state as far as [reading policy is concerned] is Margaret LaMontagne." The head of a literacy group agreed, "Certainly the Governor's Office. Margaret LaMontagne is key, is essential."

Additional examples of policy entrepreneurs working for the government include the so-called "reading goddess," Katherine Mitchell, of the Alabama State Department of Education; the "one-woman gang," Marion Joseph, of the California State Board of Education; and the "reading czar," Robin Gilchrist, of the Texas Education Agency; among others. With a strong passion for reading and an entrepreneurial spirit, these individuals played essential roles in shaping the developments in the state reading policy domain. They attested to Browne's (1998) claim that "key people make things happen in politics" (p. 238).

Policy entrepreneurs, according to Kingdon (1995), can be both in and out of government. A prominent out-of-government policy entrepreneur was Caroline Novak, the president of the A+ Education Foundation of Alabama (APEF). As explicated previously, the APEF was the most influential reading policy actor in Alabama. To a large extent, its influence had to do with the entrepreneurship of Caroline Novak. Novak was intensively involved with the Alabama Reading Initiative through her close relationship with Katherine Mitchell, the director of the Alabama Reading Initiative. Novak helped Mitchell identify and select members for the Alabama Reading Panel, a precursor to the statewide reading initiative launched in the summer of 1998. Novak herself served on both the reading panel and the steering committee of the Alabama Reading Initiative. More importantly, Novak was instrumental in securing the financial support critical to the success of the Alabama Reading Initiative. When asked who was most influential on Alabama's reading policy, a representative of a research organization responded:

> A+, Caroline raised all of the private money ... she just went out and raised the money.... So A+, I mean Caroline and Katherine are the two people that have done it all. They've just been ... not letting anybody get away from them.... They just made sure it got done.

Another respondent, a member on the Alabama Reading Panel, attributed the influence of the APEF and Caroline Novak to hard work: "[The APEF and Caroline Novak] worked hard. They brought in the right kind of consultants from out of state. They've supported the teacher forum. They've earned the respect of Alabamians through their hard work." During our interviews, few respondents mentioned the APEF without mentioning Caroline Novak. For many Alabamians, the APEF was almost synonymous with Caroline Novak, whose entrepreneurial leadership made the citizens group one of the most prominent reading policy actors in the state.

Unlike the aforementioned entrepreneurs who worked for government agencies or interest groups, the second type of policy entrepreneurs mainly act on their own. The 11 individual policy actors in this study fell into this category. The findings of our study suggest that in general, individual policy actors were of limited policy influence. As Table 3.7 shows, the highest position an individual policy actor could attain in the influence hierarchy was a fifth place (Lyons of Connecticut on centrality), and most of the individual policy actors were positioned in the lower half of the influence hierarchy in the state reading policy domain.

Evidence for the limited influence of individual policy actors also came from the multidimensional scaling scattergrams presented in the previous chapter (Figures 2.3 and 2.4). The scattergrams reveal that core actors in all the eight state reading policy networks were either

**Table 3.7.   Influence Ranks of Individual Policy Actors in
the State Reading Policy Networks**

State (N)[a]	Individual Policy Actor	Centrality Rank	Prestige Rank	Perceived Influence Rank
California (38)	Shefelbine	21	20	19
	Birdsall	26	25	27
	Krashen	27	26	15
	McQuillian	30	30	27
	Moats	31	28	11
	Moustafa	31	33	27
Connecticut (26)	Lyons	5	6	9
	Freedman	8	10	7
	Swerling	20	19	19
North Carolina (24)	Johnson	NA	NA	14
Utah (21)	Allen	7	7	12

Note: [a]The number in parentheses is the total number of actors in each state reading policy network.

government agencies or interest groups, and individual policy actors were all in the periphery of the networks. A plausible explanation for individual policy actors' peripheral status is that despite their enthusiasm in and commitment to the issue of reading, those actors generally had only limited resources (e.g., time, energy, money, and staffing) at their disposal, which put them at a power disadvantage when it came to the shaping of state reading policy.

In addition to a general lack of influence on the part of individual policy actors, Table 3.7 also indicates that actors within the government tended to be more influential than actors outside the government. It is clear from the table that the three state legislators—Lyons and Freedman of Connecticut and Allen of Utah—were all in the upper half of the influence hierarchy, whereas the eight individual policy actors outside the government were all in the lower half of the influence hierarchy, which is consistent with the overall pattern of influence that government actors were more influential than nongovernment actors in the state reading policy networks. It is also consistent with Mazzoni's (1991) observation about the constrained influence of policy entrepreneurs outside the government: "Yet for all their myriad activities and consequential impact, the outside entrepreneurs could never by themselves have produced the policy innovation. They had to have powerful insider champion their cause if it was to succeed" (p. 122).

To summarize, in this chapter, we assessed policy actors' influence on state reading policy employing both network measures (i.e., centrality and prestige) and a reputational measure (i.e., perceived influence). We discussed the results in detail using the Texas reading policy network as an example, and examined the patterns of influence across the nine states. Influence as an abstract concept, however, is not very meaningful; it assumes meaning and importance only when it is exercised to promote specific policy beliefs, ideas, and proposals, which are the focus of the next two chapters.

NOTES

1. Other types of centrality measures include closeness centrality and betweenness centrality. Although different types of centrality measures focus on somewhat different aspects of the strategic positions of network actors, most the measures are highly correlated with each other (Bolland, 1988). The same is true with prestige measures. See Wasserman and Faust (1994) for an explication of alternative centrality and prestige measures.
2. Results of actor centrality, prestige, and influence nominations in the other seven state reading policy networks are provided in Appendix C.
3. Centrality and prestige data were not available for North Carolina.

CHAPTER 4

POLICY BELIEFS ABOUT LEVEL AND TREND OF READING ACHIEVEMENT, READING PEDAGOGY, STATE STANDARDS, AND STATE TESTS

Policy theorists argue that policy actors' core values and beliefs play a significant role in their actions as well as the policies that they create (e.g., Sabatier & Jenkins-Smith, 1993). In the field of education, such core values and policy beliefs often concern a number of themes that seem omnipresent in discussions about reforming public schools in the United States. In particular, the interpretation of achievement data, ideological or research-based conjectures concerning effective pedagogy, and the benefits and shortcomings of standards-based accountability systems have consistently lied at the center of claims of both reform proponents and opponents. The reading policy community was not exempt.

Drawing upon both quantitative and qualitative data, we seek to explore, in this chapter, state reading policy actors' beliefs in three general areas: (1) level and trend of reading achievement, (2) reading pedagogy, and (3) state reading standards and tests. Each of these areas presents a special set of concerns related to the development, implemen-

Reading: Policy, Politics, and Processes, pp. 71–98
Copyright © 2008 by Information Age Publishing
All rights of reproduction in any form reserved.

tation, and evaluation of state reading policies. Before we present our findings, an explanation of the methods that we used to measure policy actors' beliefs is in order.

MEASUREMENT OF POLICY BELIEFS

Table 4.1 shows the interview questions that were specifically designed to measure policy actors' beliefs about the level and trend of reading achievement, pedagogy, state reading standards, and state reading tests (see Appendix B for complete interview schedules). Although much of the pertinent information was found in participants' responses to these inter-

Table 4.1. Interview Questions and Coding Categories Pertaining to Policy Actor Beliefs About the Level and Trend of Reading Achievement, Pedagogy, State Standards, and State Tests

Belief	Interview Questions and Coding Categories
Level of reading achievement	The NAEP percentage of [STATE NAME] fourth-grade students achieving below basic in reading is XX%. Do you think that this percentage accurately depicts your students' reading level?
	• How big of a problem do you think that the state has with its reading achievement levels? • What percentage do you think is correct for your state?
	Coding: 1 = NAEP overestimates achievement, 2 = NAEP scores are accurate, 3 = NAEP underestimates achievement
Trend of reading achievement	Over the last few decades, has reading performance increased, decreased, or stayed the same in your state?
	Coding: 1 = increased , 2 = stayed the same, 3 = decreased
Reading pedagogy	Should reading instruction be based primarily on phonics, whole language, a balanced approach, an integrated approach, or some other approach? Explain.
	Coding: 1 = phonics highly positive, 2 = phonics positive, 3 = balanced, 4 = whole language positive, and 5 = whole language highly positive
State reading standards	Do you support state standards for reading? Explain.
	Coding: 1 = highly negative, 2 = negative, 3 = neutral, 4 = positive, and 5 = highly positive
State reading tests	Do you support state tests for reading? Explain.
	Coding: 1 = highly negative, 2 = negative, 3 = neutral, 4 = positive, and 5 = highly positive

view questions, each interview transcript was coded in its entirety following the coding procedures described in Appendix A, so that relevant
information from other sections of the interview transcript would not
have been overlooked. To ensure an acceptable degree of coding reliability, both intracoder reliability and intercoder reliability were checked. The
reliability estimates ranged from 66% to 100%, with all but one estimate
above 70%.

Based on the coding results, we obtained a quantitative measure for
each of the five types of beliefs for each individual respondent. For policy
actors with more than one respondent, we averaged across the respondents to get the values at the level of policy actor. Given that the frequency distributions of the five actor-level measures did not support
treating them as continuous measures, we created a number of distinct
response categories for each measure based on the frequency distribution
of the actor-level values. The categorizations for measures based on a 3-
point coding scheme and measures based on a 5-point coding scheme are
presented in Tables 4.2 and 4.3 respectively.

In the sections to follow, we present our findings based on both
descriptive analyses of the above five quantitative measures and qualitative analyses of rich interview data regarding policy actors' beliefs about
each of the five key policy issues. Where data permitted, we also conducted chi-square tests or logistical regressions to assess whether there
were any significant differences in policy actors' beliefs between government actors and nongovernment actors. Given the limited sample size,
these tests were conducted based on the full sample across states rather
than within individual states.[1]

LEVEL OF READING ACHIEVEMENT

With regard to the level of reading achievement, an Indiana state legislator summarized it well: "I think every state has a problem with its reading

**Table 4.2. Categorization of Policy Actors' Beliefs About Level and
Trend of Reading Achievement**

	Value Categories for Actor-Level Measures		
Belief	*1.00 ~ 1.66*	*1.67 ~ 2.33*	*2.34 ~ 3.00*
Level of reading achievement	NAEP-Overestimation	NAEP-Accurate	NAEP-Underestimation
Trend of reading achievement	Increased	Stable	Decreased

Table 4.3.   Categorization of Policy Actors' Beliefs About Reading Pedagogy, State Standards, and State Tests

Belief	Value Categories for Actor-Level Measures				
	1.00 ~ 1.80	1.81 ~ 2.60	2.61 ~ 3.40	3.41 ~ 4.20	4.21 ~ 5.00
Reading pedagogy	Strong phonics	Phonics	Balanced	Whole language	Strong whole language
State reading standards	Highly negative	Negative	Neutral	Positive	Highly positive
State reading tests	Highly negative	Negative	Neutral	Positive	Highly positive

achievement levels." Indeed, in most, if not all, states, low reading achievement has been recognized as a grave problem in need of immediate policy action. Such recognition was often triggered by widespread dissatisfaction with student test scores. In all nine states that we studied, students' performance on standardized reading achievement tests served as a major "problem indicator" that led to heightened agenda status for reading (Kingdon, 1995). When asked the question "How big of a problem do you think that your state has with its reading achievement levels?," an Alabama think tank representative responded, "Oh, giant!" The response from a former president of a literacy group in North Carolina was also rather typical, "I think it's tremendously huge … I think it's still a very severe problem.… Instead of a disappearing problem, I think it's going to be an increasing problem." Although some respondents acknowledged recent improvement in reading achievement in their states, there was not a single respondent who expressed content with the current level of achievement.

During our interviews, we not only asked study participants about their general impression of the reading achievement problem in their respective states, but also asked them whether they agreed with the level of reading achievement as measured by National Assessment of Educational Progress (NAEP). As shown in Table 4.4, in every state, at least half of the policy actors agreed that NAEP scores accurately represented the reading achievement level among fourth-graders in their respective states. The level of agreement was particularly high in California, where 25 out of 32 actors believed that NAEP results were accurate. Across the nine states, about two thirds of the actors believed that NAEP results were accurate. A Texas education agency official, for instance, expressed his trust in NAEP: "The NAEP is what it is. It's a good sample. It's a good test.… It just seems reasonable." A former California state education agency official concurred:

Table 4.4. Number and Percentage of Policy Actors in Different Response Categories for the Level of Reading Achievement, by State and Response Category

State	NAEP Overestimation	NAEP Accurate	NAEP Underestimation	Number of Policy Actors
Alabama	4 (33%)	7 (58%)	1 (8%)	12
California	4 (13%)	25 (78%)	3 (9%)	32
Connecticut	0 (0%)	12 (67%)	6 (33%)	18
Indiana	3 (15%)	12 (60%)	5 (25%)	20
Maine	3 (25%)	8 (67%)	1 (8%)	12
Michigan	2 (13%)	11 (73%)	2 (13%)	15
North Carolina	4 (22%)	10 (56%)	4 (22%)	18
Texas	9 (38%)	12 (50%)	3 (13%)	24
Utah	3 (19%)	11 (69%)	2 (13%)	16
Total	32 (19%)	108(65%)	27 (16%)	167

Note: Number of policy actors is the number of actors with valid response to the relevant interview questions.

> I think the NAEP scores are an accurate reflection of what's going on here in California. Those that don't like the NAEP scores will say, "Well, it's because we have so many limited-English learners that is responsible for all of this, but I think if you look carefully at the data, that's clearly not the case. You can't say that it's all due to the Asian and Latino children that have come to this country."

While the majority of respondents believed that the NAEP scores accurately reflected the level of reading achievement in their respective states, some were dubious. A North Carolina citizens group representative, for instance, thus responded to our question about NAEP:

> To be honest with you, I really believe it's probably worse than that because one of the things that we know is that a significant number of our exceptional children or children with quote learning disabilities were not included in that testing.

A Texas education researcher also observed, "I think that the NAEP scores are worrisome and I think probably underestimate the literacy problems here in Texas because it's voluntary." A member of a conservative interest group in Texas made his point more forthrightly, "I think that [the NAEP scores] are being pumped for politics. I don't believe it. I think the numbers are cooked."

Other participants felt NAEP scores may be misleading because NAEP's focus on state average scores might have disguised the low performance of subpopulations from disadvantaged backgrounds. Such concerns were particularly pronounced amongst Connecticut policy actors. As a member of a Connecticut business association noted, "I think when you aggregate the data in Connecticut it can be very misleading because of this great disparity we have between the performance in the urban districts and in the suburban districts." A Connecticut state legislator echoed a similar theme:

> You got to be careful with these statistics. Connecticut is very much a tale of two cities. I mean, we've got, uh, three cities. We've got three of the poorest cities in the country, New Haven, Hartford and Bridgeport. Yet we have the richest state in the country on income per capita basis. So you are bound to have exceptional scores across the board from a state that has that high of socioeconomic demographic. But certainly when you look at our urban areas you can see far lower scores. You know ... so that has to all be taken into context.

There were also participants, however, holding a more optimistic view. A number of respondents in California, for instance, claimed that that the NAEP state comparisons were erroneous because the NAEP sampling procedures were not representative, and as such, NAEP underestimated achievement scores. A California state official disclosed:

> What I've been told about the most recent NAEP sample that was used is that there was a huge disproportionately large number of English language learner students represented in the sample. You know, like 25% in California compared to 2% in comparable states ... and so if you were to take out the sample and make it more comparable to similar states, then it actually shows that our scores have actually risen a bit.

Another common explanation for NAEP underestimating achievement was that many states and local school districts had recently implemented new programs and initiatives designed to raise reading achievement. Some believed that the NAEP scores were dated and did not reflect recent progress. For example, a representative from a North Carolina administrators association observed: "I would say that a lot of progress has been made since 1998 because of our testing program and our accountability. So that [NAEP scores] may be low." A Texas Congressman made a similar comment, "I don't think [NAEP scores are accurate] anymore. I don't think that was the case. We have put such an emphasis on it over the last five years, that I think we're in better than that today."

Overall, however, there was a high level of agreement among both government and non-government actors across the states on the accuracy of

NAEP results as an indicator of reading achievement levels in their respective states.[2] There was an even higher level of agreement—a consensus—among the state reading policy actors that the level of reading achievement was too low and that reading achievement was a serious problem that demanded heightened attention and effective policy actions.

TREND OF READING ACHIEVEMENT

During our interviews, study participants commented not only on the level of reading achievement, but also the trend of reading achievement in their states. Although almost all participants lamented that the level of reading achievement was not where it ought to be, they believed that reading achievement had improved in recent years. As shown in Table 4.5, with the only exception of Utah, the majority of actors in every state that we studied sensed an improvement in reading achievement. Across the nine states, 69% of the actors believed that the level of reading achievement was on the rise.

Many respondents maintained that reforms, particularly state wide reading initiatives, changes in pedagogical practices, and new or modified accountability systems, brought about needed changes that subsequently led to achievement gains. Speaking positively of the Alabama Reading Initiative, a representative of an Alabama parents group told us,

Table 4.5. Number and Percentage of Policy Actors in Different Response Categories for the Trend of Reading Achievement, by State and Response Category

State	Increased	Stable	Decreased	Number of Policy Actors
Alabama	8 (89%)	1 (11%)	0 (0%)	9
California	11 (50%)	3 (14%)	8 (36%)	22
Connecticut	18 (95%)	1 (5%)	0 (0%)	19
Indiana	16 (64%)	3 (12%)	6 (24%)	25
Maine	7 (64%)	1 (9%)	3 (27%)	11
Michigan	15 (65%)	6 (26%)	2 (9%)	23
North Carolina	11 (73%)	1 (7%)	3 (20%)	15
Texas	27 (96%)	0 (0%)	1 (4%)	28
Utah	5 (26%)	3 (16%)	11 (58%)	19
Total	118 (69%)	19 (11%)	34 (20%)	171

Note: Number of policy actors is the number of actors with valid response to the relevant interview questions.

"I would say it may get somewhat better because more schools are going through the reading initiative. Each year we're hearing good things, how good things are happening."

In addition to reading-specific initiatives, some respondents also attributed the improvement in reading achievement to the state accountability systems in general. A member of a California state agency thus described the link between accountability pressures and reading achievement:

> [Reading achievement] is getting a little bit better, slightly. It's moving. It's moving because we have a public accountability system that's driving it. People know they have to do better, so there's pressure because the scores that the kids get in our state testing system are public. It's that public system that's putting people on notice that we really can't ignore any child.

A school administrators association representative in North Carolina was obviously more satisfied with the pace of the progress in their state, proclaiming: "I would say that a lot of progress has been made since 1998 because of our testing program and our accountability."

While most participants believed that reading achievement was improving in their states, some believed it stayed the same or even declined. The past president of an Indiana citizens group, for example, commented, "I would say that reading performance, in decades, ... maybe stayed the same. I think it's stayed the same or gotten worse.... I don't think it's getting any better at all." Nowhere was the sense of decline, however, more acute than in Utah, where over half of the policy actors expressed concerns about a downward trend in reading achievement. Such concerns were in part attributable to the NAEP results that revealed Utah as one of the only two states (the other being Wyoming) experiencing continuous decline of reading scores from 1992 to 1998. These results received considerable public attention, and had become a focusing event for educational reform in Utah. It was no wonder, therefore, many Utah policy actors seemed to have unquestionably accepted the drop in reading achievement. Lamenting the "plummeting test scores," a professor told us, "In addition to not doing as well as I think they could, the trend has been downward. And I think that's got a lot of people concerned."

Such a downward trend in Utah was commonly attributed to changes in student demographics and the lack of preparedness of teachers and school systems for effectively teaching diverse student populations. When asked about the trend of reading achievement in Utah, for instance, a state education agency official responded, "Oh, well it has gone down.

Absolutely! Again, it's because a lot has changed in demographics too."
Another state official partly agreed:

> [The scores] have been declining, which is to me absolutely ... something
> that's hard to believe ... educators can claim, "Ok, our population is chang-
> ing." And it is. We have more low income. We have more minorities ... but
> we can't say that is the reason our test scores are not [high].... Our teachers
> aren't trained.

Despite a widely perceived downward achievement trend in Utah, overall, policy actors across the states tended to agree that although the current level of reading achievement was far from being satisfactory, progress
was being made and reading scores would improve because of the concerted efforts from a diverse array of actors in the reading policy community. Simply, there was an atmosphere of hope and optimism, a belief that
reading policy initiatives and education reforms in general would make a
difference in students' reading achievement. Moreover, such positive perceptions about the trend of reading achievement were similar among both
government and nongovernment actors ($p > .05$ based on a Chi-square
test), many of whom shared the sentiment of an Indiana government official, who told us, "I'm actually anxious ... we've made tremendous
improvements ... I think you will see an improvement."

READING PEDAGOGY

Reading pedagogy has been at the center of the century-long reading war.
Our interview data suggested that the once heated debate had subsided
considerably, although it had not disappeared entirely. As shown in Table
4.6, in six out of the nine states, the majority of the actors supported a
balanced approach to reading instruction. Across the nine states, slightly
over half of the actors (54%) believed that reading instruction should be
based on a balanced approach. Among the other half, there was a clear
preponderance of phonics advocates over whole language advocates—
while 39% of policy actors favored "Phonics" or "Strong Phonics," only
8% favored "Whole Language" or "Strong Whole Language." The
response pattern was similar for both government and non-government
actors ($p > .05$). A consultant for a Connecticut think tank, for example,
expressed his support for phonics most passionately:

> I've already indicated in my preference by saying that if you don't learn
> phonics, you can't read. You cannot read a word if you don't know phonics.
> It begins with the alphabet. In the literature called a balanced approach in

Table 4.6.   Number and Percentage of Policy Actors in Different Response Categories for Reading Pedagogy, by State and Response Category

State	Strong Phonics	Phonics	Balanced	Whole Language	Strong Whole Language	Number of Policy Actors
Alabama	0 (0%)	6 (40%)	7 (47%)	2 (13%)	0 (0%)	15
California	6 (15%)	15 (38%)	14 (35%)	1 (3%)	4 (10%)	40
Connecticut	3 (13%)	5 (22%)	13 (57%)	2 (9%)	0 (0%)	23
Indiana	5 (19%)	8 (30%)	12 (44%)	1 (4%)	1 (4%)	27
Maine	2 (13%)	1 (7%)	10 (67%)	1 (7%)	1 (7%)	15
Michigan	4 (14%)	5 (18%)	18 (64%)	1 (4%)	0 (0%)	28
North Carolina	4 (24%)	3 (18%)	9 (53%)	1 (6%)	0 (0%)	17
Texas	5 (17%)	5 (17%)	19 (66%)	0 (0%)	0 (0%)	29
Utah	2 (11%)	3 (16%)	13 (68%)	1 (5%)	0 (0%)	19
Total	31 (15%)	51(24%)	115 (54%)	10 (5%)	6 (3%)	213

Note: Number of policy actors is the number of actors with valid response to the relevant interview questions. Percentages in different belief categories may not add up to 100% due to rounding.

the Connecticut reading program, the word alphabet is not mentioned. How ridiculous! ... I would teach intensive phonics. Whole language is a means of collectively kidding yourself. It doesn't teach children to read.... It is all a set of expectations. There are no methods involved.... But the kids don't learn to read by themselves. Tragic! Almost criminal!

Although not as blunt as the Connecticut consultant quoted above, quite a few respondents also made disparaging remarks about the whole language approach and considered phonics the unrivaled solution to the reading achievement problem. Critics of whole language frequently cited its lack of research-based evidence as justification for not putting it into practice in classrooms. They also argued that phonics was strongly supported by scientifically-based research and was thus indisputably the legitimate approach to teaching reading. Using research findings to build a compelling case for phonics was evident in the remarks of a Congressman from North Carolina who was astonished that state legislators did not consider a bill advocating phonics:

So they still wouldn't hear the bill, even though that overwhelming body of evidence that came forward from the Houston study and all the other studies that have been conducted in the last decade have proven phonics to be superior, especially in the minority race children, and so many others.

As a matter of fact, almost every phonics advocate used research to make their argument. For example, when we asked two government officials in California about their views on reading instructional methods, the first official responded: "Well, I would not support what they [whole language proponents] do. It's not based on real research. It's based on their opinions." The second official added: "It should be based on phonics ... because the research seems to indicate that the way you learn how to read most efficiently and most successfully is by understanding the phonetic structure of the written language." A state official from Utah shared a similar view, opining:

> I mean, that is the research that I look to. To me, it's not a question of one or the other. It's just not even an issue. There is a body of research. There is. And I don' think it's debatable. I don't think it depends on the way you look at it. I think there's a clear body of research that we look to in order to give us guidelines and recommendations for practice. And that's where I stand on it. I mean, I just think the debate is a stupid debate and it seriously hurts the field of reading, as you well know.

Simply, the use of "research"—often just the term instead of specific references—seemed to make an assertion incontestable. A whole language proponent in California expressed great distress about the role of selected research in informing policy:

> The concern that only a very narrow band of research is being recognized by the state, and even of that narrow band of research, very poorly conducted studies are being used to make policy. And that prior to anyone being able to see the studies, reflect on them, investigate them, the findings of studies have driven state policy, and that's just of grave concern.... [We should take] a very wide look at a broad range of research that is credible, not poorly conducted studies that are only of empirical design. I don't know how the only research you can look at is replicable research. I don't know how human beings are replicable.

Indeed, the debate between phonics and whole language had evolved from one focusing on philosophical or ideological differences to one about what research says and what constitutes credible research. A California reading professor, for instance, refuted the research-based claims of phonics proponents with the following statement:

> Well, first of all, whole language is more effective and there is tons of research to show it, all of which is ... I mean, the people who are promoting the more traditional approaches are pointing to their research, which most professionals don't accept. And pretending there is no research to support a more contemporary approach.

Another aspect of the debate about reading instructional approach concerned student subpopulations. Some policy actors believed that the whole language approach was ineffective for students with special needs, limited English proficiency students, and socially and economically disadvantaged students. Phonics, several actors argued, facilitated learning for all students, as evident in the statement of a member of the North Carolina state education agency, "Some students just can't learn except the direct way," and the remarks of a member of an educational advisory board in Texas:

> Now I'm convinced that the data is overwhelming and your kids who come to school without knowing how to read, our data is just overwhelming. You're going to have to give them a lot of direct instruction, including nuts and bolts phonics, then you want something else, but you've got to do that. It's not something that you can skip over.

A former state policymaker in California also held that whole language benefited some students but hindered the learning of other students, claiming, "I think the whole language approach ... works much more effectively with middle-class kids who have parents who read to them in their homes, and their exposure to reading begins much earlier."

For many whole language proponents, the debate about pedagogy was based on erroneous ideas about whole language. This view of a widespread misconception of whole language was clearly expressed by a reading researcher in California:

> I think the whole language/phonics debate is a false dichotomy, which the press drums in again and again so that even educators begin to think that way. Phonics is part of the whole language approach. I think the press has not understood what whole language is ... and people outside the field don't understand the difference between whole word and whole language.... The set of discoveries that gave rise to the whole language approach was that children who are learning how to read can read better in the context of familiar language than in the context of unfamiliar language or words in isolation because language is another cueing system. This was the fundamental discovery that led to the whole language instructional approach. That included phonics, but it included a healthy skepticism for traditional phonics and applied phonics in context.

Several respondents further pointed out that it was not only the misconception of the public and the media that was problematic, but also the misunderstandings of the classroom teachers who were implementing their ideas of "whole language" that incurred substantial setbacks for champions of whole language. Certainly, teacher modifications of instructional programs and practices are universal and often necessary. However, undermining the integrity of an instructional approach by altering its critical features becomes particularly troublesome when assessing its effectiveness. In fact, California's former State Superintendent of Public Instruction, Bill Honig, testified before the state legislature that teachers and administrators misinterpreted the whole-language-inspired literature-based English and language arts framework, and this misinterpretation, though inadvertent, subsequently led to the decline of test scores.

With the prolonged debate centering around a dichotomy, false or otherwise, and advocacy backed by supportive research evidence from both sides, it should come as no surprise that many found an eclectic approach incorporating elements from both sides a more reasonable and also intuitively appealing one. This approach, commonly referred to as "the balanced approach" or "integrated approach," was espoused by the majority of policy actors in all nine states. For instance, when asked about his opinion on reading instructional approach, the executive director of a school administrators association replied, "We think it ought to be balanced. I don't think that's one approach. It's really a blending of the two extremes." The response from the head of a state education agency was particularly insightful:

> It seems like we aren't really learning from our history. Any time the pendulum goes ... if it swings too far all it's going to do is get the momentum to swing back and swing too far in the other direction. So if we really do things right and if we don't want to repeat history, I think what we have to do is stop this extreme debating and say, "You know, there's merit to both sides of this. Of course, there's merit to code instruction. And of course there's merit to good literature and getting kids excited about what they read and focusing on comprehension." Why do those things have to be mutually exclusive? Why can't the focus embrace both of those things and maybe then, I think when we see that, then maybe the debate will ease up a little bit.

While most respondents expressed support for a balanced approach to teaching reading, the exact definition of a balanced approach may be different for different people. As a California researcher pointed out, "'Balanced' assumed multiple meanings.... Everyone says, 'I'm for balanced approach,' but what does 'balanced approach' actually mean? It is subject to, I think, very different interpretations." Some actors believed that "balanced approach" was really a code word for "whole language." A representative of a Texas-based foundation told us, "In theory we believe the balanced approach sounds reasonable; in practice what that means is all whole language and lip service only to phonics." This assertion was substantiated by a professor in North Carolina, who claimed, "I'm a real whole language advocate. And I think that whole language is a real balanced approach." A teachers organization representative in Indiana similarly claimed, "I think whole language means balanced."

Partly out of the concern that the term "balanced" may be associated with "whole language," the Early Reading Success Panel convened by the Connecticut State Department of Education chose to adopt the more "politically correct" term "comprehensive approach" instead of "balanced approach," according to a reading consultant for the department. Obviously, the Connecticut State Department of Education and its reading panel were very successful in distinguishing their comprehensive approach from the whole language approach, as the comprehensive approach that they advocated for was viewed by some as "phonics-heavy," as indicated by the following comment on the panel report (Connecticut State Department of Education, 2000) made by a newspaper reporter:

> It's very heavy on language development. And they will tell you, they will argue to the end that this is a balanced approach, and it is, but it's very heavily influenced by the folks at Yale and U Conn.... I was struck by how phonics-heavy the state's new report on teaching reading is.

In addition to the ambiguity in defining balance, many respondents noted that effective reading instruction should attend to the needs of individual students. From this perspective, a balanced approach would require teachers to possess a toolkit of instructional strategies and be able to put "differential emphasis," in a respondent's terms, on different skills based on the unique needs of individual students at different stages of language development. As a representative of a Connecticut education association explained:

> The one thing that we would presume to know is there is no one method that's appropriate for every child. So phonics, whole language, whatever they'll come up with next month ... you need a package and educators need a package of techniques and resources if we really are serious about making sure every kid reads by third grade.

A leader of a private foundation provided a more succinct definition for this prevalent perspective, stating: "What I mean by balanced is whatever that child needs to get them to read."

Many respondents also recognized that this student-centered perspective put a great deal of demand on teachers as instructional decision-makers. It requires teachers to not only possess both content and pedagogical knowledge for teaching a variety of skills, but also be able to identify the strengths and weaknesses of each child and make instructional decisions accordingly. A professor in Maine, for instance, observed that while the emphasis on balanced instruction was a good legacy of the reading wars, it is really up to the teacher to figure out what to do and what that balance is. A California policy actor made a similar comment:

> Everybody seems to be in favor of a balanced approach. That seems like the very common, sensible, reasonable thing to say. But as I said, I think the devil is in the details and what that actually means in terms of what occurs in the classroom. If the child is having a problem, what are alternative strategies that ought to be employed to try to assist that child or what needs to be done to put together, you know, a program in a systematic fashion that has the best chance of working? I think it's at that level that we need more attention and that the consensus begins to break down on those kinds of issues.

Speaking of the role of teachers, many respondents, particularly faculty members from schools of education, noted that the relatively recent emphasis on a balanced reading instructional approach also had implications for teacher preparation programs. A Connecticut reading professor, for example, explained:

> We try to represent a balanced approach. We have people within the department who are both fairly traditional and we have people who are committed to whole language. We do that [i.e., represent a balanced approach] because the department feels that our role is to prepare teachers to do it all.

An Alabama state education official also indicated that colleges of education should teach future teachers to be able to decide what method they need to use to best help their students to read. College professors in Indiana would particularly welcome the following statement from a state legislator:

> From my window I feel that the school of education has to have those dollars to teach those potential teachers how to teach reading. It cannot be a six-hour course.... We need to arm them with the tools to have complete reading programs.

Overall, our interview data showed that the balanced approach had drawn many people to a middle ground from opposite sides. As a faculty member at an Alabama university noted:

> The Alabama Reading Association has probably come more to the center just as ... most experts in reading have during the last few years. This whole language versus phonics battle I think has ... I won't say it has been

resolved. I think it has been negotiated, however, to the point where the old phonics people and the old whole language people can agree that some kind of balanced approach is preferable.

One interesting thing about the above observation is the reference to "some kind of balanced approach," which conveys the ambiguity about the term "balanced approach." Such ambiguity actually may have partly contributed to the popularity of the balanced approach. As Stone (2002) contends, ambiguity allows policy actors to (a) aggregate support for a policy proposal, (b) unite actors with different opinions, (c) satisfy demands to take action, (d) placate both sides of the conflict, and (e) facilitate compromise. Indeed, although the balanced approach by no means represented total consensus, it did facilitate reconciliation and compromise, and provided a reasonable middle ground for people holding conflicting ideologies so that no one would feel completely defeated and everyone could claim triumph to some extent.

STATE READING STANDARDS

Consensus of belief among state reading policy actors was most evident in the area of state reading standards. As shown in Tables 4.7 and 4.8, policy actors' views about state standards were overwhelmingly positive. In all but one state (North Carolina), over half of the actors held "highly positive" views about state reading standards; in all nine states, over 80% of the actors were supportive of state standards (i.e., either "positive" or "highly positive"). Support for state standards was particularly strong among government actors as compared with nongovernment actors (83% vs. 57% for "highly positive," $p < .01$),[3] which is not surprising given that the standards were developed mostly by government actors. In contrast, only 5% of the actors across the nine states expressed either "negative" or "highly negative" opinions about state standards, and another 5% took a neutral position on this issue. When asked whether he supported state standards, for example, a teachers association representative in Alabama readily admitted:

> Oh, yes, definitely! As a matter of fact, I support the entire standards movement. I think that in order to measure achievement, there must be some type of barometer, and that barometer is either your national standards or state standards that are carved from national standards.

While policy actors across the nine states overwhelmingly expressed support for statewide reading standards, their support was not unconditional. Many respondents qualified their support by indicating

Table 4.7. Number and Percentage of Policy Actors in Different Response Categories for State Reading Standards, by State and Response Category

State	Highly Negative	Negative	Neutral	Positive	Highly Positive	Number of Policy Actors
Alabama	1 (6%)	0 (0%)	0 (0%)	5 (31%)	10 (63%)	16
California	3 (7%)	2 (5%)	3 (7%)	11 (27%)	22 (54%)	41
Connecticut	1 (5%)	1 (5%)	0 (0%)	6 (27%)	14 (64%)	22
Indiana	0 (0%)	0 (0%)	2 (7%)	5 (19%)	20 (74%)	27
Maine	0 (0%)	0 (0%)	2 (13%)	4 (25%)	10 (63%)	16
Michigan	0 (0%)	1 (3%)	1 (3%)	9 (31%)	18 (62%)	29
North Carolina	0 (0%)	0 (0%)	1 (5%)	10 (50%)	9 (45%)	20
Texas	2 (7%)	1 (3%)	0 (0%)	5 (17%)	21 (72%)	29
Utah	0 (0%)	0 (0%)	1 (5%)	5 (25%)	14 (70%)	20
Total	7 (3%)	5 (2%)	10 (5%)	60 (27%)	138 (63%)	220

Note: Number of policy actors is the number of actors with valid response to the relevant interview questions. Percentages in different belief categories may not add up to 100% due to rounding.

that standards per se might not be effective at improving achievement. Rather, improved student achievement would only result from faithful implementation of "quality" standards in conjunction with related policies that serve as precursors or facilitators for standards-based reforms. According to many actors, clarity and specificity were two essential features of quality standards. For example, a representative of an educational association in California claimed, "So I'm a big fan of standards, as long as they're clear, not vague and not broad." A policy advisor inside the Michigan government remarked likewise, "So hopefully, a strong supporter of state standards, but state standards to the

Table 4.8. Number and Percentage of Policy Actors in Different Response Categories for State Reading Standards, by Actor Type and Response Category

Actor Type	Highly Negative	Negative	Neutral	Positive	Highly Positive	Number of Policy Actors
Government	0 (0%)	1 (2%)	1 (2%)	6 (13%)	39 (83%)	47
Nongovernment	7 (4%)	4 (2%)	9 (5%)	54 (31%)	99 (57%)	173
Total	7 (3%)	5 (2%)	10 (5%)	60 (27%)	138 (63%)	220

Note: Number of policy actors is the number of actors with valid response to the relevant interview questions. Percentages in different belief categories may not add up to 100% due to rounding.

extent that they're not written in a way that they can't be used professionally in the field or of little value."

In addition to the clarity and specificity of standards, some respondents also expressed concerns about the way state standards were created in some places. Inputs from various reading policy community actors were widely viewed as desirable as they would inform and facilitate the development of quality standards. In contrast, standards development dominated by a small selected group was seen as silencing divergent perspectives. As one Michigan official noted of the standards development and adoption process:

> We adopted these standards and it's a terrible way to do it because what happens is the standards are drawn up by a core of insiders. They come to the State Board. You then have to reject it, and if you don't have the vote, you can't reject it. And you're not in a position usually to rewrite the standards at [the] State Board meeting.... The mechanics of the system make it very difficult for you to deny them ... I mean your alternative is no standards.

The executive director of a conservative group in Connecticut also voiced his doubts about state standards: "How do you set the standard that's going to be the standard? And who are the standard-makers? I'm not sure there's a good way to do that." Echoing the sentiments, a California reading scholar made an interesting metaphor:

> [Standards]—as created by who? When the states are sending their standards to Achieve, the Achieve organization run by non-educators, um ... you know... would doctors accept engineers deciding what medicine is good for their patients?... It's just incredible that people without an educational background are calling the shots and we have to question what is their motive.

Another common concern about state standards, as one would expect, was the "teaching to the standards" problem and the consequent narrowing of curriculum. Some standards proponents believed that standards specified the minimum level of knowledge or skill acquisition, and as such, assumed teachers would expand the curriculum beyond the basic standards. A member of an Indiana state agency, for example, explained, "I think that it has a certain consistency so that schools know what students should learn as basic minimum at least, and then make and expand that curriculum beyond." Others, however, were more skeptical. They surmised that instead of building upon the standards, teachers would simply focus on them exclusively. Such a concern was evident in the observation made by a Texas interest group representative: "Once you set a state standard, you teach to those standards. I think there should be a lot more freedom for the teachers as well as the students."

The concerns that we heard most frequently, however, pertained to the implementation of the standards. Quite a few respondents noted that it was one thing to establish a set of standards and it was another thing to have the standards effectively implemented in classrooms. A North Carolina state representative, for instance, remarked:

> Of course [I support standards]! But standards are unfortunately worthless although they look good when they're pretty much ignored by those responsible for implementing them. When words have no meaning and measurements are meaningless, why pretend we have standards? The state reading standard for K-2 is a joke when testing is done using predictable texts and no one tells parents what is actually going on in the classroom. Putting standards in writing that are not followed is nothing more than a hoax.

In particular, policy actors held that adequate support—in terms of both fiscal resources and teacher professional development—was crucial for the standards to be implemented as intended and to achieve the outcomes as desired. A member of an educational professionals association in Connecticut made the following comment on the need for fiscal support: "I think standards are good. I have nothing really against them as long as the money is eventually put in to help districts carry out those standards, especially when there are new thrusts." With regard to professional development, a Maine media representative maintained that it was "absolutely crucial" because of all the changes that occurred in the recent years. He also told us that the biggest complaint among teachers was that there were not enough time and money put into professional development and that they were not getting enough training in how to meet the state standards. A representative of a Texas research organization made a similar argument:

> I think, if you're going to set standards, you also have to be able to make sure that teachers know those standards and are able to incorporate them into their instruction. So I don't think it's fair just to develop the standards and say, "Now teach them."

Other concerns conveyed by the state reading policy actors about state standards included pressures for teachers and school administrators, loss of local control, and lack of attention to individual differences when mandating common standards. Nevertheless, all in all, policy actors were supportive of state standards, believing that standards would promote both excellence and equity—high learning expectations for all learners. This viewpoint is evident in the comments of a Michigan policy actor who stated: "I think they are important because it insures that all kids are getting opportunities for equal kind of instruction and learning opportunities."

Finally, it is worth noting that many policy actors were not only supportive of standards in general, but also especially pleased with their state standards in particular. A member of an Indiana business association, for instance, expressed great pride in Indiana's standards:

> We want world class standards in regard to reading.... We had Achieve, which is a bipartisan organization out of D.C. that did an analysis. We had ... Sandra Stotsky who is a reading specialist out in New York who is sort of the premier in standards and said that Indiana's standards now in English language arts are the highest in the nation.

Also citing Achieve, a North Carolina policy actor spoke proudly of North Carolina's reading standards:

> Well, we just revised them and I'm very pleased with the way they are now. In fact, Achieve, a national organization, uses our English language arts as a model for other states. We have received good ratings from both conservative and liberal groups.

On the whole, although state reading policy actors expressed various concerns about and potential problems with state reading standards, the overall tone was clearly on the positive side. The issue of state tests, often talked about in tandem with state standards, however, appeared more controversial.

STATE READING TESTS

Policy actors were generally supportive of state reading tests as well, although to a lesser extent than they were of state reading standards. While 63% of the actors across the nine states held "highly positive" views about state standards (see Table 4.7), only 39% held "highly positive" views about state tests (see Table 4.9). On the other hand, while only 5% of actors held "negative" or "highly negative" views about state standards, more than twice as many (12%) held such views about state tests. Overall, policy actors' responses about state tests were somewhat more spread out across the different response categories and less concentrated on the positive side compared with their responses about state standards.

Another difference in policy actors' beliefs about these two issues was that there were greater variations between states in policy actors' beliefs about state tests than in their beliefs about state standards. With regard to

Table 4.9. Number and Percentage of Policy Actors in Different Response Categories for State Reading Tests, by State and Response Category

State	Highly Negative	Negative	Neutral	Positive	Highly Positive	Number of Policy Actors
Alabama	1 (6%)	0 (0%)	6 (38%)	5 (31%)	4 (25%)	16
California	3 (8%)	7 (18%)	3 (8%)	18 (45%)	9 (23%)	40
Connecticut	0 (0%)	1 (4%)	2 (8%)	14 (58%)	7 (29%)	24
Indiana	0 (0%)	2 (8%)	5 (19%)	9 (35%)	10 (39%)	26
Maine	1 (7%)	1 (7%)	1 (7%)	7 (44%)	6 (38%)	16
Michigan	0 (0%)	5 (17%)	3 (10%)	9 (30%)	13 (43%)	30
North Carolina	0 (0%)	3 (13%)	4 (17%)	8 (33%)	9 (38%)	24
Texas	2 (7%)	1 (4%)	2 (7%)	6 (21%)	17 (61%)	28
Utah	0 (0%)	0 (0%)	1 (5%)	7 (35%)	12 (60%)	20
Total	7 (3%)	20 (9%)	27 (12%)	83 (37%)	87 (39%)	224

Note: Number of policy actors is the number of actors with valid response to the relevant interview questions. Percentages in different belief categories may not add up to 100% due to rounding.

state standards, the percentage of actors holding either "positive" or "highly positive" views ranged between 81% and 95%, the percentage of actors holding "neutral" views between 0% and 13%, and the percentage of actors holding "negative" or "highly negative" views between 0% and 12% across the nine states. The corresponding ranges for state tests, however, were much wider: 56% ~ 95%, 5% ~ 38%, and 0% ~ 26% respectively across the states. These findings suggest that there was generally a lower level of agreement about state reading tests than about state reading standards among policy actors both within and across states.

Nevertheless, the overall pattern of response for state tests was similar to that for state standards in that the majority of the actors (76%) spoke favorably of state tests (i.e., "positive" or "highly positive"). Moreover, as was the case with state standards, support for state tests was significantly stronger among government actors than among nongovernment actors as shown in Table 4.10 (63% vs. 32% for "highly positive," $p < .001$). Policy actors, on the whole, believed that tests were necessary benchmarks to measure students learning and an important part of the accountability system. When asked whether he supported state reading standards, an Indiana house representative, for example, answered:

Oh, definitely! Oh, there has to be! And we're talking about accountability and also we need to have measurements of that accountability, and the greatest efforts are being made right now nationally to put down standard-

Table 4.10.   Number and Percentage of Policy Actors in Different Response Categories for State Reading Tests, by Actor Type and Response Category

Actor Type	Highly Negative	Negative	Neutral	Positive	Highly Positive	Number of Policy Actors
Government	1 (2%)	1 (2%)	2 (4%)	14 (29%)	31 (63%)	49
Nongovernment	6 (3%)	19 (11%)	25 (14%)	69 (39%)	56 (32%)	175
Total	7 (3%)	20 (9%)	27 (12%)	83 (37%)	87 (39%)	224

Note: Number of policy actors is the number of actors with valid response to the relevant interview questions. Percentages in different belief categories may not add up to 100% due to rounding.

ized tests.... Once there are standardized tests, then they will measure and show accountability in the classroom.... If they can get rid of that, then everything is relative, and there are no absolute criteria or standards of measurement by which to hold the schools and the teachers accountable. Testing is very, very important.

Indeed, for most policy actors, standards and tests went hand in hand and were both integral parts of an accountability system. As a Michigan state education official observed, "I think standards without some form of assessment are really only half of the package. Standards have meaning when there is an assessment. That's an external audit that provides some clean information in regard to pupil progress." Similarly, a respondent from Connecticut described standards not accompanied by tests as "floating standards or ad hoc standards—they are totally without meaning because there are no meaningful rewards for meeting them nor are there penalties for not meeting them."

Supporters of state tests also argued that tests were essential tools for diagnosing students' weaknesses and guiding instructional decisions. As an Indiana state education official put it plainly: "If you're going to teach something, you're going to have to test it. Otherwise, you're not going to know whether students are getting anywhere with it or not. You can't assume that they know things." State tests were considered essential not only for teachers to accurately gauge their students' learning, but also for keeping parents well informed of their children's progress in school. Dubious about the reliability of school grades, a Connecticut think tank consultant opined:

it seems to me every school district in this state claims to be above average, of course, like everybody in the country. And from the grades the children are getting on their report cards and from what teachers tell parents at those meetings that they have, there isn't a kid in the state who isn't doing wonderfully. But the nationally administered or statewide administered standardized tests tell a different story.... I find that a huge problem for parents.... The bottom line is parents have no idea how the school is doing ... or how the kids are doing by reading their report card because everybody gets As and Bs.

A member of a research organization in Connecticut perceived the problem similarly:

Standardized tests are needed so that parents and communities know how their town's schools are stacking up against others. If the public school employees were better educated themselves, and were more honest in self-assessment, standardized tests would not be needed.

While proponents for state tests often claimed that tests were important diagnostic tools that helped teachers to identify students' problems and adjust their instruction accordingly, others were skeptical about whether state tests could adequately serve a diagnostic function. In some instances, they argued, the tests were not designed to be diagnostic. In other instances, diagnosing was simply not the focus for users of the test results. As a member of a Connecticut business association observed:

You have to have the data. But it's really what you do with that information that's far more important. We've sometimes gotten caught up in reporting instead of getting caught up in figuring out from the information how to address the problem.

According to some policy actors, diagnosing reading problems was not really the intention of high stakes tests, because the impetus of testing was politically motivated, and certain stakeholders, such as politicians, the media, and real estate investors had a vested interest in test scores. A Connecticut reading researcher voiced his frustration poignantly: "Where I'm discouraged by the testing is that it's almost taken to a level that's beyond caring for the child or the development of literacy to evaluating the community and setting the real estate prices."

Indeed, although policy actors generally agreed that state tests were needed, they were quick to point out various potential problems associated with state tests. Another recurrent theme that we heard from state reading policy actors was the role of state tests within an accountability system. An overwhelming majority of actors saw state tests as only "one piece of the puzzle" and, as such, an incomplete and perhaps inaccurate representation of the true achievement levels of individual students or schools. They firmly believed that no single measure could adequately represent student achievement. The stance that an Alabama educational interest group took was fairly typical among the policy actors that we interviewed: "We are in support of state reading assessments.... We're not in support of an accountability system that's based on one measure." A California policy actor echoed, "I wouldn't rely on one single instrument to determine or make high stakes decisions, but I do think there's an important place for standardized tests in that system."

Local assessments and performance-based assessments, some believed, should also have a place in the accountability system. Such a perspective was particularly prevalent among policy actors in Maine, a state with a long-standing tradition of local control. A university researcher in Maine, for example, commented, "I would not support the state test as the only means of accountability. I do very much favor the development of local assessment systems." A representative from a Maine teachers' advocacy group felt even more strongly about local assessments: "The most powerful tests and assessments are ones that are given by a classroom teacher, one-on-one with a student to diagnose what that student needs and make plans for instruction." A conservative citizens group in Maine just opposed outright to any state mandates, as its executive director claimed, "I don't believe that there is anywhere in our state or federal Constitutions where education is a mandated issue. I believe in home rule and in local education. I would be opposed to state mandates." A lobbyist for a Michigan teachers organization similarly claimed, "Our position is "no" on [state tests]. We prefer that each individual school district would make that decision. I think we're bound into local control."

The concern that we heard most frequently about state tests during our interviews was their high stakes nature. Most of the respondents believed that state tests were given too much emphasis and drove almost everything in school. They had serious reservations about using high-stakes tests as the only factor in determining student promotion or retention and school rewards or penalties. As a member of a Connecticut educational professionals association remarked, "I would support a state test at the end of third grade. What I don't support is using that state test as a gatekeeper for kids and saying this is the sole reason for promotion or retention of a third grader."

Policy actors were particularly concerned that under the pressure of high-stakes tests, teachers were spending an inordinate amount of instructional time teaching to the tests and preparing students for the tests. A literacy professor in Michigan, for instance, opined:

> I'm not opposed to there being statewide assessment.... It is the abuses of those assessments that I think are problematic ... because they drive some very negative practices. I think the MEAP is an interesting case in point—it

has now become a verb.... We are "meaping." Meaping doesn't just mean taking the test; it means all the preparation.

Predictably, one major consequence of "meaping" or the like was the narrowing of the curriculum. Some policy actors even went so far as to say that in many schools and districts, the tests were becoming the curriculum. Concerned about the negative impact of high-stakes tests on curriculum, a Texas teachers association representative lamented:

> And whether that's leading to a general dumbing down of the curriculum across the state or not has been a subject of debate. But I think from the perspective of classroom teachers, as the focus narrows and the bar becomes sort of the lowest common denominator, a lot of other things are, in effect, being squeezed out of the curriculum.

Some respondents also pointed out that the overemphasis on test results might lead to unethical practices on the part of teachers and schools. A representative of a Connecticut conservative group mentioned that some principals had come under fire for assisting students during the standardized tests to make the results look better. A member of a Utah educational association also observed, "When you begin to tie teachers' salaries and everything to test results, then you get all of this cheating that is taking place, and there are significant problems, which I think are counter-productive."

While deploring teaching to the test and any unethical practices, policy actors did not blame it on teachers. As a matter of fact, many respondents were sympathetic towards teachers. A Maine professor, for instance, noted,

> I think [state test] does terrible things, not only to the kids in terms of anxiety level and negative learning, but also to teachers who then are not free to teach what they know they should be doing. They're trying to get everybody to pass the test so they won't be fired or whatever.

A Texas interest group member shared similar sentiments:

> The pressure on the teachers.... They feel their jobs are in jeopardy. They feel their raises are in jeopardy because there is so much emphasis placed on their ability to get these kids to spit out TAAS information. Somehow, that piece needs to be de-escalated. To the benefit of the children, you need to look and see how to implement that information; how to integrate it into curriculum without stripping the teachers entirely of their power or their ability to function independently.

In addition to pressure on teachers, our respondents also mentioned the pressure of state tests on schools and expressed concerns particularly about the fairness of rank-ordering schools and judging school performance solely on the basis of test results. Some respondents warned against "looking at any data in education in a vacuum." Schools in affluent neighborhoods, they maintained, were of course going to do better on test scores compared with schools in high-poverty neighborhoods. A former school superintendent in Connecticut made his point most aptly:

> I mean, the two biggest indicators of success are family and economic background and the highest level of education of the mother. Not the color of some kid's skin, but it's poverty and family background. And I look at, taking tests and doing those kinds of ranking is, like somebody described to me, it's like coming down the hill at the end of a battle and shooting the wounded.

In sum, state reading policy actors saw state tests as a "two-edged sword." They generally agreed that tests were necessary and could serve useful purposes in standards-based accountability systems. On the other hand, state tests were also seen as having a variety of problems and unintended consequences on students, teachers, and schools. Although overall, policy actors' support for state reading tests was strong, it was not as strong as their support for state reading standards, and it was often qualified by serious concerns and reservations.

DISCUSSION

All in all, our data reveal that the state reading policy communities demonstrated high levels of consensus on key policy issues both within and across states. The majority of the actors, for example, agreed that the NAEP results accurately represented the level of reading achievement in their respective states. Almost every actor thought that the reading achievement level was unacceptably low, although most actors, with the exception of those from Utah, believed that reading achievement was on the rise. Where pedagogy was concerned, over 90% of the actors favored a balanced approach or a balanced approach with an emphasis on phonics. About 90% of the actors also indicated positive and highly positive dispositions towards state reading standards. Policy actors' views toward state reading tests were somewhat more spread out than their views towards standards, but the overall consensus was still quite strong, with over three quarters of actors expressing positive or highly positive opinions about state tests. These findings suggest that the once highly contentious and polarized reading policy arena was settling down, and that disagreements were gradually giving way to consensus.

Another shared belief of the state reading policy actors was that good policy should not only improve student achievement in general but also promote equity. We heard repeatedly during our interviews that statewide standards and curriculum frameworks would ensure that all students be held to the same set of expectations and spur schools to provide students with equal opportunities to acquire the same knowledge and skills. Furthermore, many actors believed that statewide assessments are essential tools for evaluating student learning against the common standards, and an important means to hold teachers and schools accountable for the learning of all students. Equity was also brought up in discussions about pedagogy. In particular, many phonics proponents maintained that phonics instruction would be particularly beneficial for English language learners and socioeconomically disadvantaged students, and would help them to catch up with their more advantaged peers.

Interestingly, when it came to achievement levels, many actors had a somewhat different notion of equity. While policy actors overwhelmingly supported high expectations and common standards for all students and the closing of achievement gaps, many of the same actors argued that test results should account for differences in student demographics. A common refrain amongst the state reading policy actors was that state and district comparisons were inappropriate and unfair because of demographic differences in their student populations, and that we should not really expect the same level of achievement for students from different backgrounds. It seems that the state reading policy actors generally supported equity as it relates to equal educational expectations and reducing achievement gaps, but many did not want to be held accountable for inequitable distribution of student outcomes.

Finally, we would like to point out that although we analyzed the key reading policy beliefs separately, those beliefs were often interconnected. Participants in our study, for example, rarely explicated their viewpoints on state standards without bringing up the issue of state tests, and vice versa. For many, standards and tests are as inseparable as two sides of the same coin. Achievement levels and reading pedagogy were also often discussed within the context of standards and assessment. The interrelatedness of key policy issues in the perceptions of state reading policy actors is reflective of the systemic approach to standards-based education reform, which emerged in the early 1990s and laid the foundation for the accountability provisions of the No Child Left Behind Act of 2001 (Smith & O'Day, 1991). Proponents of systemic reform view policy fragmentation as the major problem with the education system, and argue for coherent policy systems with well-aligned and integrated components promoting ambitious outcomes for all students. Apparently, these ideas had taken hold among state reading policy actors.

NOTES

1. Valid Chi-square tests, however, could not be conducted to test the differences between states in the response patterns for the belief measures because of low frequency count (fewer than five) in many of the cells in the response-category-by-state cross-tabulations.

2. A Chi-square test showed no significant difference between government actors and nongovernment actors in their responses regarding the accuracy of NAEP results ($p > .05$).

3. We ran a logistic regression to compare government and nongovernment actors in their likelihood of demonstrating "highly positive" views about state reading standards, and found that government actors were significantly more likely to hold "highly positive" views than nongovernment actors ($p < .01$). A valid Chi-square test comparing the response patterns of government and nongovernment actors could not be conducted because 40% of the cells had a frequency count less than five.

CHAPTER 5

CAUSAL STORIES AND PROPOSED SOLUTIONS

In the previous chapter, we explored state reading policy actors' beliefs on a number of key policy issues—level and trend of reading achievement, reading pedagogy, state reading standards, and state reading tests. In this chapter, we shift our focus to a special type of policy belief: beliefs about the causes of the reading achievement problem. Beliefs about problem cause, or "causal stories," according to Stone (2002), are integral to the transformation of difficult conditions to policy problems, and to the definition or portrayal of the policy problems. Moreover, perceptions about the causes of a problem play a key role in the formulation and selection of policy solutions, as policy solutions are intended to resolve or alleviate the policy problem by eliminating, modifying, reducing, suppressing, or neutralizing the causes of the problem. Thus, understanding the causal stories put forward by state reading policy actors is essential to understanding the development of proposed policy solutions.

The purpose of this chapter is to examine state reading policy actors' causal stories and proposed policy solutions, as well as the linkage between the two. Our exploration of policy actors' causal stories is grounded in Stone's (2002) work about causal stories and agenda formation, which is briefly reviewed before we present our findings.

Reading: Policy, Politics, and Processes, pp. 99–139
Copyright © 2008 by Information Age Publishing
All rights of reproduction in any form reserved.

STONE'S FRAMEWORK OF CAUSAL THEORIES

Stone (2002) argues that problem definition is inherently a process of image making, during which policy actors deliberately portray societal conditions in ways calculated to gain support for their side, and compose stories that attribute cause, blame, and responsibility. Making a distinction between actions that have a purpose and actions that do not, and a distinction between intended consequences and unintended consequences, Stone proposes a typology of causal stories that classifies causal explanations commonly used in politics into four categories: accidental, mechanical, intentional, and inadvertent.

The first category, accidental causes, involves unguided actions and unintended consequences, which may include natural disasters, accidents, and occurrences in the realm of fate. The second category, mechanical causes, entails unguided actions and intended consequences. Causal stories of a mechanical nature may be created, for example, when "somebody acts purposefully, but their will is carried out through other people, through machines, or through 'automatic' social procedures and routines" (Stone, 2002, p. 193). Inadvertent causes, the third category, pertain to unintended consequences resulting from purposeful actions. Stories about inadvertent causes may spotlight the damaging side effects of well intentioned policies, avoidable ignorance, and carelessness or recklessness. The final category in the typology, intentional causes, concerns purposeful actions with intended consequences. Examples include rational actions when the consequences are perceived as good, and oppression and conspiracies when the consequences are perceived as bad.

In addition to these four types of relatively simple causal theories, Stone (2002) offers three types of more complex models of causal explanations: complex systems, institutional causes, and historical causes. Briefly, causal theories based on complex systems presume that failures or accidents are inevitable, because in the inherently complex interactive social systems, it is "impossible to anticipate all possible events and effects" (p. 195). When a problem is attributed to established patterns of behavior of large and longstanding organizations, the cause is thought to be institutional. Finally, historical or structural causes hold that social patterns tend to reproduce themselves, and that problems persist because: (a) those with power and resources to address the problem benefit from the status quo that keeps them in power, and therefore do not seek to address the problem, and (b) those victimized by the problem do not seek change because they do not see the problem as changeable and need the resources provided by existing conditions. Such complex causal explanations, according to Stone, are less likely to be employed in politics than are simple causal explanations, because they do not offer a single locus of control, a plausible candidate to take responsibility for the problem, or a point of leverage to fix the problem.

It is important to note that our focus for this chapter is on describing and understanding policy actors' causal beliefs about the reading problem, not on evaluating the credibility of their causal stories; nor do we seek to ascertain the "true" causes of the reading problem. As Stone (2002) contends, true causes must, in principle, be verified by scientific research. Claiming any cause for the reading achievement problem as categorically true is a challenge for at least four reasons. First, there is a lack of research examining the link between many of the perceived causes and reading achievement. The paucity of research is likely to result from the difficulty both in developing adequate measures of the relevant concepts and in designing methodologically rigorous studies with strong causal validity. Second, for potential causes that have been studied, the research evidence often fall short of being conclusive (e.g., studies of the effectiveness of different reading instructional methods). Third, learning is complex and state policy environments are multifaceted. As such, it is especially difficult to discern what factors in the state policy environment may have negatively impacted student learning. Last, some policy actors contend that there is no problem, and hence, there are no causes. In fact, some claim that the reading *problem* is an artifice crafted by actors with political, financial, or research agendas.

Clearly, an assessment of the credibility of various causal stories is beyond the scope of our research. We choose to focus instead on an understanding of the potential causes of the reading achievement problem as perceived by the state reading policy actors, which are documented in the section to follow.

PERCEIVED CAUSES OF THE READING ACHIEVEMENT PROBLEM

Our interviews with state reading policy actors generated rich data on their perceptions of the potential causes of the reading achievement problem. Drawing upon Stone's (2002) framework of causal theories, we coded the interview transcripts for themes that reflect the four categories of simple causal stories and the three complex causal models proposed by Stone. Table 5.1 presents the causal stories that we heard most frequently from the state reading policy actors, which are organized according to Stone's typology of simple causal stories. Note that we relabeled "accidental cause" in Stone's typology as "sociocultural cause" in order to more accurately depict the nature of the causal stories about the reading achievement problem.

**Table 5.1.   Simple Causal Stories of
the Reading Achievement Problem**

	Consequences	
Actions	*Intended*	*Unintended*
Unguided	*Mechanical Causes*	*Sociocultural Causes (Accidental Cause)*
	• [NONE]	• Demographic changes • Demographic conditions • Media influence • Cultural values and attitudes
Purposeful	*Intentional Causes*	*Inadvertent Causes*

	• Political deception
	• High stakes tests
	• Permissive immigration
	  policies
		• Pedagogy
		• Teacher preparedness (preservice and
		  inservice)
		• Resources
		• Response to demographic challenges
		• Parental involvement

Note: This table is adapted from the typology of simple causal theories presented in Table 8.1 on p. 191 in Stone (2002).

As Table 5.1 shows, state reading policy actors offered a variety of explanations for students' poor reading performance. Most of the causal stories portray the reading problem as an unintended consequence of purposeful or unguided human actions or government policies, and fall under the categories of sociocultural (accidental) causes and inadvertent causes. We did not hear any stories that described the reading problem as an intended consequence of unguided human actions (i.e., mechanical cause). We did hear, however, some actors asserting that the reading problem was an intended consequence of purposeful human actions (i.e., intentional cause), although such radical views were relatively rare. In the section to follow, we recount the causal stories most frequently told by state reading policy actors in the categories of sociocultural causes, inadvertent cause, and intentional causes.

Sociocultural Causes

Stories about sociocultural causes, or "accidental causes" in Stone's terminology, pertain to phenomena that are "devoid of purpose, either in their actions or consequences" (Stone, 2002, p. 190). Typical examples in this category given by Stone are often "in the realm of accident and fate" such as hurricanes, earthquakes, and machines that run amok. Where the reading achievement problem is concerned, many causal stories that we heard were about unintended consequences resulting from causes that were unguided and beyond human control, and thus clearly fit into the category of accidental causes. However, those causal stories were often about social and cultural factors, and it does not seem quite accurate to characterize them in terms of accident or fate. Therefore we changed Stone's label for accidental causes to "sociocultural causes" in order to better depict the nature of causal stories about demographic changes, demographic conditions, media influence, cultural values, and attitudes, among others.

Demographic Changes

Causal stories that attribute the reading problem to demographic changes fall under this category. According to such causal stories, declining reading achievement was a by-product of larger societal changes and population shifts, most notably the influx of students with limited English proficiency (LEP) or English language learners. Many study participants believed that the growing population of English language learners posed tremendous challenges to schools and teachers and "dragged down" the test scores, in the words of a California newspaper reporter.

While concerns about the impact of English language learners were particularly wide-spread among policy actors in California, we also heard them from respondents in every other state in our study. The director of an Indiana literacy group, for instance, believed that reading achievement in their state had probably decreased, and that "a lot of that might be attributed to the high influx of the Hispanic population primarily." A Utah state education official, for instance, commented:

> I think [the reading problems] have only become more dramatic in Utah because of the changing demographics we have within our state. We have a lot more ESL children coming into the state. And we have been unprepared to address those kinds of things and all of a sudden 21 languages might be in an elementary school and trying to teach those children to read has been certainly a challenge.

A member of a Texas educational association further noted that very often students who are limited English proficient also come from households with limited social and economic resources, further exacerbating the situation. He remarked:

> Clearly some of the factors are just our mushrooming student population and an awful lot of the new students coming in are coming from Mexico. They are now a majority minority student population.... We have a population, I think, that is disproportionately low income, bilingual, don't have the advantages maybe that some other students have had when they arrive at

the schoolhouse door ... [we try to] catch the problems as early as we can and get those folks up to speed, because we do have a more challenging student population to work with.

Demographic Conditions

Where demographics were concerned, causal stories were told not only about demographic changes, but also about demographic conditions, the latter of which relate to the general composition, rather than changes in the composition, of the student population. Frequently, participants cited the well-documented correlations between student achievement and their socioeconomic status, andclaimed that the high concentration of African American and Latino students, English language learners, or students from low-income families in their states was the primary reason for the low reading scores. For example, when asked whether the National Assessment of Educational Progress (NAEP) scores were an accurate portrayal of the reading problem in her state, an Alabama professor replied:

> Probably, because we are a poor state. I mean, I happen to believe that vocabulary and experiences are terribly tied ... closely tied, as everybody thinks, to socioeconomic level. So I guess I think we've done real well to just have 44%, given the poverty in the state.

A university faculty member in Michigan expressed a similar opinion, although in language that might be less accessible to people outside the academia:

> You gonna find that it's mostly societal factors.... I believe, I'm not a complete deterministist. I believe the data from reports like the Coleman report basically gave the school maybe 10% to 20% of the variance, but the other 80% variance comes from community, class, things like that.

In addition to socioeconomic status, "ruralness" was also seen as related to low academic achievement, as implied by the remark from a member of a North Carolina interest group: "We're a very rural state and we have pockets of just really poor performing schools." Implicit in such observations was the suggestion that the school system did not have control over the influence of students' demographic background on their achievement, and hence could not be held fully accountable for the reading problem or achievement problems in general. A literacy professor in Maine thus elaborated on this idea:

> The fact of the matter is we have not been able to change the demographics. You know, Maine is a poor state with many schools rural, small, and very poor funding for education.... Well, poverty of course is a major contributor because many of our families are rural families. They don't have access to

quality day-care ... all the kids do is sit in front of the TV. They don't go any-where. They don't do anything. Poor language development. No access to transportation. So I think it has to do with ruralness.

Media Influence

Another recurrent theme in the sociocultural causal stories told by the state reading policy actors was the influence of the media, particularly television and video games, which was mentioned by participants from every state in our study. A Utah government actor, for instance, blamed electronic media for diverting childrens' attention away from printed media, opining: "The TV is on. The video games are on. The Internet is on. All of those are taking kids away from reading.... You're off doing all kinds of activities and reading isn't a priority or focus." A member of a Texas citizens organization similarly attributed low reading achievement to the pervasiveness of electronic media, remarking: "It's the fact that the kids are watching so much television, they are not so interested in read-ing, and they get so involved in those video games and all that."

The sociocultural nature of causal stories about media influence was most clearly revealed in the observation made by a Michigan business group representative, who bemoaned, "We've created an entertainment culture that doesn't challenge kids to get out and do the hard work of reading anymore." Also speaking from a cultural perspective, a Maine lit-eracy professor commented:

> Another change teachers are seeing is children being so much more involved in media events before school that this results in less work with books and exposure to books and reading and writing. That's part of the culture we live in and also part of the phenomenon of more and more parents working. You know, single parent families or two-parent families who are both people working, there's less time devoted to the children. I think that day care and childcare programs and providers have not always been ... have not bucked this trend in general. There's a lot of use of TV, video and so forth.

Cultural Values and Attitudes

Although not as frequently mentioned as the demographic factors or media influence, value systems that did not emphasize the importance of education were also seen as contributing to the reading problem in a few states. The director of an Indiana foundation, for instance, claimed, "Collective brainstorming is needed to challenge Indiana's environ-ment, which does not support a learning culture." The executive direc-tor of an Indiana government agency further elaborated:

> It's definitely a problem.... It's more of a southern kind of attitude towards education that education really isn't valued in this state.... [T]he majority of

the state is rural and a lot of folks think that, just graduate from high school and go get yourself a factory job. That is just changing, but the attitude as far as you're not really valuing education, it's still prevalent. So until you can convince the seven and a half million people who live here that education is important for everyone, there's going to be this reading problem.

The representative of a Texas teacher organization noted a similar problem in their state:

[W]e were also a state that not only didn't value education, had more scorn for education than respect for a long time. The strategy in Texas for most of the century for economic success was to strike oil on the family farm. And the thinking was that as long as you were willing to work hard, you could make a fortune in Texas if you had the gumption, and education was maybe a nice add-on, but maybe not.

A similar observation was also made by a past president of a Maine literacy organization, who linked students' lack of aspiration and their lack of appreciation for the value of education to the unique geographic location of the state, remarking:

One of the things in Maine that we really have to talk about and work on is aspirations. How our students see themselves in a bigger world and what their place is in the bigger world. And we're up in the Northeast corner and there's an isolation that goes with that. You're sort of protected. You have this simply little world here that's not very complicated and a lack of appreciation for the complexities of life beyond our border. And a lot of our kids still don't know the value of their education; don't know where that might take them.

Causal stories about demographic changes, demographic conditions, media influence, and cultural values and attitudes as described above were the most frequently heard sociocultural explanations for the reading achievement problem. Additional causal stories in this category included increased expectations for what students should be able to do and higher demand for literacy skills in an information-driven society, among others. Common among such stories was the belief that the causes of the reading problem were natural occurrences or phenomena that were largely beyond human control. Therefore, school systems, teachers, or anyone else, were not to blame for the problems due to such causes.

It is interesting to note that while many study participants believed that sociocultural factors were the causes of the reading problem, others framed the issue somewhat differently. From their perspective, certain sociocultural factors, demographic shifts and demographic conditions in particular, were not really the causes of the problem, but were actually explanations for why reading achievement was not a problem in their state or at least was not as big of a problem as it appeared. A California state education official, for instance, downplayed the reading problem in the state by saying:

> I think it is true that a lot of kids in California have had some difficulty reading; that that is tied to the heavy, heavy immigration we had during the late '80s and '90s; and that I believe that they have looked at the NAEP scores with the English language learners extracted and that we don't look that bad under those circumstances. So I think part of it is a language phenomenon. I think part of it may be ... what the construct is of basic and proficient. And I've heard it is said that even Connecticut didn't do that well in terms of, if you look at how many are proficient.

An academic similarly suggested that California's reading problem as highlighted by the NAEP state comparisons was largely exaggerated given the way English language learners were treated in NAEP, stating:

> [The decision to make state comparisons on NAEP] set the trap for the drum that was being beaten in 1995 of California's children were failing to learn how to read. The ... feds defined limited English proficient children as children who have been in the system 3 or less years. So once they have been in the system 4 years, the feds reclassify limited English proficient children in with the English-only scores.... So if the feds lump in children who have been in the country 4 to 5 years to 6 years with the English-only scores, then if California serves 40% of the limited English speaking proficient children in the country, we are naturally going to look bad compared to any other state, except Alaska.

Clearly, depending on the spin of the story teller, the same facts could be used to compose very different stories. Some used the demographic data to explain the existence of a problem, whereas others used the same data to explain the lack of a problem. Nevertheless, those discounting the reading problem were certainly in the minority; the majority of the policy actors did not express any doubt about the reading problem and easily related various causal stories. While policy actors often linked the reading achievement problem to social and cultural factors that were largely beyond human control, many also believed that the reading problem was attributable to purposeful human actions as indicated by the inadvertent causal stories that they told.

Inadvertent Causes

Inadvertent causes pertain to unintended consequences caused by purposeful human actions (Stone, 2002). Inadvertent causal explanations commonly involve: (a) harmful side effects of well-intentioned policy, where consequences are predictable but unforeseen (e.g., minimum wage policies); (b) harmful consequences due to actions of uninformed individuals, which often reflects ignorance (e.g., poverty or diseases related to lifestyle choices); and (c) harmful consequences brought about by entities that understand the consequences but engage in the behavior anyway (e.g., carelessness or recklessness). Of the four basic categories of causal stories proposed by Stone, most of the stories told by state reading policy actors fit into this category, and typically centered around the following themes: pedagogy, teacher preparedness, resources, responses to demographic challenges, and parental involvement.

Pedagogy

Of the various types of inadvertent causes mentioned by state reading policy actors, pedagogy was mentioned most frequently, and were discussed, often fervently, by respondents in all nine states in our study. Flawed pedagogy was featured as the primary culprit for the reading problem in some stories, and played a secondary role in others, particularly stories about the ill preparation of teachers.

What is particularly noticeable about such stories is that they overwhelmingly blamed whole language as the cause for low reading achievement levels, and few, if any, pointed fingers to phonics. The most vehement criticism of whole language came from a conservative think tank member in Connecticut:

> Whole language is a means of collective kidding yourself. It doesn't teach children to read. There's nothing in the language of whole language that says, "Here's how to teach a child to read." It is all a set of expectations. There are no methods involved.... Whole language teachers say, "Well, my kids can't read, but they love books." Exactly! They have been taught to appreciate that there are books, but they have not been taught how to read them.... But the kids don't learn to read by themselves. Tragic! Almost criminal!... English is a Phonetic language. It cannot be learned when it is taught as a pictographic language. Whole language teachings are causing 99% of the reading problems in our schools. That has been proven for decades. Today's children are the victims of whole language.

Other actors faulted low reading achievement to the lack of phonics instruction. As the president of a North Carolina professional association claimed, "We got away from doing the phonics, and it killed us." A North Carolina state house representative also asserted:

> We haven't made tremendous gains because basically phonics is not being taught in North Carolina public schools.... I think as long as they have

whole language as the foundation for teaching reading, they are going to come up short and not make the progress that they need to make.

Rather than blaming a particular instructional approach, some actors criticized the ideological discord. They maintained that focusing on either approach was counterproductive and recommended a comprehensive approach that best accommodates the needs of individual students. The comments from the director of an Indiana governmental agency illustrate this viewpoint:

> The problem is that people have gotten religion about this. When in fact it really is an issue that has to do with the way different children read or learn to read, and it's highly probably that in almost every classroom, if not every classroom, there are kids that learn both ways and in some combination of those ways. So what we've done is to reduce a very complex problem to an ideological war and that's really sad.

A Maine professor also held that the reading wars promote a strategy-centered rather than a child-centered discussion, observing:

> We were seeing kids struggling to learn to read under fairly rigid and sometimes totally contradictory reading strategies.... [The] dichotomy that is really bogus, but it seemed like in the '80's it took on a life of its own. We found the dichotomy growing and not serving kids well because while some kids will respond and do well under either of those approaches, there are a lot of kids who won't do well under just one approach.

Instead of focusing on the appropriate approach to teaching reading, some causal stories focused on the incoherence of instructional methods, and the negative impact of education fads and idiosyncratic practices. A Michigan business group representative, for instance related:

> Well, unfortunately, I think we've gotten into a lot of trends, or a lot of what's stylish, or is the reading program du jour sort of thing and it comes and goes, and education sort of goes, "What new theory do we want to try today? This new program?" and that sort of thing. So I think we've been susceptible to that and I think that's had an impact. And once again how reading is taught in School A and three blocks down, School B, may be completely different.

Incoherent instructional methods existed not only between schools, but also within schools, as indicated by the following observation from a member of a California educational association:

> What we found in Oakland was every teacher had his or her own reading approach. There was no school approach. There was no district approach.

And there's an increasing view that you just can't do that. You have to have, maybe at the school level, it doesn't have to be district-wide, you have to have some thought about what your teachers are trying to do in reading.

Although the nuances of the pedagogical causal stories varied, the theme persisted—no matter how well-intentioned the instructional methods were, they failed to foster the acquisition of basic and comprehensive reading skills. It is to note that few study participants put the blame for flawed instructional methods squarely on teachers. A couple of education policymakers actually took the blame themselves. A formal California state education official, for instance, acknowledged:

It was about mid-80's that [the report *Becoming a Nation of Readers*] came out. It basically said, "Dear phonics, get it over with and get them on so they can read." We sent that out to every principal in California a year before the framework. So we figured there was not going to be really an issue, but this skills stuff. Well, what happened is people interpreted the literature framework as saying, "You don't have to teach skills." And a lot of our people did that; the ones in the department and so forth. So we were at fault by not being closer to it and watching it closely enough.

Most participants, however, traced teachers' ineffectual instructional practices to substandard preservice preparation programs and inadequate inservice training, among others, as detailed below.

Teacher Preparedness

While flawed instructional approach was widely perceived as contributing to the reading achievement problem, many study participants did not think it fair to blame it all on teachers. They argued instead that inadequate preservice and inservice training left teachers ill-prepared for effective teaching, which in turn led to the reading problem. The causal chain was thus extended by one link, and traced the origin of the problem to teacher preparation programs that did not equip future teachers with the essential knowledge and skills that they needed, and to school systems that did not provide adequate inservice training to help teachers implement effective instructional practices. A school district representative from California, for instance, thus explained the reason for the low reading achievement in their state:

Our colleges and universities haven't done a good job of preparing teachers to teach reading…. Teachers don't really come out of the colleges and universities with a good sense of how to teach reading. They come out with more of … I don't want to call it skill … they come out with how to plan for reading games and reading centers and you know, how to nurture children to a love of reading, but not in teaching reading. And I think that's contributed to the dismal statistics.

An Alabama state education official told a similar story and made a poignant comment: "Sometimes teachers are victims too." A state education official in Connecticut was more forthright in her criticism of higher education institutions, asserting: "They are a disaster. An absolute disaster! They're not teaching anything. They don't have any curriculum and you can't get them to move on this." Even a university professor from Utah acknowledged higher education institutions' responsibility for the reading problem, admitting: "[One] problem [was] with we as the people who prepare teachers. I don't think we've given them the tools that they need ... to adequately teach reading."

Other than general criticisms about the inadequacy of preservice programs for preparing effective reading teachers, our respondents also noted three specific problems with those programs: (1) promotion of unproven or unsubstantiated practices, (2) insufficient coursework in reading; and (3) professors' partiality toward certain strategies. The first problem was evident in the remarks made by a university professor in Alabama, who stated, "I think the universities have been promoting some reading education policies that haven't been research-based and philosophy-based." A governmental actor in California concurred: "The content of the preparation has not been founded on current and confirmed research, but more on the opinions and theories of the particular professors." A Connecticut respondent affiliated with a policy foundation made a similar comment, but in harsher terms. She opined, "Schools of education and teachers colleges. That's where the dumbing down starts. They enroll low-quality students and faculties and teach low-quality information and misinformation. They perpetuate beliefs whose errors have long been exposed."

In addition to the view that teacher preparation courses were not grounded in research-based practices, actors expressed concerns over the amount of reading coursework that teachers were required to take in their teacher preparation programs. This concern is evident in the remarks of an Indiana educational association policy actor:

> I think that one of the controversies that's come about or questions that have been raised by the General Assembly is the amount of reading courses elementary teachers are required to take to become licensed. There's some concern that they aren't prepared enough to do the diagnostics and that sort of thing, in order to help students read.

A member of a North Carolina state education agency also indicated that a major issue yet to be resolved is that teacher preparation programs did not spend sufficient time in the teaching of how to teach reading.

Finally, many study participants were critical of the ideological inclinations of university professors. They held that many professors did not teach a full range of instructional approaches and skills because they favored particular approaches. In most instances, the blame was laid at the feet of professors who supported whole language or literature-based approaches. The director of an Indiana reading organization, for instance, stated, "We really have the child who is losing out, and of course, the major problem [is] this is a guru land or the Shangri-La land of whole language professors." Even a professor from Indiana criticized his colleagues' inability to achieve consensus and insistence on promoting their favored instructional approach, commenting:

> Every freaking faculty member has their own solution and goes down in flames yelling that "I have the answer." And if we only get some consistency, we'd be one hell of a lot better off; and if we got the faculty members with the egos out of the problem we'd be a lot better off.

Although less frequently mentioned than weak preservice training, inadequate inservice training was also seen as a factor contributing to ineffective teaching and low reading achievement. The president-elect of an Indiana literacy organization, for instance, lamented: "I think our biggest problem in Indiana is we have no professional development, systematic professional development for teachers. So school systems tend to spend their money on programs rather than professional development." A Michigan education official likewise noted, "We have had no commitment to professional development in this state for the last ten years.... We have wasted a lot of money because we didn't know how to target professional development to changing teaching behavior. And that's what we should have done." The problem of insufficient teacher training was also present in Maine, as a representative of a media organization from the state commented:

> In some cases though teachers end up being bewildered.... They're not getting a whole lot of training.... In general the biggest complaint I hear from teachers in Maine is that there is not enough time and money put into professional development. And in the case of reading, it's absolutely crucial because so much has changed in the past five years and teachers will say: "We have these standards now that we're supposed to meet, but we're not getting training in how to do that."

While the above observation could be interpreted as a causal story about teacher preparedness, it could also be interpreted as a story about resources, in particularly, the lack of money for professional development. This latter view is clearer in the following remark made by a Michigan state education official: "We never really had money to define what we mean by comprehension strategies and to systematically help teachers to implement it in their classroom." Indeed, the boundaries between different types of causal stories are sometimes fuzzy and blurred; the same issue could be framed and interpreted in multiple ways, depending on the slant of the story teller and the listener.

Resources

State reading policy actors' causal stories about resources were not limited to the lack of funding for professional development, but covered a variety of areas. It seems, according to our respondents, that resources— both fiscal and nonfiscal—for schools were nearly always insufficient. In addition to the lack of funding for professional development, participants repeatedly attributed the reading problem to deficit of resources with respect to class size, qualified teachers, and books and libraries, to name just a few.

The class size issue is a double-edged sword. On one hand, actors contended that large classes made it difficult for teachers to deliver effective instruction that met the unique needs of individual students. On the other hand, as in the case of California in particular, reducing class sizes generated a greater shortage of teachers. As a result, as a California policy actor observed, "California has many, many more inexperienced, uncredentialed teachers because of the class size reduction."

Concerns about teacher qualifications were not unique to California, but shared by actors across all nine states. Some actors held that good teachers were in short supply because teaching was an underpaid yet demanding profession. As a consequence of teacher shortage, the number of unlicensed teachers and inexperienced teachers grew tremendously in many states. A North Carolina policy actor, for example, observed, "We don't have enough teachers, and right now we have a lot of people entering the profession through lateral entry ... with a lower level of teaching expertise." A member of a Maine educational association shared an anecdotal story that revealed her grave concerns about teacher quality:

> You know, the old idea, "Those who can't, teach." And of course now anybody can teach, right? Because they're going to be taking donkeys off the street to teach school because they won't have enough qualified teachers to do it. And so everybody is in a panic. We have a person who comes in and substitutes here occasionally who went through the fast track in New York City and I'm sorry ... this person does not know how to teach kids. This person is a babysitter.... Teaching is a human endeavor and human resources are important.

Another type of resources that was a topic of policy actors' causal stories was books and libraries. A well-known reading scholar in California, for instance, linked students' reading achievement to their access to libraries, and lamented, "California's children have little access to books. The worst school libraries in the country, among the worst public libraries." A member of an educational association in Indiana likewise remarked, "Indiana libraries are horrifically behind where they should be."

Other than what was discussed above, participants also mentioned additional resource-related barriers to effective teaching and learning, such as lack of investment in preschool programs, low teacher salaries, poor working conditions, and lack of reading consultants. There were also participants who attributed the reading problem to a lack of resources in general, as indicated by the executive director of a North Carolina professional association:

> You've got to get the resources into those schools to [address the reading problems]. So we still have clumps of schools where over half the kids are below grade level, and everybody knows it's resources, but they don't seem to be quite getting there.

Responses to Demographic Challenges

Another common theme in inadvertent causal stories pertains to school system's lack of adequate response to demographic challenges. As is clear from our earlier discussion about sociocultural causal stories, many policy actors perceived demographic factors—demographic shifts and demographic conditions—as the cause of the reading achievement problem. Other actors, however, framed the issue differently. While recognizing the influence of demographic factors on student achievement, these actors believed that the cause of the problem was not demographics per se, but rather school system's lack of adequate response to various challenges related to demographics. The nature of the causal story was thus no longer sociocultural, but inadvertent.

When asked what factors contributed to the declining reading scores in Utah, for example, a state education official answered: "What I think has been happening is that our kids have been changing and teachers have not changed their teaching behaviors to match the needs of kids." He further elaborated:

> We have not adapted to meet the needs of diverse learners. We just haven't done it in the state, and teachers don't know how to do it ... they have a child with a second language, or speak English as a second language. They are stuck dead in their tracks. They don't know what to do.... And there's no doubt in my mind that that has hurt us. One of the single biggest things that I hear from teachers is, "Tell me what to do with the children who come into

my classroom not knowing English.... I don't know what to do." ... [W]e
need to be really careful not to imply that that means our diverse learners
were causing the low scores, it's teachers who are not able to adapt to individual student needs that are different from what they have traditionally
worked with.

As such, the reading problem in Utah was not blamed on demographic shifts, but on the failure of the school system to adequately
address the challenges brought about by the demographic shifts. Challenges to effective teaching stemmed not only from demographic shifts,
but also from existing demographic conditions. Many actors pointed
out the challenges associated with students living in poverty and
English language learners, and argued that schools had not been able
to meet the unique needs of those students. A Utah state education official, for instance, observed:

Children who live in high socioeconomic areas do just fine. Our children
who live in poverty are the ones who are scoring below basic for the most
part. And so it really is an SES factor and whatever we've done to try to mitigate those circumstances, and we have tried to with our highly impacted
dollars going to those schools in the most need, Title I dollars going, but
you know what?, we obviously are not doing some of the things right that we
ought to be doing.

Among the things that ought to be done but are not done right to
mitigate the negative impact of socioeconomic factors are effective
instructional methods and sufficient resources targeted to students from
disadvantaged backgrounds, according to some study participants.
These participants spoke about an "interaction effect" between demographics and certain inadvertent causes, suggesting that inadvertent
causes such as ineffective pedagogy and lack of resources are particularly detrimental to disadvantaged students. A California researcher, for
example, opined:

On the NAEP, I believe, that the percentage of kids who were African-
American and Hispanic who were scoring extremely low on NAEP, where
it was quite astronomical. I'm thinking it's like between 70 and 80 per-
cent were scoring below basic; and, therefore, it was evident that they
weren't getting the type of instruction that they should have been. And
one can only make the connection that it was because of that whole lan-
guage-type of instruction they were probably getting from the 1980s and
1990s.

Additionally, some study participants pointed out that when resources
(e.g., funding, instructional materials and libraries, professional

development opportunities, special instructional programs, and highly qualified teachers) are scarce, students most in need are often disproportionately affected. A Texas professor commented:

> I think we've made progress in getting more funds into minority schools. It still continues to be a problem. I think Texas is one of the places where this whole issue of the equity of school funding continues to be played in the courts. We've got our Robin Hood plan right now that we're working under, and I suspect that that's not going to hold up and work very long.

An Alabama interest group member made a similar statement:

> We ought to be spending more on education, but instead we spend less, and so as a result, what we get out is basically what we put in.... [I]f you're an Alabama student and you're upper middle-class you can go through our school system and get as good an education probably as you could anywhere else cause your parents are going to see to it. But if you're a poor student, you're going to be much worse off because we have no money to help that.

Parental Involvement

The statement from the Alabama respondent quoted above mentioned another important character in causal stories about the reading problem: parents. Policy actors frequently blamed parents for not paying adequate attention to their children's educational needs and for not providing a supportive home environment conducive to their children's reading development. A Utah legislator, for instance, believed that the declining reading achievement in Utah was at least in part due to the failure of parents to do their share for their children's learning. He said:

> I think the parents have tremendous responsibility to look out for their own children's education. And I think there's a prevalent attitude of considering public education as a babysitter and for parents of elementary-aged children not to take individual responsibility for the reading performance of their children.

A Michigan education association representative voiced his criticism of parents in even harsher terms: "There's a certain selfishness about adults and parents these days in terms of childrearing today, like 'I want my time. I want my career.... And I don't want to spend all the time [with my kids].'"

Many study participants acknowledged that in today's fast-paced society, parents, particular working parents, are just too busy to spend time with their children. A member of an education association in Michigan, for example, observed:

> We've got more busy parents. It doesn't necessarily have to be low socioeco-
> nomic. If you've got both parents working and they're not taking the time
> with their kids and reading to them, which we know is effective, then you are
> going to see the results in kids when they start school.

A Texas interest group representative concurred:

> I think that it really has a lot to do with what parents put as a priority. We
> know very definitely that the children who have been encouraged to read
> and who are read to and read with, that those are the children that really
> do succeed with their reading. I think that part of our problem is that
> everyone has just gotten so busy and rush, rush, rush here and there, that
> we have not taken the time to do that kind of reading preparedness that
> we need.

Another reason for the lack of parental involvement, according to our respondents, was that some parents themselves were illiterate, unedu-cated, or nonnative English speakers, and as such, did not have the ability or skills to provide preliteracy experiences for their children. Some respondents spoke about "cycles of illiteracy in the family." A professor from California, for instance, remarked:

> I think it's somewhat a vicious circle that the education level of the parent ...
> doesn't allow them to assist their child as well as they might.... There is less
> access to books. The books aren't in the home. And just overcoming the
> other poverty factors, which seem to be a major hurdle.

An Indiana state education official similarly attributed some children's reading problem to the literacy level of their parents, claiming: "Partially [the reading problem is] an adult literacy problem. I mean we've got par-ents who can't read themselves, let alone read to their kids."

While the above causal stories all blame parents for their lack of sup-port for their children's reading development, others believed that the school system should have done a better job in promoting parental involvement in student learning. A North Carolina state education offi-cial, for instance, pointed out, "[O]ne of the key needs that we have is probably parent education and parent involvement and also probably ongoing staff development for teachers." A Maine citizens group repre-sentative also acknowledged:

> I would say a big component of any achievement problem would have to
> do with how we're involving parents at the local level, beginning at the

preschool level and immediately upon entry into the school. We are not doing that well at all. We're not involving parents in the important things around education. It's unfortunate, but that really is the case here in Maine.

Less prevalent than the inadvertent causal stories discussed above were causal explanations concerning social promotion, lack of rigorous standards and accountability, and overcrowded curricula, among others. A California policy maker, for instance, held that social promotion policies "pushed [students] through the grades" even though they had failed to learn basic reading skills, the result of which was persistent reading difficulties. Some actors also indicated that state standards and accountability systems were not rigorous enough to push schools to ensure learning for all students. Finally, some actors criticized overcrowded school curricula, which they believed did not allow sufficient time and resources to be devoted to reading instruction.

These causal explanations, like causal stories about pedagogy, teacher preparedness, resources, responses to demographic challenges, and parental involvement, all construed the reading problem as an unintended, although often predictable, consequence of purposeful human actions. Thus, they also fell under the category of inadvertent causes, according to Stone's (2002) typology. Next, we move on to another type of causal story that has a very different connotation than those that we just reviewed.

Intentional Causes

Unlike stories about sociocultural and inadvertent causes that view the reading problem as an unintended consequence, stories about intentional causes portray the reading problem as an intended consequence of deliberate human actions that were willfully taken in order to bring about the consequence or taken with full knowledge of what the consequence would be. Intentional causal stories thus convey strong causality and represent the most forceful allegation of blame. It would seem that of the four types of causal stories that Stone (2002) proposes, intentional causes would be the least likely to be mentioned where the reading problem is concerned. After all, who would willfully or knowingly act to hinder students' acquisition of reading skills—the fundamental building block to all learning? Indeed, we rarely heard stories about intentional causes of the reading problem, but a few study participants did voice their concern that the decline or the seeming decline in reading achievement was directly traceable to deliberate decisions and activities of persons or groups with special agendas.

These participants described three types of intentional causes for the reading problems in their respective states—political deception, high stakes tests, and permissive immigration policies. The first two types of intentional causes are interlinked and fit into a conspiracy story purported by some of our participants. Specifically, some participants believe that much like the issue of education in general, reading achievement was political. Simply, a reading problem made for interesting political fodder. A Utah school district representative noted that the reading problem was a point of leverage to address concerns about public education, remarking: "Well, it's just become a political football. I think the right-wing conservatives have taken it on as an example of how schools are failing." A Utah right-wing conservative likewise observed:

> [They are] always talking about the fact that test scores are going down, that Utah is not doing as well as they had hoped they would be doing, that as a nation we are doing horrible and that we have fallen from the top to almost the bottom as a nation in literacy. So, that always creates politics; that always creates agendas. And of course the last ten years, all of your politicians have used education as their platform.... It's interesting how very few politicians ever come up with solutions, they just come up with platforms.

Additionally, some actors hold that high stakes tests were intentionally used to highlight failure. Responding to our question about the magnitude of the reading achievement problem, for example, the president of a Texas citizens group claimed, "I think that it's being pumped right now for politics. I don't believe it. I think the numbers are cooked." According to some respondents, were a variety of ways in which tests could be manipulated to point to low reading achievement. The test cut points, for instance, could be selected to make passing the tests or achieving a certain level difficult, might have exaggerated the reading problem. Inappropriate comparisons of test results across schools, states, and time might also misrepresent the reading problem. A member of a Maine citizens group, for example, made the following comment on the political aspects of testing: "The tests are not just educational tests, but they become also an element of social engineering. So I think one has to be very careful when they talk about achievement testing."

A Michigan public official moved beyond the interpretation of the tests and argued that the very development of tests was a political process, sharing: "State testing can only be done through what? The political process! So politics will determine what the standards are and what the test questions are." To these actors, the much-talked-about reading problem did not necessarily reflect the lack of reading skills, but were more likely to result from the intentional misrepresentation of reading achievement by those with a special political agenda.[1]

Also falling under the category of intentional causes are permissive immigration policies adopted by politicians who knew well the likely consequences. Some study participants, particularly those from Texas, believed that the growing number of English language learners from families of illegal immigrants, the reading difficulties that they experienced, and the challenges that they posed to schools largely resulted from the actions of politicians who chose not to enforce existing immigration policies or supported permissive immigration rules and underpayment of illegal workers. When asked what contributed to the reading problem in Texas, the president of a Texas conservative group answered:

> Well, we have a runaway immigration issue. Actually, it's an illegal alien issue. Regretfully, those Hispanic speakers do not learn then to read or write in their own native tongue, Spanish. And when they are given a test in English, they can't read it; and they're given a test in Spanish, they can't read it.

A Texas legislator also spoke about the immigration problem, or, the "border" problem:

> I think Texas has some unique problems with the long border and a lot of kids coming across that maybe haven't even been in school. We get kids moving in that are fourth or fifth grade age and have never been to school in their life and can't speak English.

A member of a Texas educational professional association echoed:

> The only thing that has really changed is that we continue to have kids with more and more needs because of the kind of state where we are, being on the border and the kinds of birthrates that come with people in poverty.

Complex Causes

The sociocultural, inadvertent, and intentional causes discussed above are all considered *simple causes* in that they imply a single actor (who may be a collective entity) and an identifiable action as the causal agent (Stone,

2002). Our study participants also offered more complex causal stories that are consistent with the complex causal models proposed by Stone: complex systems, institutional causes, and historical causes. Such stories, however, were relatively rare.

Complex Systems

Complex systems causal stories underscore the convoluted and interactive nature of social systems, which makes it impossible to anticipate all possible events and effects. Thus, malfunctions and mishaps are unavoidable. In the context of reading policy, a number of study participants noted the complexities in developing and implementing sound and effective state reading policy. A governmental actor from Indiana, for instance, remarked of Indiana's policy milieu: "It's all piecemeal; there isn't one systemic initiative that is touching everybody. It's everybody scrambling to figure out their own little part of the puzzle."

One reason that the policy development process is so complex, according to an Indiana professor, is that there is no single state entity solely responsible for developing educational policy. The professor made the following comment on the fragmented nature of policy development in Indiana:

> I do think the policy environment in Indiana, the education policy environment, is complex if not convoluted. We don't have a single state voice that speaks to or about education. We have several, and they tend to overlap. They tend not always to agree with each other, and at the very least, they fragment the state influence. And it may affect what's going on with regard to reading or any other curriculum area in schools.

Other actors indicated that there was no easy explanation for the reading problem because it was "such a complex issue," if not, as one respondent noted, "extremely complex." A prominent policymaker in California, for example, remarked, "It just breaks my heart to say, 'Kids in California can't read.' ... [T]he problem is so complex in this huge and diverse state, it's just ... there's no black and white about it." Another respondent from California pointed out that because learning to read is complex, complex and thoughtful solutions are necessary, relating:

> You know I would just emphasize I think the point ... is ... how children learn to read or not to read is, I think, a complex undertaking. I don't think that there are any magic bullets and I think we sometimes simplify this process and it requires an enormous commitment not only of resources, but I think thoughtful attention to some of these issues.

Institutional/Historical Causes

According to Stone (2002), institutional casual stories attribute a problem to "a web of large, longstanding organization with ingrained patterns of behavior" (p. 195), and historical causal stories seek explanations in the reproduction of social patterns. Stone recognizes, however, these two types of complex causes are very similar. We, too, found that they are often difficult to distinguish. Therefore we collapsed the two categories for the purpose of this study. The following observation from a consultant for a Connecticut conservative citizens group illustrates how institutional and historical causal explanations are often intertwined:

> People within the education establishment have created the problem and will not solve it because they thrive on the problem, not any solution. Solutions will ONLY come from people OUTSIDE the establishment. If the state of Connecticut becomes interested in improving reading in the state-run schools, it should contact me end I can refer it to many others who can help a lot.... Government agencies—including all education-related associations and agencies—should be removed from education policymaking. They are the creators, and enlargers, of the problems.

Maintaining that the education establishment was unwilling to "react to challenges" and often simply "trying to make some modest marginal changes in the existing status quo," a Michigan governmental actor also believed that the education establishment was an impediment to resolving the reading problem. Additionally, actors pointed out specific groups as institutions resistant to changes and reforms, most notably departments of education, colleges and universities, and teacher associations.

The relationship between education establishment and social reproduction is also evident in the remarks from a member of a Connecticut educational association, who lamented, "The achievement gap, what it's doing is cementing into place a socioeconomic and social gap. And it means that the children of the poor are being conditioned to be the parents of the next generation of the poor." A Connecticut legislator even contended that schooling's contribution to social reproduction is the intent of the federal government, asserting:

> The federal government uses the public school system to create and maintain a docile, undereducated majority in our population. Actual education is not, and has never been, the goal of the public schools. The schools are warehouses of mediocrity and centers of government indoctrination for the country's children, and sinks for the employment of poorly trained "teachers" and other adults.

Such radical views about the education establishment, however, were rare among our respondents. Although institutional/historical causal stories often blamed the reading achievement problem on the education establishment, some stories focused more on the institutional aspect, criticizing the establishment for trying to maintain the status quo and protecting existing power structure rather than accusing the establishment of intentionally engaging in social reproduction.

Diversified Causal Stories for a Multifaceted Problem

Overall, complex causal stories were told far less often than simple causal stories, which is consistent with Stone's (2002) argument that complex causal explanations are not very useful in politics because they do not offer a single locus of control and therefore no one could be held accountable for the problem. Moreover, by the very nature of complex causes, they are not amenable to policy solutions. Although sociocultural causal stories are similar in this aspect (i.e., no one is held accountable), other types of simple causal stories (inadvertent and intentional) delineate a clear causal link, attribute responsibility to specific person, individuals, or groups, and thereby often offer, or at least imply, a clear solution or solutions to the problem.

That being said, simple causal stories do not necessarily imply simple solutions, particularly when multiple simple stories are told about the same problem, as was the case with reading. While some actors attributed the reading problem to a specific cause (e.g., demographic shift or flawed pedagogy), many attributed it to a host of causes. As a professor in California observed, "[T]here's no one variable. There are many" that are related to the reading problem. Similarly, the president of a Utah professional association acknowledged that there were "many sides" to the reading problem. He went on to explain:

> We have the largest pupil/teacher ratio in the whole nation and we have the lowest expenditure per pupil in the whole nation. That has created some problems. I think we have a significant number of our students that aren't reading as well as they should be reading. And I think there's a whole multitude of reasons for that. We don't have the parental support that we wish we had. There's too much television going on and not enough emphasis on reading. I don't think there are enough partnerships between parents and teachers. All of those things, I think, contribute.

The most comprehensive list of potential causes of the reading problem was provided by a prominent reading scholar from California:

A combination of things, but certainly the curriculum frameworks that were in use at the time. I mean, number one on my list would be um, the very misinformed practice in reading instruction, going back to the adoption of the frameworks in 1987 under Bill Honig that were directing teachers to do stuff that was just [laughs] sort of the opposite of what good practice calls for. And I would say in conjunction with that, very poor teacher preparation, and then in conjunction with that, conditions in the schools that always undermine performance.

Very large class size, very poor professional development programs, very low levels of support, insufficient instructional materials. And the instructional materials that teachers had were poorly … I mean, just … were not good tools. And then add to that a poor accountability system. We had very little accountability on the right things. And then some demographic variables. I don't put a lot of emphasis on these, but certainly a great, rapid influx of kids into city schools who speak other languages, very rapid shifting patterns of school populations and concentrations of kids with special needs in urban schools, particularly second language issues, poverty, all that.

Indeed, according to our study participants, it seems that everyone was to blame to some extent for the reading achievement problem. There are a number of political advantages associated with telling multiple causal stories and specifying multiple causal agents. First, attributing the problem to multiple causal agents disperses blame and subsequently responsibility. With the blame spread out across many causal agents, no one is to be singled out and scrutinized particularly intensively, and responsibility for addressing the problem has to be shared. More importantly, it is often incredibly difficult to develop policies that could adequately address multiple sources of problems simultaneously. Resource constraints alone would probably undermine such efforts. As such, certain existing social orders may simply maintain their status quo. Furthermore, should reform initiatives fail, no single actor could be held entirely responsible.

The nature of many causal stories told by the state reading policy actors also helped to mitigate blames. First, while some of the causes depicted in those stories are malleable to policy actions (e.g., pedagogy and professional development), others are difficult to address with formal policy instruments (e.g., demographic shifts and cultural values). The implicit message here is that there is a limit to what could be done via policy and expectations for policymakers as problem solvers should not be unrealistically high. Second, most of the causal stories for the reading problem pertained to sociocultural and inadvertent causes, both construing the problem as an unintended consequence. In sociocultural causal stories, the causes of the problem (e.g., demographic and cultural factors) were largely beyond human control and hence no one was to blame. In inadvertent causal stories, although the problem results from purposeful human actions (e.g., flawed instruction and ineffective teacher training), these actions were believed to be well-intended and the harmful consequence was unanticipated. The unintended nature of the consequence by no means totally exonerates those involved in the purposeful actions, but it does soften the criticism against them.

In sum, low reading achievement was perceived as an extremely complex problem that arose from a multitude of factors. In a sense, we are all responsible to some extent for the problem and we all share the responsibility for addressing the problem. In the next section, we turn to the various solutions that were proposed in the nine states for addressing the reading achievement problem.

PROBLEM SOLUTIONS: STATE READING POLICIES

Ever since the reading achievement problem was brought to the front burner by results from NAEP as well as state tests in the early 1990s, a slew of major federal and state reading initiatives have been launched with millions of dollars invested in programs designed to raise reading achievement. Landmark federal reading legislations include the America Reads program of 1996, The Reading Excellence Act of 1998, and more recently, the Reading First initiative under the No Child Left Behind Act of 2001. At the state level, 35 states had created or were developing major reading initiatives to improve early reading achievement by the year 2002 (Manzo, 2002). In the remainder of this section, we review reading policy developments in the nine states that occurred during the time period covered in our study (1995-2001), drawing upon the work of McDonnell and Elmore (1987) and Schneider and Ingram (1990) on alternative policy instruments.

Policy Instruments

According to McDonnell and Elmore (1987), policy instruments involve the use of government resources (i.e., money, rules, and authority) to compel individuals and institutions to act in a way that serves the political objectives of the government. McDonnell and Elmore propose four generic categories of policy instruments: mandates, inducements, capacity-building, and system-changing. Mandates, such as nondiscrimination requirements, are rules that govern the actions of individuals and agencies.

Inducements are transfers of money to individuals or agencies in return for the production of goods or services. Examples include grants-in-aid to governments and in-kind grants to individuals. Mandates differ from inducements in three ways. First, mandates employ coercion to affect action, whereas inducements use money as an incentive for performance. Second, the expected outcome of mandates is compliance, whereas that of inducements is the production of something of value. Third, mandates expect actions from all individuals and agencies regardless of differences in capacities; inducements, however, assume that individuals and agencies vary in their ability to produce things of value and that monetary incentive is one way to elicit performance.

Similar to inducements, capacity-building as a type of policy instruments also has money as a primary element (McDonnell & Elmore, 1987). While both mandates and inducements focus on short-term tangible effects, capacity-building aims at long-term intangible effects and future returns through investments in material, intellectual, and human resources (e.g., basic research and preservation). The final category of policy instruments in McDonnell and Elmore's framework, system-changing, changes the distribution of official authority among individuals and agencies in order to alter the system by which public goods and services are delivered. Policies that permit more competitive public-private market for education, such as vouchers, are examples of system-changing policy instruments.

What is missing in McDonnell and Elmore's (1987) framework is the type of instruments labeled "symbolic or hortatory tools" in Schneider and Ingram's (1990) classification scheme. Hortatory policies, according to Schneider and Ingram, assume that people are motivated from within and appeal to the values and beliefs of target constituents. These symbolic tools attempt to not only provoke certain values and beliefs, but also mobilize people to act on the very values and beliefs they arouse. The drug prevention campaign, "Just Say No," is one such example.

Taken together, the five types of policy instruments described above provide a useful framework for examining state reading policies, and facilitate cross-state comparisons of policies intended to address similar problems and enacted within a similar time frame (1995-2001). In addition, our analysis of state reading policies allows us to empirically test whether the framework of policy instruments proposed by McDonnell and Elmore (1987) and Schneider and Ingram (1990) adequately represents the different types of state policies enacted to address the reading achievement problem.

Reading Policies in Nine States

Table 5.2 summarizes the types of instruments, the originating agencies, and the foci of major reading-related policies enacted in each of the nine states during the time period covered by our study (1995-2001) (see Appendix D for a list of the actual policies). Although reading policies were developed under the unique sociocultural, political, and historical context of each state, our analysis revealed strong similarities in the policy instruments adopted by different states to address the reading problem. Certainly, important differences between the states also existed. In the remainder of this section, we discuss five major themes that emerged from our analysis.

The Policy Instrument Mix

As is clear from Table 5.2 and Appendix D, every state in our study employed a mix of different types of policy instruments to address the reading problem. Among the five types of instruments, mandates, inducements, and capacity-building were the most common, which were found in all nine states. Across the states, the majority of reading policy initiatives relied on mandates, which often pertained to standards, assessment, accountability, and teacher certification/licensure (see Appendix D). Every state in our study also provided inducements, such as special grants or award programs, to encourage efforts to improve reading achievement. Capacity-building instruments were popular among state reading policymakers as well. It is to note that for the purpose of our analysis, we generally considered policies with a focus on professional development and instructional improvement as capacity-building instruments, although one could argue that all education policies could be construed as capacity-building in a broad sense for both individuals and the public.

Compared with mandates, inducements, and capacity-building, hortatory and system-changing policies were less common, both of which were found in five states during the period 1995-2001. Hortatory policies typically took the form of reading awareness campaigns, such as READ California, Governor's Summer Reading Challenge in Connecticut, and Read With ME in Maine. These campaigns sought to raise people's awareness of the importance of reading skills, encourage reading both in school and at home, and promote reading achievement as a matter of public interest.

Typical system-changing instruments—those that involve a shift of authority among actors—were typically seen in legislations that established the first statewide accountability system in a state (e.g., North Carolina's Senate Bill 1139: The School-Based Management and

Table 5.2. Reading Policy Instruments in Nine States (1995-2001)

State	Instrument Type	Originating State Government Agency	Focus
Alabama	• Mandates • Inducement • Capacity-building • System-changing	• Legislature • State Board of Education • State Department of Education	• accountability • standards • assessment • professional development • literacy demonstration sites
California	• Mandates • Inducement • Capacity-building • System-changing • Hortatory	• Governor • State Senate • State Assembly • State Board of Education	• accountability • standards • assessment • instructional materials • pedagogy • professional development • preservice training • class size reduction • low-performing schools • school library • alignment of standards with curriculum and instruction • reading campaign "READ California" • classroom libraries • teacher licensure

State	Policy instruments	Actors	Focus areas
Connecticut	• Mandates • Inducement • Capacity-building • Hortatory	• Governor • General Assembly • State Department of Education	• accountability • standards • assessment • state grants to needy districts and schools • early reading programs • summer reading programs • social promotion • class size reduction • teacher training • professional development • school-readiness plans • curriculum and instruction • reading awareness campaign
Indiana	• Mandates • Inducement • Capacity-building • System-changing	• Governor • Legislature • General Assembly • State Department of Education	• accountability • standards • assessment • early literacy grants • school libraries • adult education • professional development • pedagogy • teacher licensure
Maine	• Mandates • Inducement • Capacity-building • Hortatory	• Legislature • Office of The First Lady	• standards • assessment • reading awareness campaign

Table continues on next page.

Table 5.2. Reading Policy Instruments in Nine States (1995-2001) Continued

State	Instrument Type	Originating State Government Agency	Focus
Michigan	• Mandates • Inducement • Capacity-building • Hortatory	• Governor	• assessment • professional development • summer reading programs • teacher licensure • Reading awareness campaign
North Carolina	• Mandates • Inducement • Capacity-building • System-changing	• Senate	• accountability • standards • pedagogy • professional development
Texas	• Mandates • Inducement • Capacity-building	• Governor • Senate • House of Representatives • Office of The First Lady • Office of the Lieutenant Governor	• accountability • standards • assessment • research-based instruction • reading programs • reading academies • early literacy • family literacy • social promotion • professional development • teacher certification
Utah	• Mandates • Inducement • Capacity-building • System-changing • Hortatory	• Governor • House of Representatives • Office of the Lieutenant • Office of The First Lady	• standards • assessment • pedagogy • remediation • professional development • school-community based literacy programs • reading readiness campaign • reading center • reading awards program • teacher licensure

Accountability Program (also referred to as "ABCs of Public Education"). They were rarely used otherwise, which is not surprising given the political tension and conflict that are likely to result from any redistribution of power and authority. One exception is Utah House Bill 177 (Assessing, Reporting and Evaluating Student Performance) introduced in 2000, which stripped local school boards of their control over testing and transferred their performance assessment duties entirely to the Utah State Board of Education in an effort to tighten state control over assessments.

The mix of policy instruments occurred not only at the state level, but also at the individual policy level, as many polices were comprehensive in scope and designed to serve multiple functions through multiple means. The above-mentioned Utah House Bill 177 (2000), for example, was both a system-changing policy and a mandate, as it not only tightened state control over testing (system-changing), but also established the Utah Performance Assessment System for Students as the new statewide testing program (mandate). As another example, Connecticut's Public Act 98-243 (An Act Concerning Early Reading Success) required each school district in the state to develop and implement a 3-year plan to improve the reading skills of students in early grades (mandate). It also established the Early Reading Success Grant program that provided $20 million each year to the 14 "priority districts" to improve early reading achievement (inducement and capacity-building). In addition, the act required the state department of education to convene a panel to review research on how children learn to read and to identify professional development and competencies for effective reading instruction required for K-3 teachers, school administrators, and librarians (mandate and capacity-building).

Multiple Policy Foci

Similarly, a mix of policy foci, or topics addressed, also occurred at both the state and the individual policy level. As shown in Table 5.2 and Appendix D, reading policies in the nine states covered a comprehensive set of issues. Indeed, state reading policymakers generally took a systemic approach and attempted to tackle the reading problem from multiple dimensions simultaneously—from standards and assessments to curriculum and instruction, from professional development to teacher certification or licensure, and from instructional materials to class size reduction. These policies were generally coherent and congruent, intertextual (cf. Chrispeels, 1997) and interdependent. That is, a policy could not be fully understood or properly implemented without knowledge of other relevant policies, and different policies or different components of the same policy were often intended to operate in synergy towards the common goal of improving student achievement and closing achievement gaps. It is also worth noting that although a policy was usually formally introduced or enacted by a specific government agency, the policy development process was often characterized by concerted efforts and collaborations among multiple government agencies, which were likely to have contributed to the coherence of difference policies.[2]

State Impact on Curriculum and Instruction

Among the array of issues addressed by state reading policies, curriculum and instruction received particular attention. In every state that we studied, the reading policy initiatives not only stated their grand goals in broad terms, but also stipulated in explicit language what specific reading skills students are expected to master and how reading should be taught inside the classrooms. The state impact on reading curriculum and instruction was exerted through a variety of channels. Other than revising existing curriculum standards in their desired directions, most, if not all, state education agencies (e.g., Connecticut and Texas), often with legislative support, made heavy investment in statewide professional development programs to help teachers to align instruction to new state standards. Moreover, some states (e.g., California and Indiana) also added specific requirements regarding reading pedagogy to teacher licensure laws. Additional means through which states influenced what to teach and how to teach in early reading included updating state assessment programs to highlight the essential skills of reading, disseminating research-based reports on reading pedagogy drafted by expert panels, posing specific requirements for teacher education programs, and imposing restrictions on textbook adoptions. A detailed discussion with more recent data on how states have established firm control over reading curriculum and instruction since the 1990s can be found in Song (forthcoming).

The Not-So-Hidden Hand of Federal Funding

Not clearly evident from Table 5.2 and Appendix D or to those outside of the state reading policy loop is the not-so-hidden hand of the federal government in the enactment and implementation of state-level policies. Specifically, some of the state reading policies were adopted on the premise that federal policy instruments, in particular, Goals 2000, The Reading Excellence Act of 1998 (REA), and at the end of our study, Reading First of the No Child Left Behind Act of 2001, would fund various reading initiatives in the states. REA, for example, awarded grants to state education agencies, which in turn awarded subgrants to eligible local school districts to help improve the reading skills of prekindergarten through third-grade children. REA grants, which may be construed as both inducements and capacity-building instruments, financed many professional development and remediation programs throughout the states in our study with the only exception of Michigan. While Goals 2000 had some flexibility in terms of the use of the funds, the REA and Reading First[3] grants were only intended to fund research-based or scientifically-based programs, restricting to some extent how the money should be spent and which reading programs could be adopted.

Research, Research, Research

As explained earlier, reading policies in the nine states that we studied were designed to address a wide range of issues, particularly curriculum and instruction—the core of schooling. When it came to curriculum and instruction, however, little consensus existed on the best way to teach reading at the time states were considering initiating new policies or modifying existing policies in their attempt to tackle the reading problem. As different sides of the reading wars strove to sway policy in their favored directions, state policymakers made use of research to bring people with divergent perspectives to the same table, to reach common understandings about how reading should be taught, and to inform state reading policy development.

Although what counts as credible research or the so-called "scientifically based research" has been a topic of debate particularly within the research community, to most policymakers and the general public, research connotes a sense of objectivity, credibility, and legitimacy. It thus came as no surprise that just about every state relied on research for consensus building and informed policymaking and policy implementation. Research has clearly played a critical role in shaping the policy directions of the state reading policy arena in the past decade and in garnering broad support for those policy directions.

Most notably, with the exceptions of North Carolina and Utah, seven of the nine states in our study convened some kind of expert panel, task force, or advisory committee to examine research-based evidence for effective reading instruction and to make recommendations to state policymakers (see Table 5.3). These panels often included renowned researchers and various stakeholders from diverse backgrounds and embracing diverse perspectives. A Connecticut state representative, for instance, made the following comment on Connecticut's Early Reading Success Panel:

> [Phonic vs. whole language] was a very contentious issue, ... we did let it reach the level of a huge, full-blown debate because I think by putting together this reading panel where we literally found the most ardent whole language supporter, the most ardent phonemic awareness supporter, and put them all in a room with a bunch of people in between ... I think that did make everybody grapple with it.

Table 5.3. State Reading Policy Task Forces (1995–2001)

State	Task Force or Panel	Convened by	Report/Product
Alabama	Alabama Reading Panel (1996)	State Department of Education at the behest of State Board of Education.	*Report on the Review of the Research.* Alabama Department of Education (1998a); *Knowledge and Skills Teachers Need to Deliver Effective Reading Instruction.* Alabama Department of Education (1998b).
California	California Reading Task Force (1995)	State Superintendent of Public Instruction.	*Every Child A Reader: The Report of the California Reading Task Force.*[a] California Department of Education (1995).
Connecticut	Connecticut Early Reading Success Panel (2000)	State Department of Education in compliance with PA 99-227.	*Connecticut's Blueprint for Reading Achievement: A Report by the Early Reading Success Panel.* Connecticut State Department of Education (2000).
Indiana	Phonics Task Force (2000)	State Superintendent of Public Instruction; Indiana Association of Public School Superintendents	*Phonics Tool Kit.* Indiana Department of Education (2000a); *Phonics Online.* Indiana Department of Education (2000b).
Maine	Early Literacy Workgroup (1998)	State Department of Education.	*A Solid Foundation: Supportive Contexts for Early Literacy in Maine.* Maine Department of Education (2000).
Michigan	Governor's Advisory Council on the Reading Plan for Michigan (1998).	Governor	NA
Texas	Governor's Focus on Reading Task Force (1996)	Governor and Education Commissioner	*Good Practice: Implications for Reading Instruction–A Consensus Document of Texas Literacy Professional Organizations.* Texas Education Agency (1997a); *Beginning Reading Instruction: Components and Features of a Research-Based Reading Program.*[b] Texas Education Agency (1997b).

Note. [a] This report was supplemented by a reading program advisory published by the California Department of Education in 1996: *Teaching Reading: A Balanced, Comprehensive Approach to Teaching Reading in Pre-kindergarten Through Grade Three.*
[b] This report has been commonly referred to as the "Red Book." The Texas Education Agency released a revised edition in 2002 and has developed companion documents to the "Red Book." These documents are collectively referred to as the "Red Book Series."

The Early Reading Success Panel, according to this representative, was instrumental in generating consensus and ending the reading wars. He told us, "So we never really had those divisive debates, except you know around that panel table, where there were debates." A respondent from a California education association similarly noted the ideological diversity of the California Reading Task Force and its role in consensus-building, remarking,

> She [Delaine Eastin, former State Superintendent] had two chairs that were different in their approaches. It was a very eclectic group. I mean, we had great difficulty reaching agreement ... it took a lot of testimony. It did create a forum for a while to at least get people talking about reading.... The power of that though, was eventually we got agreement, as difficult as it was.... There were members from all of the different perspectives.

Indeed, these high-profile panels or task forces were crucial in states' efforts to combat the reading achievement problem. They not only facilitated consensus building, but also helped to create an ideologically pluralistic decision-making process, prevent potential criticisms of exclusivity, and add to the legitimacy of proposed policy solutions (Young & Miskel, 2006). The reports based on the work of those panels (see Table 5.3) were often deemed the official position statement of the state government on reading policy. They were disseminated widely and provided important guidance for both policy development and implementation as well as instructional practices in classrooms across the states.

Clearly, those panel reports served as a significant mechanism through which the state government sought to influence citizen behavior and to achieve policy goals, and as such may also be viewed as policy instruments (McDonnell & Elmore, 1987; Schneider & Ingram, 1990). In particular, we construe panel reports as a special type of capacity-building instruments. They embody capacity-building because they focus on intangible results and future returns through investment in intellectual resources. However, panel reports are not the typical type of capacity-building instruments as defined by McDonnell and Elmore (1987) because they do not involve money as a primary element. They do, however, fit into the category of "capacity tools" proposed by Schneider and Ingram (1990), which is a broader conception of capacity-building instruments and are defined as policy tools that "provide information, training, education, and resources to enable individuals, groups, or agencies to make decisions or carry out activities" (p. 517). Thus, panel reports can be appropriately characterized as *knowledge-based capacity-building* policy instruments.

Variations in Scope, State Control, and Prescriptiveness

Similarities and differences always coexist. While our review of state reading policies identified a number of common themes, it also revealed significant differences among the states. An obvious difference is scope, as reflected in both the quantity and the issue coverage of reading-related policies. Among the nine states we studied, California clearly toped the list in terms the of scope of its reading policies. Between 1995 and 2001, California enacted about two dozen reading-related legislations (see Appendix D), and its policy activism continued after the completion of our study.[4] In contrast, the state governments of Alabama, Maine, and North Carolina passed a very limited number of policies during the same time period with more focused issue coverage. In these three states, reading policies dealt primarily with standards, assessment, pedagogy, and professional development, whereas policies in states such as California, Connecticut, and Texas were much broader in scope, covering a wide array of issues, from instructional materials to class size reduction, and from teacher licensure to social promotion.

It is also worth noting that reading policies in different states reflected varying degrees of state control and prescriptiveness. Again, California and Maine provide the best illustration. Reading policy development in California since the mid-90s was characterized by tight state control, particularly in the area of curriculum and instruction. As part of the California Reading Initiative, Assembly Bills 170 and 1504 (1995), nicknamed the "ABC bills" for their sponsors, mandated that reading instructional materials in grades K-8 should include "systematic, explicit phonics" and spelling, and that instructional materials purchased with state funds must contain "systematic, explicit phonics." Similarly, Assembly Bill 3075 (1996) stipulated that the reading requirement for teaching credentials shall include satisfactory completion of reading instruction that is research-based and that includes "both a strong comprehension component and the study of direct, systematic, explicit phonics." Where professional development was concerned, Assembly Bill 1086 (1997) required school districts to certify that no less than 90% of employees who provide direct reading instruction in grades K-3 have received specified in-service training. The training must include 12 specific components, including phoneme awareness, systematic explicit phonics, decoding, word-attack skills, spelling and vocabulary instruction, and comprehension skills, among others.

On the other end of the spectrum of state control and prescriptiveness is Maine. With its long-standing tradition of local control, Maine was not as active as most of the other states in mandating state education policy, and the limited number of polices that it did enact were generally drafted in broad terms, leaving much room for local autonomy and flexibility. The

Learning Results Standards passed by the Maine State Legislature in 1997, for instance, were fairly general and ranked 28th in "specificity" according to the Quality Counts survey conducted by *Educational Week* (2000). Notably missing from the 11-page English language arts standards are "phonics" or "phonemic awareness," terms that appeared in the standards or curriculum frameworks of every other state in our study, although the phrase "letter-sound relationships" did appear in three places.

There has been evidence, however, that state control over reading curriculum and instruction in Maine as well as other states has been on the rise. The Maine Department of Education, for example, recently revised the 1997 Learning Results Standards. The revised standards are much more concrete, and feature phonemic awareness and phonics much more prominently than the previous standards (Song, forthcomin). With the passage of the No Child Left Behind Act of 2001 and the hefty sums of money attached to it, as Song notes, states have been given both strong incentives and tremendous pressure to take firm control of their K-12 education systems. It thus seems safe to predict that state control over reading policy, or education policy in general, is unlikely to subside, and the between-state variations in state control over reading policy and policy prescriptiveness are likely to diminish to some extent in the years to come. A potentially fruitful area of future investigation is to explore how increased state control and policy prescriptiveness affect policy implementation, sustainability, and outcomes.

CONGRUENCE BETWEEN CAUSAL STORIES AND PROPOSED SOLUTIONS

Our review of state reading policy actors' causal stories and state reading policy developments during the latter half of the 1990s and early 2000s reveals a high degree of congruence. Consistent with the diversified nature of the causal stories about an extremely complex problem, a large number of policy solutions were adopted by the states, which represented different types of policy instruments and embodied multiple policy foci. Moreover, almost every policy focus could be linked to a causal story (although the converse did not hold), and those that were the most common targets of policy actions also tended to be those most frequently mentioned in state reading policy actors' causal stories. As a case in point, among causes amenable to policy actions, flawed pedagogy and ill-preparedness of teachers were by and large the most pervasive explanations for low reading achievement. These two inadvertent causes were also the most common foci of state policy actions, which emphasized heavily on curriculum and instruction.

Other types of inadvertent causes perceived by the state reading policy actors were also addressed in various policy initiatives. Policies that provided funding for purchasing instructional materials and class size reduction, for instance, helped to alleviate resource deficits. Special grant programs that targeted students most in need allowed schools to respond more effectively to demographic challenges. Reading awareness campaigns and family literacy programs helped to raise people's awareness of the importance of reading readiness and promote parent involvement in their children's reading development.

Not all problem causes, however, are amenable to policy solutions. Although stories about sociocultural causes—demographic shifts, demographic conditions, media influence, and cultural values and attitudes—were as frequently told as were stories about inadvertent causes, sociocultural causes were often largely beyond the control of education policymakers, and much harder, if not impossible, to tackle. Similarly, policy solutions for addressing intentional causes and complex causes (i.e., complex systems and institutional/historical causes) were also elusive to policymakers by the very nature of such causes.

While certain causes were yet to find a policy solution, almost every policy solution proposed in the nine states could be coupled with at least one causal story. Very often, the linkage between policy solutions and causal stories were not one-to-one, but one-to-many (i.e., one policy addressing different issues) or many-to-one (i.e., different policies addressing the same issue). The policy formation, or "alternative specification," process, according to Kingdon's (1995) multiple streams model, takes place largely independently from developments in the problem stream. Kingdon further argues that policy development is guided more by recombination of familiar ideas into new proposals than by rational problem solving, and that policy entrepreneurs couple their pet solutions to appropriate problems at an open policy window, which represents a propitious time for policy change.

Our data suggest, however, that the policy formation process in the state reading policy arena may be more rational, and the problem stream and the policy stream may be more interdependent than what Kingdon (1995) postulates.[5] There seems to be clear connections between state reading policy actors' beliefs about problem cause and proposed policy solutions, and it seems reasonable to assume that in many instances, solutions were designed in response to perceived problem causes. On the other hand, it is also possible, as Kingdon argues, that some policy solutions did not necessarily result from a rational problem-solving process, and their connections to certain problem causes may simply reflect post hoc coupling by policy entrepreneurs promoting the ideas and beliefs embodied in those solutions. After all, policymaking is an extremely complex process, which is characterized by both order and irrationality, both predictability and uncertainty, and both design and serendipity.

NOTES

1. Misrepresentation of and myths about achievement as a causal story are not a new phenomenon (cf. Berliner & Biddle, 1995).
2. For details about collaborative activities among state reading policy actors, see reports for individual states based on the State Reading Policy Study (Coggshall, 2002; Coggshall & Osguthorpe, 2002; DeYoung, 2002; DeYoung & Athan, 2002; Osguthorpe, 2002; Shepley, 2002a, 2002b; Song, 2002; Young, 2002), and Young & Miskel (2006).
3. Reading First has provided unprecedented funding (one billion a year) for reading programs; however, grants associated with this program are outside of the timeframe covered in this study.
4. Since 2001, California state legislature passed another 10 reading/literacy policies, of which 6 were signed into law, 1 adopted as an emergency rule, and 3 vetoed (Education Commission of the States, 2007). No major reading legislations have been enacted in Alabama, Maine, North Carolina, or Michigan since 2001.
5. See DeYoung (2004) and Young, Shepley, Miskel, and Song (2002) for an application of Kingdon's multiple streams model to the development of reading policy.

CHAPTER 6

INTEREST GROUPS' LOBBYING TACTICS IN THE STATE READING POLICY DOMAIN

Having reviewed the structural system, influence system, and belief system of the state reading policy domain, we now turn to the lobbying system—the behavioral aspect—of the policy domain. We will examine what policy actors did to promote what they believed and to attain and exercise influence over state reading policy. Specifically, we will focus on interest groups' use of various lobbying tactics, and assess the extent to which their use of lobbying tactics was related to their policy influence.

LOBBYING TACTICS

With the advocacy explosion, there has not only been an increase in both the number and diversity of interest groups, but each group has been doing more in more ways than ever before (Petracca, 1992). Based on interviews with 175 Washington interests, Schlozman and Tierney

Reading: Policy, Politics, and Processes, pp. 141–165
Copyright © 2008 by Information Age Publishing
All rights of reproduction in any form reserved.

(1986) compiled a comprehensive list of 27 influence strategies, or lobbying tactics.[1] They found that testifying at hearings, contacting government officials directly, and engaging in informal contacts with officials were the most commonly used tactics; whereas contributing finances and manpower to electoral campaigns, protests, and demonstrations the least used ones. Similar results were also obtained in studies conducted by Berry (1977), Knoke (1990a), Walker (1991), Heinz, Laumann, Nelson, and Salisbury (1993), and Nownes and Freeman (1998), among others (see Baumgartner & Leech, 1998, p. 152, for a list of 12 types of lobbying tactics that are fairly consistent across the studies).

Salisbury (1990) makes a distinction between inside and outside strate-gies that interest groups employ to maximize their impact. By inside strategies, Salisbury refers to the "principal means of action" for interest groups, such as hiring independent agents, establishing Washington offices, creating political action committees, and building coalitions (p. 215). Interest groups may also go outside the policy community, seek-ing to influence government policy by arousing public opinion, using mass media and indirect marketing techniques to attract attention and broad support for their causes. However, Salisbury believes that the odds are generally against outside strategies, given the "tendency for their appeals to decay swiftly," and that outside strategies may be expected to have only a short-term effect on policy (p. 216). Similar distinctions were also made by Schlozman and Tierney (1986) (i.e., direct versus indirect forms of influence), and Smith (1986) (i.e., old inside game of lobbying versus new outside game of lobbying).

Kollman (1998) adopts a more finely defined classification scheme of group lobbying tactics. To inside and outside lobbying tactics, Kollman adds a third category: group maintenance. According to Kollman, inside lobbying tactics involve communication or interaction directed at policymakers or their staffs that aims to directly influence the decisions of policymakers, such as contacting legislators personally, testifying at Congress, and presenting research to government officials. Outside lobbying tactics are attempts by interest group leaders to mobilize citizens outside the policymaking community to contact or pressure public officials inside the policymaking community. They are often targeted at undecided policymakers and involve more intense activities than inside lobbying tactics. Specific examples include talking with the press, mobilizing group members, and organizing letter-writing campaigns.

Kollman (1998) further articulates that outside lobbying has two purposes corresponding to the two interdependent audiences targeted: communicating public support to policymakers or "signaling" in

Kollman's terms, and increasing that public support among constituents or "conflict expansion." The dual purposes reinforce each other and make outside lobbying "a viable and effective strategy" and "a powerful tool" in the hands of interest group leaders. In this respect, Kollman's view clearly differs from that of Salisbury (1990), who contends that outside lobbying has rapidly-fading appeals and is generally ineffective in the long run.

Kollman's (1998) third category, organizational maintenance, include tactics intended to help the group, or a coalition of groups, solve collective action problems. Typical examples include entering coalition with other groups, raising funds, sending letters to group members, advertising for new members, and polling group members on policy issues. Of those tactics, Kollman found forming coalitions to be the most common, used by 98% of the groups that he surveyed. Other large-scale surveys have produced similar findings (e.g., Heinz et al., 1993; Nownes & Freeman, 1998, Schlozman & Tierney, 1986).

In comparing the types of tactics used by different groups, Kollman (1998) found that inside lobbying was ubiquitous among groups, while outside lobbying was less common but still fairly prevalent. Moreover, certain types of groups, labor unions and public interest groups in particular, used a wider variety of outside lobbying tactics more consistently than did their business and professional counterparts. Overall, successful groups use their extensive knowledge of the political environment to adopt strategies that fit specific situations (Heinz et al., 1993).

While those studies conducted by political scientists have considerably advanced our understanding of interest groups' lobbying activities, significant gaps in the literature remain. Specifically, most large-scale studies of interest groups' lobbying activities have been looking at lobbying across issue areas and policy domains, even though a given group's targets and tactics typically differ dramatically from issue to issue (Baumgartner & Leech, 1998). Indeed, we know very little about the lobbying tactics that interest groups employ in the field of education, let alone in the specific subject area of reading. Moreover, as Nownes and Freeman (1998) note, although considerable progress has been made in understanding lobbying at the national level, we have little systematic empirical data on group activities at the state level, nor do we have much information on how group activities differ across group types. Nownes and Freeman further point out that existing studies of lobbying have mostly relied on dichotomous data, which help us to understand whether specific tactics are used, but not the extent to which they are used. By assessing the extent to which various types of lobbying tactics were used by interest groups in the state reading policy domain, and by examining interest groups' tactic use across states and across group types, our study has helped to fill a void in this literature.

INTEREST GROUPS' USE OF LOBBYING TACTICS IN THE STATE READING POLICY DOMAIN

Measurement of Interest Groups' Use of Lobbying Tactics

In developing the interview schedule for interest groups, we compiled a list of 12 lobbying tactics that were likely to be used by interest groups in the state reading policy domain based on prior work by Baumgartner and Leech (1998) and Kollman (1998), among others (see Table 6.1).[2] These tactics fall into three broad categories—inside lobbying, outside lobbying, and organizational maintenance—according to Kollman's (1998) classification scheme. During the interviews, we asked the interest group representatives whether and how often they used each tactic in attempts to influence state reading policy. Their responses were entered into an SPSS data set with the following coding categories for each type of tactic: $0 =$ never, $1 =$ occasionally, $2 =$ sometimes, and $3 =$ frequently. Where multiple individuals from a given group were interviewed, individual responses were aggregated to the group level to represent the frequency with which the group used the tactics.

In addition to the set of variables representing the intensity of tactic use, we created a set of dummy variables to indicate whether the groups had ever employed the tactics to influence state reading policy. These dummy variables were summed up to obtain the total number of different types of tactics that each group used. We further created another three dummy variables to indicate whether the groups had engaged in inside lobbying, outside lobbying, and organizational maintenance activities respectively; we also created three continuous variables to represent the average frequencies with which each group engaged in the three categories of lobbying activities. In the sections to follow, we report our findings about both the types of lobbying tactics used and the intensity of tactic use in the nine state reading policy networks.

Types of Lobbying Tactics Used

General Patterns

Our interview data revealed that interest groups in the state reading policy domain had in their toolboxes a diverse yet fairly common set of

Table 6.1. Comparison of Findings from Studies of Interest Groups' Lobbying Tactics

Lobbying Tactics	Percentage of Interest Groups Using the Tactic						
	Schlozman & Tierney (1986)	Knoke (1990a)	Heinz et al. (1993)	Nownes & Freeman (1998)	Kollman (1998)	State Reading Policy Study
Inside Lobbying						
• Contacting government officials	98	65	95/92 [a]	97	100	98
• Presenting research findings	92				100	92
• Testifying at legislative or agency hearings	99	49	95/87 [a]	99	100	88
• Serving on commissions	76			76	79	87
• Drafting legislation	85		80	88		81
						64
Outside Lobbying						
• Engaging the mass media	86	15		74	98	75
• Organizing phone and letter writing campaigns	84	67		83	90	63
• Endorsing officials for public office	22	5		24	24	34
Organizational Maintenance						
• Forming coalitions	90	58	99 [b]	93	98	92
• Monitoring officials for policy developments			99			87
• Raising funds					32	84
• Advertising for new members	31			21	32	41
						35

Note: Table sources: Schlozman & Tierney, 1983, p. 150; Knoke, 1990a, p. 208; Heinz et al., 1993, p. 65; Nownes & Freeman, 1998, p. 92; and Kollman, 1998, p. 35.

[a] The first percentage refers to legislative lobbying activities, and the second to executive and agency activities.

[b] Heinz et al. asked about "maintaining contacts with other organizations" rather than "forming coalitions."

lobbying tactics. Across the nine states, about 80% of the groups reported using at least half of the 12 types of tactics we identified, and nearly half (43%) of the groups reported using at least 10 different types of tactics to influence reading policy. Among the 12 types of lobbying tactics, contacting government officials was the most commonly used one, with 92% of the groups across the nine states reporting using the tactic (see the shaded column in Table 6.1). Next in popularity were presenting research findings, testifying at legislative or agency hearings, and forming coalitions, which were used by 88%, 87%, and 87% of the groups respectively. The least commonly used tactics were endorsing policy allies for elective office and advertising for new members, which were used by only about one third of the groups in the full sample. Given that many interest groups desire to maintain their tax status as nonpolitical organizations, the low percentage of groups endorsing political candidates was not surprising (Kollman, 1998). Moreover, many of the groups in our study were non-membership groups (e.g., research organizations and high education institutions); the low percentage of groups advertising for new members was not unexpected either.

With regard to the general categories of lobbying tactics, Table 6.1 shows that the three categories of lobbying tactics—inside lobbying, outside lobbying, and organizational maintenance—were all used by the majority of the groups. Across the nine states we studied, 84% of the groups tapped into all three categories of lobbying tactics in efforts to shape reading policy. In support of Kollman's (1998) claim that "all groups inside lobby to some extent all the time" (p. 36), we found that in seven of the nine states, 100% of the groups used some types of inside lobbying tactics to influence reading policy, and that overall, 98% of the groups engaged in inside lobbying across the states. Outside lobbying and organizational maintenance, although not as prevalent as inside lobbying, were still used by an overwhelming majority of the groups (87% and 92% respectively across states).

Table 6.1 also lists the findings from prior large-scale surveys of interest groups' lobbying activities. As Baumgartner and Leech (1998) note, although these surveys differ substantially in terms of question wording, sampling frame, and study purpose, they have generated remarkably consistent findings. All these surveys, as well as ours, show that contacting government officials, testifying at legislative or agency hearings, and forming coalitions were among the most commonly used lobbying tactics, and that endorsing public officials was the least commonly used one. The pattern even holds true in Knoke's (1990a) survey, which was distinct from other surveys in that its sample was restricted to membership organizations and included a large number of apolitical organizations and organizations from outside Washington.

Differences in the Types of Tactics Used Across States

Having examined the general patterns in the types of lobbying tactics used by interest groups in the state reading policy domain, we further explored whether there existed any systematic differences across states in the types of tactics used (see Table 6.2 for percentage of groups using each type of tactic by state). Specifically, we constructed a tactic-by-state cross-tabulation table for each type of tactic, and calculated the chi-square statistic. It turned out that for all but two types of tactics, interest groups in different states did not differ significantly in terms of the likelihood for adopting the tactics, which suggests that interest groups in different states were generally engaged in the same types of activities to influence reading policy.

We did find, however, significant overall between-state variations for two specific types of tactics (i.e., contacting government officials and presenting research findings) and two general categories of lobbying activities (i.e., inside lobbying and group maintenance) ($p < .05$). To ascertain where the differences lay exactly, we constructed a logistic regression model, in which the dependent variable was the log odds for using a particular type of tactic or category of lobbying activities, and the predictors were a set of dummy variables representing the states.[3] We ran the regression for each type of tactic or category of lobbying activities for which we identified an overall significant between-state variation based on the chi-square statistic. Results of the logistic regressions suggest that interest groups in the California reading policy network were significantly more likely to present research findings than groups in the Maine network, and that interest groups in both the Michigan and Texas networks were significantly more likely to engage in organizational maintenance activities than groups in the Maine network ($p < .05$). Groups in North Carolina were also more likely to adopt organizational maintenance tactics than groups in Maine, although the difference was only marginally significant ($p < .10$). The logistic regression results failed to reveal any significant differences in the likelihood of contacting government officials or using inside lobbying tactics between any particular pair of states.[4]

Table 6.2 also lists the mean number of different types of tactics that interest groups in different states employed in their lobbying efforts. Overall, interest groups on average employed about eight different types of tactics to influence reading policy across the nine states. Of the nine states, Alabama interest groups used the most diverse set of tactics: on average each group used about nine different types of tactics. The number for Maine interest groups (6.1), although the lowest among the states, was not far below. An analysis of variance (ANOVA) suggests that the

Table 6.2. Percentage of Reading Interest Groups Using Different Types of Lobbying Tactics by State

Lobbying Tactics	AL (N=12)	CA (N=23)	CT (N=17)	IN (N=20)	ME (N=11)	MI (N=21)	NC (N=18)	TX (N=21)	UT (N=13)	Total (N=156)
*Inside Lobbying**	100	100	94	100	82	100	100	100	100	98
• Contacting government officials*	92	91	76	95	73	100	100	100	92	92
• Presenting research findings*	83	91	81	100	55	81	100	100	85	88
• Testifying at legislative or agency hearings	92	95	80	95	64	81	88	90	92	87
• Serving on commissions	83	82	88	85	64	90	82	70	77	81
• Drafting legislation and regulations	73	64	69	60	36	67	65	75	62	64
Outside Lobbying	100	91	69	90	64	86	94	85	100	87
• Engaging the mass media	100	81	60	85	55	71	71	80	69	75
• Organizing letter-writing and telephone campaigns	67	50	56	79	45	62	82	55	69	63
• Endorsing policy allies for elective office	33	32	19	30	36	38	41	20	62	34
*Organizational Maintenance**	92	91	87	100	64	95	94	95	100	92
• Forming coalitions	83	91	87	95	64	95	76	80	100	87
• Monitoring officials for policy developments	75	91	86	90	45	81	94	90	85	84
• Raising funds to promote policy issues	67	27	38	40	36	43	31	55	38	41
• Advertising for new members	36	27	31	25	36	38	38	45	46	35
Mean Number of Different Types of Tactics Used	9.2	8.2	7.6	8.8	6.1	8.5	8.6	8.6	8.8	8.3

Note: *Between-state variation was significant at the .05 level.

states did not differ significantly in terms of the total number of different types of tactics used by reading interest groups ($p > .05$).

Differences in the Types of Tactics Used Across Group Types

In addition to cross-state variations, we also examined variations across group types in the types of tactics interest groups used in the state reading policy domain. We classified the 156 non-media interest groups in our sample into the following five broad categories in light of the interests that they represented: citizens groups, educational associations/school districts, higher education institutions, business groups/foundations/firms, and research organizations/policy institutes. The sample size and the percentage of groups using different types of lobbying tactics for each of the five types of groups were presented in Table 6.3. For each type of tactic, we calculated the Chi-square statistic based on a tactic-by-group type cross-tabulation table. For most types of tactics, we found no significant variation across group types, which suggests that different types of groups had similar preferences in the choice of lobbying tactics, regardless of whom they represented. We did find, however, significant variations across group types in the likelihood for engaging in the following lobbying activities: Engaging the mass media ($p < .05$), organizing letter-writing and telephone campaigns ($p < .001$), forming coalitions ($p < .01$), and raising funds ($p < .05$), and outside lobbying ($p < .05$). Employing logistic regression, we identified a number of significant differences between specific types of interest groups in their likelihood of engaging in those types of activities (see Table 6.4).

In terms of the number of different types of lobbying tactics that different types of groups employed, ANOVA analysis suggests that there was a significant overall difference across group types ($F_{(4, 140)} = 2.59$, $p < .05$). Specifically, citizens groups and educational associations/school districts tended to adopt more types of lobbying tactics to influence state reading policy than research organizations/policy institutes. Both differences were marginally significant ($p < .10$) based on Bonferroni post hoc tests.

Intensity of Interest Groups' Use of Lobbying Tactics

One strength of our study compared with prior studies on interest groups' lobbying tactics is that we not only explored whether the groups used particular tactics, but also the intensity or frequency with which the groups used the tactics. The frequency of tactic use was measured on a

Table 6.3. Percentage of Reading Interest Groups Using Different Types of Lobbying Tactics by Group Type

Lobbying Tactics	Citizens Groups (N=21)	Education Associations (N=79)	Higher Education Institutions (N=22)	Business/ Foundations/ Firms (N=14)	Research Organizations (N=20)	Total (N=156)
Inside Lobbying	95	99	100	100	95	98
• Contacting government officials	95	94	95	93	80	92
• Presenting research findings	90	86	95	93	85	88
• Testifying at legislative or agency hearings	90	90	75	93	85	87
• Serving on commissions	85	86	75	79	65	81
• Drafting legislation and regulations	75	64	58	86	45	64
*Outside Lobbying**	90	88	95	93	65	87
• Engaging the mass media*	90	68	95	79	65	75
• Organizing letter-writing and telephone campaigns***	84	73	50	57	20	63
• Endorsing policy allies for elective office	30	40	35	21	20	34
Organizational Maintenance	95	95	85	100	80	92
• Forming coalitions**	90	92	75	100	65	87
• Monitoring officials for policy developments	85	89	75	93	65	84
• Raising funds to promote policy issues*	65	32	35	71	35	41
• Advertising for new members	40	39	25	36	25	35
Mean Number Of Different Types Of Tactics Used	9.2	8.5	8	9	6.6	8.3

Note: Statistical significance of variation across group types: * $p < .05$; ** $p < .01$; *** $p < .001$.

**Table 6.4. Significant Differences in
the Types of Lobbying Tactics Used
Between Different Types of Interest Groups in
the State Reading Policy Domain**

Lobbying Tactics	*Difference Between Group Types*
Engaging the mass media	Higher education institutions were more likely to engage the mass media than education associations/school districts and research organizations/policy institutes ($p < .05$).
Organizing letter-writing and telephone campaigns	Citizens groups were significantly more likely to organize letter-writing and telephone campaigns than higher education institutions ($p < .05$) and research organizations/policy institutes ($p < .001$). Education associations/school districts and business groups/foundations/ firms were more likely to organize letter-writing and telephone campaigns than research organizations/policy institutes ($p < .001$ and $p < .05$ respectively).
Forming coalitions	Education associations/school districts were more likely to form coalitions than higher education institutions ($p < .05$) and research organizations/policy institutes ($p < .01$).
Raising funds to promote policy issues	Citizens groups and business groups/foundations/firms were more likely to raise funds than education associations/school districts institutes ($p < .05$). Business groups/foundations/firms were more likely to raise funds than higher education institutions and research organizations/policy ($p < .05$).
Outside Lobbying	Educational associations/school districts and higher education institutions were more likely to engage in outside lobbying than research organizations/policy institutes ($p < .05$).

scale from 0 to 3, with 0 = never, 1 = occasionally, 2 = sometimes, and 3 = frequently. In the remainder of this section, we discuss the general patterns of the intensity of interest groups' tactic use as well as the variations in tactic use across states and across group types.

General Patterns

Table 6.5 lists the average frequency with which different types of lobbying tactics were used in each state and across states. A comparison of the last column in Table 6.5 with that in Table 6.2 shows that those more commonly used tactics also tended to be used with higher levels of frequency. Specifically, contacting government officials was the most frequently used tactic, which were used by interest groups with an average

Table 6.5. Average Frequency of Interest Groups' Use of Lobbying Tactics by State

Lobbying Tactics	Citizens Groups (N=21)	Education Associations (N=79)	Higher Education Institutions (N=22)	Business/Foundation/Firms (N=14)	Research Organizations (N=20)	Total (N=156)
Inside Lobbying	2.0	1.9	1.4	2.0	1.4	1.8
• Testifying at legislative or agency hearings	2.2	2.2	1.1	2.2	1.3	2.3
• Contacting government officials	2.6	2.4	1.7	2.6	1.9	1.9
• Presenting research findings	2.0	1.7	2.3	1.8	2.1	1.9
• Drafting legislation and regulations	1.4	1.3	0.5	1.7	0.7	1.8
• Serving on commissions	1.7	2.1	1.5	1.7	1.2	1.2
Outside Lobbying	1.3	1.1	0.9	1.0	0.7	1.1
• Engaging the mass media	1.7	1.1	1.6	1.8	1.5	1.4
• Organizing letter-writing and telephone campaigns	1.6	1.4	0.5	0.9	0.3	1.1
• Endorsing policy allies for elective office	0.6	0.9	0.5	0.5	0.3	0.7
Organizational Maintenance	1.7	1.4	0.7	1.8	1.2	1.4
• Monitoring officials for policy developments	2.2	2.2	1.0	2.5	1.6	2.0
• Forming coalitions	2.3	2.1	1.2	2.4	1.8	2.0
• Raising funds to promote policy issues	1.4	0.6	0.5	1.8	1.1	0.9
• Advertising for new members	0.9	0.8	0.2	0.6	0.6	0.7

Note: Frequency of tactic use was measured on a scale from 0 to 3: 0 = never; 1 = occasionally; 2 = sometimes; 3 = frequently.

frequency somewhat higher than "sometimes." The next two most frequently used tactics were forming coalitions and monitoring officials for new policy developments, both of which were "sometimes" used by groups in the state reading policy networks. The two tactics used by the fewest number of groups, endorsing policy allies for elective office and advertising for new members, were also the ones used most rarely, each with an average frequency rating between "never" and "occasionally." Overall, interest groups most intensely engaged in inside lobbying activities (with an average frequency rating slightly below "sometimes"), somewhat less intensely engaged in organizational maintenance activities (with an average frequency rating between "occasionally" and "sometimes"), and only "occasionally" engaged in outside lobbying activities.

Differences in the Intensity of Tactic Use Across States

With the frequency data, we performed analyses of variance (ANOVA) to examine whether state variations existed in terms of the intensity with which interest groups made use of various lobbying tactics. We found significant differences between states in interest groups' use of the following three types of tactics: presenting research findings (Welch-statistic = 3.17, $p < .01$),[5] monitoring officials for policy developments ($F_{(8, 140)} = .215$, $p < .05$), and engaging the mass media ($F_{(8, 141)} = 2.06, p < .05$). No significant between-state variations were found in the intensity of tactic use for the other nine types of tactics, or for inside lobbying, outside lobbying, or organizational maintenance in general.

To pin down the sources of the significant between-state variations, we conducted pairwise comparisons using post hoc tests selected based on whether the assumption of homogeneity of variance was met. Employing Tamhane's T2 tests, we found that interest groups in the Texas reading policy networks presented research findings significantly more often than groups in the Michigan reading policy network ($p < .01$). Employing Bonferroni tests, we found that interest groups in California and Texas monitored officials for policy developments on a significantly more frequent basis than did interest groups in Maine ($p < .05$). Interest groups in Indiana and North Carolina also used the monitoring tactic more frequently than groups in Maine, although the differences were only marginally significant ($p < .10$). With regard to engaging the mass media, the Bonferroni test results revealed that none of the differences between pairs of states were significant at the .05 level, although the difference between Alabama and Connecticut approached statistic significance ($p < .10$).

Differences in the Intensity of Tactic Use Across Group Types

Table 6.6 presents the average frequency of interest groups' use of lobbying tactics for citizens groups, education associations/school districts, higher education institutions, business groups/foundations/firms, and research organizations/policy institutes respectively. To determine whether any of the differences across group types were statistically significant, we performed ANOVAs, the results of which were provided in Table 6.7.

As Table 6.7 shows, significant or marginally significant differences in the frequency of tactic use across group types were evident for all types of tactics except presenting research findings, which suggests that although different types of groups used similar types of lobbying tactics, they used those tactics with different degrees of intensity. We further performed post hoc tests to identify the differences between specific types of groups for each type of tactic. We employed Bonferroni tests where the homogeneity of variance assumption was met, and Tamhane's T2 tests where the assumption was not met. Significant differences in the intensity of tactic use between specific types of groups were presented in Table 6.8.

The most noticeable feature of Table 6.8 is the low intensity of tactic use of higher education institutions. For 7 of the 12 types of tactics, higher education institutions reported significantly lower frequencies of tactic use than at least one other type of groups. These institutions' engagement in organizational maintenance activities was also significantly less frequent than all other types of groups except research organizations/policy institutes. Another recurring pattern in the results presented in Table 6.8 is that education associations/school districts used certain types of tactics significantly more frequently than research organizations/policy institutes. As a general pattern, all the between-group-type differences in the intensity of tactic use we identified were between research-oriented organizations—higher education institutions and research organizations/policy institutes—and other types of groups. In all cases, research-oriented organizations made less use of the lobbying tactics in their repertoire than other types of groups.

INTEREST GROUPS' USE OF LOBBYING TACTICS AND THEIR INFLUENCE ON STATE READING POLICY

General Patterns

In the interest group literature, lobbying tactics have been variously called influence tactics or influence strategies. A question that naturally arises is how interest groups' use of influence tactics is related to their pol-

Table 6.6. Average Frequency of Interest Groups' Use of Lobbying Tactics by Group Type

Lobbying Tactics	Citizens Groups (N=21)	Education Associations (N=79)	Higher Education Institutions (N=22)	Business/ Foundation/ Firms (N=14)	Research Organizations (N=20)	Total (N=156)
Inside Lobbying	2.0	1.9	1.4	2.0	1.4	1.8
• Testifying at legislative or agency hearings	2.2	2.2	1.1	2.2	1.3	2.3
• Contacting government officials	2.6	2.4	1.7	2.6	1.9	1.9
• Presenting research findings	2.0	1.7	2.3	1.8	2.1	1.9
• Drafting legislation and regulations	1.4	1.3	0.5	1.7	0.7	1.8
• Serving on commissions	1.7	2.1	1.5	1.7	1.2	1.2
Outside Lobbying	1.3	1.1	0.9	1.0	0.7	1.1
• Engaging the mass media	1.7	1.1	1.6	1.8	1.5	1.4
• Organizing letter-writing and telephone campaigns	1.6	1.4	0.5	0.9	0.3	1.1
• Endorsing policy allies for elective office	0.6	0.9	0.5	0.5	0.3	0.7
Organizational Maintenance	1.7	1.4	0.7	1.8	1.2	1.4
• Monitoring officials for policy developments	2.2	2.2	1.0	2.5	1.6	2.0
• Forming coalitions	2.3	2.1	1.2	2.4	1.8	2.0
• Raising funds to promote policy issues	1.4	0.6	0.5	1.8	1.1	0.9
• Advertising for new members	0.9	0.8	0.2	0.6	0.6	0.7

Note: Frequency of tactic use was measured on a scale from 0 to 3: 0 = never; 1 = occasionally; 2 = sometimes; 3 = frequently.

Table 6.7. ANOVA Results for Differences in the Frequency of Interest Groups' Use of Lobbying Tactics Across Group Types

Lobbying Tactics		df	Mean Square	F
		Equal Variance Assumed		
Testifying at legislative hearings	Between Groups	4	6.82	6.59***
	Within Groups	146	1.03	
Presenting research findings	Between Groups	4	1.66	1.57
	Within Groups	145	1.06	
Serving on commissions	Between Groups	4	4.19	3.33*
	Within Groups	146	1.26	
Inside Lobbying	Between Groups	4	1.98	3.61**
	Within Groups	142	0.55	
Outside Lobbying	Between Groups	4	3.41	5.50***
	Within Groups	142	0.62	
Organizational Maintenance	Between Groups	4	1.30	2.14~
	Within Groups	144	0.61	

	df1	df2	Welch Statistic
		Equal Variance Not Assumed	
Contacting government officials	4	44.49	4.40**
Organizing phone and letter writing campaigns	4	45.04	11.29***
Monitoring officials for policy developments	4	44.00	7.25***
Drafting legislation	4	45.41	8.07***
Engaging the mass media	4	42.51	2.91*
Endorsing officials for public office	4	45.81	2.17~
Forming coalitions	4	44.20	5.47**
Raising funds	4	41.13	3.63*
Advertising for new members	4	44.82	3.60*

Note: F-statistics were used for significance tests where the assumption of homogeneity of variance was met; and Welch-statistics were used where the assumption was not met.

$\sim p < .10$ * $p < .05$, ** $p < .01$, *** $p < .001$.

Table 6.8. Differences in the Frequency of Tactic Use Between Different Types of Interest Groups in the State Reading Policy Domain

Lobbying Tactics	Difference Between Group Types
Inside Lobbying	
• Testifying at legislative or agency hearings	ns
• Contacting government officials	Citizens groups, education associations/school districts, and business groups/foundations/firms testified more frequently than higher education institutions ($p < .05$, $p < .01$, and $p < .05$ respectively). Education associations/school districts testified more often than research organizations/policy institutes ($p < .05$).
• Presenting research findings	Citizens groups, educational associations/school districts, and business groups/foundations/firms contacted government officials more frequently than higher education institutions ($p < .05$).
• Drafting legislation and regulations	Citizens groups, education associations/school districts, and business groups/foundations/firms drafted legislation and regulations more frequently than higher education institutions ($p < .05$, $p < .001$, and $p < .05$ respectively).
• Serving on commissions	Education associations/school districts served on commissions more frequently than research organizations/policy institutes ($p < .05$).
Outside Lobbying	
• Engaging the mass media	ns
• Organizing letter-writing and telephone campaigns	Citizens groups and education associations/school districts organized campaigns more frequently than higher education institutions ($p < .05$ and $p < .001$ respectively) and research organizations/policy institutes ($p < .05$ and $p < .001$ respectively).
• Endorsing policy allies for elective office	Education associations/school districts endorsed policy allies more frequently than research organizations/policy institutes ($p < .05$).
Organizational Maintenance	
• Monitoring officials for policy developments	Citizens groups, education associations/school districts, and business groups/foundations/firms engaged in organizational maintenance activities more frequently than higher education institutions ($p < .01$). Citizens groups, education associations/school districts, and business groups/foundations/firms monitored officials more frequently than higher education institutions ($p < .01$, $p < .001$, and $p < .01$ respectively).
• Forming coalitions	Citizens groups, education associations/school districts, and business groups/foundations/firms formed coalitions more frequently than higher education institutions ($p < .01$).
• Raising funds to promote policy issues	ns
• Advertising for new members	Education associations/school districts advertised for new members more frequently than higher education institutions ($p < .01$).

Note: ns: No significant difference between different types of groups was detected.

icy influence. Our study provided rich data to address this question. Table 6.9 lists the Pearson's correlation coefficients between the frequency of tactic use and three types of influence indicators—centrality, prestige, and perceived influence—based on data from 154 interest groups from the nine states. Several features of the table are particularly noteworthy. First, for most types of lobbying tactics, the frequency of their usage was significantly related to the two network measures of influence: actor centrality and actor prestige (see chapter 3 for definitions of the measures). Of the 12 types of tactics examined, for example, only raising funds was not sig-

Table 6.9.   Correlations Between the Frequency of Interest Groups' Use of Lobbying Tactics and Their Policy Influence in the State Reading Policy Domain

Lobbying Tactics	*Policy Influence*		
	Actor Centrality (N = 146)	*Actor Prestige (N = 146)*	*Perceived Influence (N = 164)*
Inside Lobbying	.47***	.42***	.21*
• Testifying at legislative or agency hearings	.41***	.34***	.22**
• Serving on commissions	.37***	.37***	.20*
• Contacting government officials	.32***	.23***	.12
• Drafting legislation and regulations	.31***	.29***	.09
• Presenting research findings	.26**	.25***	.19
Outside Lobbying	.37***	.28***	.18*
• Engaging the mass media	.33***	.31***	.17*
• Endorsing policy allies for elective office	.22*	.17*	.16~
• Organizing letter-writing and telephone campaigns	.22*	.12	.10
Organizational Maintenance	.34***	.27***	.20*
• Monitoring officials for policy developments	.36***	.30***	.15~
• Forming coalitions	.32***	.25***	.20*
• Advertising for new members	.17*	.13	.09
• Raising funds to promote policy issues	.15~	.12	.12
Total Number of Different Types of Tactics Used	.53***	.45***	.26**

Note: Frequency of tactic use was measured on a scale from 0 to 3: 0 = never; 1 = occasionally; 2 = sometimes; 3 = frequently.
~ $p < .10$, * $p < .05$, ** $p < .01$, *** $p < .001$.

nificantly related to actor centrality, although the relationship approached statistical significance (p < .10). These findings support Nownes and Freeman's (1998) claim that "while more activity does not necessarily mean more influence, it probably helps" (p. 110).

Second, for every type of tactic, the correlation between tactic use and actor centrality was higher than that between tactic use and actor prestige, which was in turn higher than the correlation between tactic use and perceived influence. It is clear from Table 6.9 that while the correlation between tactic use and actor centrality or prestige was significant for the majority of the tactics, the correlation between tactic use and perceived influence was not significant in most of the cases. A plausible explanation is that both actor centrality and prestige are activity-based measures, which were therefore likely to be more strongly correlated with lobbying activities than perceived influence, a perception- or reputation-based measure of influence. Moreover, the variation in the measure of perceived influence (standard deviation = .11) was much less than that in centrality and prestige (standard deviation = .21 for both), which also likely contributed to the weaker association between tactic use and perceived influence than between tactic use and the two network measures.

With regard to the two network measures, actor centrality was based on both relationships initiated by an actor and relationships received by an actor, whereas actor prestige was only based on relationships received by an actor. Hence actor centrality was more likely to be associated with the use of lobbying tactics than was actor prestige, as lobbying tactics generally represent activities on a group's own initiative and both tactic use and the initiation of network contacts reflect an actor's active participation in the policy processes.

Third, although a few of the correlation coefficients reported in Table 6.9 were not reach statistically significant, all the correlations were positive, suggesting that the higher the frequency of tactic use, the stronger the policy influence. The results also show that the magnitude of the correlations between tactic use and influence varied considerably. The correlation between testifying at legislative and agency hearings and actor centrality (.41), for example, was almost three times as strong as that between raising funds and actor centrality (.15), and was over four times as strong as that between advertising for new members and perceived influence (.09). Overall, the use of inside lobbying tactics was more strongly associated with policy influence than the use of outside lobbying tactics or organizational maintenance tactics based on all the three influence indicators.

Positive associations existed not only between the intensity of tactic use and policy influence, but also between the diversity of tactics used and policy influence. As shown in the bottom row of Table 6.9, the correlations between the total number of different types of tactics used and the three indictors of policy influence were all positive and statistically significant. The correlation between the diversity of tactics used and actor centrality was particularly strong (.53), which was over twice as high as that between the diversity of tactics used and perceived influence (.26). These findings suggest that interest groups with stronger policy influence on state reading policy tended to employ a more diverse set of lobbying tactics. They support Baumgartner and Leech's (1998) claim:

> The most effective groups may not be those that are best at a given strategy but rather those that have the greatest repertoire of strategies available to them and who are most skillful at choosing the right strategy for the issues at hand. (p. 148)

Differences in the Relationship Between Tactic Use and Policy Influence Across States

Although overall there was clear evidence for positive associations between the use of lobbying tactics and policy influence, the results disaggregated by state were not as clear-cut. As shown in Table 6.10, only about a quarter of the correlations between the frequency of tactic use and actor centrality were significant at the .05 level, and a few of the correlations were even negative, although none of which were significant. That said, we probably should not put too much emphasis on statistical significance with disaggregated data, because our within-state sample sizes were small and hence the power of statistical tests was low. As a matter of fact, in many cases, the within-state correlations exceeded those for the full sample in magnitude, but still failed to achieve statistical significance although the overall correlations did.

What is clear from the Table 6.10 is the substantial variations across states in the relationship between tactic use and influence as measured by actor centrality. Texas, for example, stood in sharp contrast with Alabama in that while none of the correlations were significant in Texas, over half of the correlations were significant in Alabama. Moreover, in terms of magnitude, the correlations between tactic use and centrality for Alabama actors were considerably higher than those for Texas actors for the majority of the tactics. Contacting government officials and actor centrality, for instance, was highly correlated for Alabama actors ($r = .68, p < .05$), but was virtually unrelated for Texas actors ($r = -.03, p > .05$).

Such wide variations between states were seen in the correlations between tactic use and all three types of influence indicators (see Appendix E for correlations between tactic use and actor prestige and correla-

Table 6.10. Correlations Between the Frequency of Interest Groups' Use of Lobbying Tactics and Actor Centrality by State

Lobbying Tactics	AL (N=13)	CA (N=25)	CT (N=17)	IN (N=21)	ME (N=14)	MI (N=21)	TX (N=21)	UT (N=14)	Total (N=146)
Inside Lobbying	.85**	.42~	.57*	.70**	.53	.33	.27	.72**	.47***
• Testifying at legislative or agency hearings	.35	.36	.49~	.68**	.37	.51*	.27	.83***	.41***
• Serving on commissions	.74***	.29	−.04	.63***	.46	.40~	.32	.42	.37***
• Contacting government officials	.68*	.39~	.54*	.22	.51	.12	−.03	.37	.32***
• Drafting legislation and regulations	.37	.25	.52*	.68**	.10	.24	.05	.61*	.31***
• Presenting research findings	.67*	.18	.67**	.23	.49	−.20	.23	.23	.26**
Outside Lobbying	.66*	.38~	.64*	.49*	.54	.11	.03	.52~	.37***
• Engaging the mass media	−.12	.50*	.65**	.35	.80**	−.09	.02	.76**	.33***
• Endorsing policy allies for elective office	.61*	.33	.39	.33	.31	.15	.08	.08	.22*
• Organizing letter-writing and telephone campaigns	.58*	−.06	.45~	.47*	.27	.16	−.03	.38	.22*
Organizational Maintenance	.50	.42~	.57*	.45*	.30	.23	.14	.55~	.34***
• Monitoring officials for policy developments	.79**	.14	.52~	.65***	.32	.30	.42~	.10	.36***
• Forming coalitions	.45	.51*	.50~	.22	.29	.18	.08	.61*	.32***
• Advertising for new members	.01	.22	.50*	.37	.20	.07	−.14	.61*	.17*
• Raising funds to promote policy issues	.16	.20	.29	.00	−.03	.15	.12	.43	.15
Total Number of Different Types of Tactics Used	.84**	.45*	.70**	.48**	.81**	.44*	.23	.64**	.53**

Note: Frequency of tactic use was measured on a scale from 0 to 3: 0 = never; 1 = occasionally; 2 = sometimes; 3 = frequently.
~ *p* < .10, * *p* < .05, ** *p* < .01, *** *p* < .001

tions between tactic use and perceived influence by state). Overall, the relationship between tactic use and the two network measures of influence appeared to be the weakest in the states of Michigan and Texas, and stronger in the other states, particularly Alabama. The relationship between tactic use and perceived influence was also low in Michigan and Texas, but not as low as in California; the relationship was much stronger in Indiana and Utah.

Considerable variations across states also existed in the relationship between the diversity of tactics used and policy influence. The correlation between the number of different types of tactics used and perceived influence, for instance, ranged between -.01 at the lowest (California) to .62 at the highest (Utah, $p < .05$) (see Table E.2 in Appendix E). The correlations between the diversity of tactics used and actor centrality and prestige varied not as much and were generally much stronger, particularly in the states of Alabama, Connecticut, and Maine.

Differences in the Relationship Between Tactic Use and Policy Influence Across Group Types

Results on the relationship between the frequency of tactic use and policy influence disaggregated by group type were also mixed. As Table 6.11 shows, although the correlations between the frequency of tactic use and actor centrality were significant for all but one type of tactic (i.e., advertising for new members) for the full sample, only about one third of the correlations were significant based on data disaggregated by group type. However, as noted previously, the statistical significance very often was a function of sample size rather than the actual strength of the relationships.

Again, with disaggregated data, the correlation results displayed substantial variations across sub-groups. The relationship between raising funds and actor centrality, for example, was positive and fairly strong for citizens groups ($r = .53$, $p < .05$), but negative for research organizations/policy institutes ($r = -.15$, $p > .10$). The correlations between tactic use and actor centrality for other types of tactics, however, were generally fairly strong for this latter type of groups. As shown in Table 6.11, among the five types of groups, research organizations/policy institutes had the highest correlations for 5 of the 12 types of tactics and for both inside and outside lobbying. In contrast, the correlations between tactic use and actor centrality were generally lower for business groups/foundation/firms, which had the lowest for correlations five types of tactics as well as outside lobbying among the five types of groups. Similar pattern was seen in the correlations between tactic use and actor prestige (see Table E.3 in

Table 6.11. Correlations Between the Frequency of Interest Groups' Use of Lobbying Tactics and Actor Centrality by Group Type

Lobbying Tactics	Citizens Groups (N=16)	Education Associations (N=75)	Higher Education Institutions (N=20)	Business/ Foundations/ Firms (N=16)	Research Organizations (N=19)	Total (N=146)
Inside Lobbying	.57*	.45***	.54*	.40	.61**	.47***
• Testifying at legislative or agency hearings	.38	.48***	.49*	.28	.41~	.41***
• Contacting government officials	.40	.41**	.23	-.03	.30	.37***
• Presenting research findings	.48~	.10	.44~	.48~	.37	.32***
• Drafting legislation and regulations	.54*	.27*	.33	.28	.56**	.31***
• Serving on commissions	.39	.33**	.21	.47~	.55*	.26**
Outside Lobbying	.30	.34**	.47~	.23	.54*	.37***
• Engaging the mass media	.39	.37**	.39	.18	.39	.33***
• Organizing letter-writing and telephone campaigns	.27	.16	.39	.12	.38	.22*
• Endorsing policy allies for elective office	.03	.19	.29	.21	.52*	.22*
Organizational Maintenance	.63**	.45***	.15	.22	.21	.34***
• Monitoring officials for policy developments	.45*	.43***	.08	.32	.51**	.36***
• Forming coalitions	.53*	.40**	.06	.42	.33	.32***
• Raising funds to promote policy issues	.53*	.21	.17	.11	-.15	.17*
• Advertising for new members	.43~	.30*	.04	-.10	-.19	.15
Total Number of Different Types of Tactics Used	.61*	.53***	.48~	.41	.56*	.53**

Note: Frequency of tactic use was measured on a scale from 0 to 3: 0 = never; 1 = occasionally; 2 = sometimes; 3 = frequently.
~ $p < .10$, * $p < .05$, ** $p < .01$, *** $p < .001$.

Appendix E). The correlations between tactic use and perceived influence, however, manifested a different pattern: the correlations were generally stronger in business groups/foundations/firms than for research organizations/policy institutes (see Table E.4 in Appendix E).

With regard to the relationships between the diversity of tactics used and policy influence, the variations across group types appear modest when actor centrality or prestige was used, and larger when perceived influence was used as the influence indicator (see Tables E.3 and E.4 in Appendix E). In terms of the strength of the relationship, the correlations between the diversity of tactics used and influence were strongest based on actor centrality, slightly weaker but still fairly strong based on actor prestige, and weakest based on perceived influence for all types of groups.

DISCUSSION

In the previous section, we reported our findings on the relationship between interest groups' use of lobbying tactics and their policy influence. The most salient theme that emerged from our data was the variations across types of tactics, across types of influence indicators, across states, and across types of groups. Such variations are understandable when we consider the complex nature of policy influence. As widely agreed, power and influence are affected by a multitude of factors, and are dynamic, transitory, and issue/context-specific (Greenwald, 1977; Knoke, 1990b; Mitchell, Agle, & Wood, 1997). What actors do is just one of the many factors related to their power and influence. Other than the characteristics of the actors (e.g., money, knowledge, skills, and credibility), the political and institutional environments of the states, such as the power of the governor and legislature and the level of socioeconomic development, may all account for the influence of interest groups (Thomas & Hrebenar, 1990, 1992). The presence of opposition forces (Browne, 1998), media and public attention surrounding the issue of interest (Chubb, 1983; Jones & Keiser, 1987; Schattschneider, 1960), and support from public officials (Fowler & Shaiko, 1987; Schlozman & Tierney, 1986), among others, would also affect the ability of various interest groups to exert influence on public policy.

Related to the complexity of the notion of influence is the difficulty in its measurement. Indeed, the measurement of the slippery albeit crucial concept of influence has been troubling political scientists for decades and has been regarded as a methodological challenge of the highest order. As Baumgartner and Leech (1998) observe, those studies that have been designed around the false premise that we can observe the actions of influence and power are doomed to fail because they are organized on "the chimerical promise of measuring the unmeasurable" (p. 37). Therefore influence has always been assessed using indirect and hence imperfect measures, such as actor centrality, actor prestige, and perceived influence as were used in this study. Both the multifaceted nature of influence and the imperfect measurement of the concept explain why we should not expect consistently strong relationships between interest groups' lobbying activities and their policy influence.

Nevertheless, despite the variations in the relationship between tactic use and policy influence across tactics, influence indicators, states, and group types, the correlations were overwhelmingly positive, and quite strong in many cases, which suggests that intensive lobbying activities may indeed contribute to policy influence.[6] As Browne (1998) puts it, "Any interest whose lobbyists wait diligently for their invitations from government to arrive in the mail are either hopelessly naïve or just ignorant" (p. 71). Although lobbying efforts do not necessarily translate to influence, being proactive will likely help interest groups have their voices heard and their opinions taken seriously considered by policymakers.

NOTES

1. Following Nownes and Freeman (1998), we define lobbying as any attempt to influence public policy.
2. Given the distinct nature of media organizations, we did not examine their use of lobbying tactics.
3. It should be noted that given data availability, the logistic regression model that we constructed did not include any control variables other than the set of dummy variables representing states (see Nownes & Freeman, 1998, p. 99, for potential control variables for such models). It is likely that the state effect, if any, may reflect the effect of other factors unaccounted for in our model. Therefore, our results about state differences were descriptive and exploratory in nature and should be interpreted with caution.
4. Given the relatively large number of states and the relatively small within-state sample sizes, the regression analyses were of low statistic power, which might explain the lack of significant state effects for contacting government officials and inside lobbying even though the chi-square tests suggest significant overall between-state differences in the use of these two types of activities.
5. Because the assumption of homogeneity of variance was not met for presenting research findings, Welch- statistic was used instead of F-statistic, the former of which is more robust to violation of the homogeneity assumption.
6. It should be noted that the results that we have reported were largely descriptive and exploratory, which do not warrant strict causal inference about the relationship between the use of lobbying tactics and policy influence. The inferences that we have drawn are not meant to be definitive, but are only suggestive in nature.

CHAPTER 7

RECAP AND CONCLUDING OBSERVATIONS

In the preceding chapters, we have conducted a comprehensive investigation of the reading policy system in nine states, drawing on both interview and archival data collected in the State Reading Policy Study. To conclude our investigation, we recapitulate the state reading policy processes, reflect on policy theories and research methodology, and discuss the implications of our study for both policy researchers and policy actors in the field of education.

RECAP OF THE STATE READING POLICY PROCESSES

Kingdon's (1995) multiple streams model of policymaking provides a useful tool for piecing together the different elements of the policy processes into a coherent picture, as shown in Figure 7.1. Although policymaking rarely proceeds in a rational fashion or follow a clear temporal sequence, happenings in the processes could be appropriately conceptualized as falling into two major areas: agenda setting and alternative specification. Agenda setting deals primarily with the question how certain issues have garnered policymakers' attention and acquired a salient agenda status. Alternative specification is concerned with how various policy ideas and

Reading: Policy, Politics, and Processes, pp. 167–181
Copyright © 2008 by Information Age Publishing
All rights of reproduction in any form reserved.

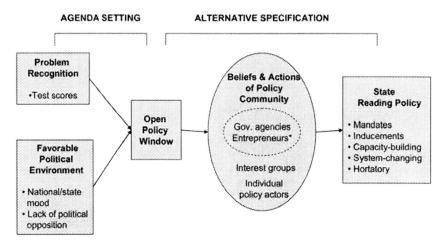

Note: * "Entrepreneurs" in the chart represent policy entrepreneurs affiliated with government agencies or interest groups. Entrepreneurs in the broader sense also include individual policy actors not affiliated with any organization.

Figure 7.1.   A schematic recap of the state reading policy processes.

proposals are generated from the policy community and why certain ideas are taken seriously whereas others are ignored.

Agenda Setting: Problem Recognition, Political Environment, and Policy Windows

A key aspect of agenda setting is problem recognition. In the state reading policy domain, reading was widely recognized as a compelling problem needing prompt policy actions in the 1990s. Although Kingdon (1995) specifies three major mechanisms for problem recognition—problem indicators, focusing events, and feedback, the recognition of the reading problem was primarily triggered by disappointing test scores as problem indicators, which raised policymakers' awareness of the reading problem and helped to move reading to the top of their political agenda.

Reading's high agenda status in the 1990s also had to do with a favorable political environment. Under a prevalent national mood that placed strong emphasis on education in general and on reading in particular, politicians on both sides of the political fence identified themselves as supporters of education reform and considered reading a good political issue. For policymakers, advocating policies to improve reading achievement offered them an opportunity for political accomplishment that was likely to be achieved with minimum opposition and little political risk. Thus, the issue of reading enjoyed strong political support and was able to sail to the top of the policy agenda with little opposition from organized political forces along the way.

The recognition of reading as a pressing problem in need of a solution combined with a favorable political environment led to the opening of a "window" for policy change in many states in the 1990s. A "policy window," according to Kingdon (1995), opens at critical junctures of the policy development process, and represents a propitious time during which policy entrepreneurs are most likely to couple their pet solutions to compelling problems. The open policy windows in the state reading policy domain galvanized into action diverse actors in the reading policy community, who interacted and exchanged ideas with one another, formulated and reformulated policy alternatives, and employed a variety of strategies to "soften up" both the policy community and the larger publics in efforts to build acceptance to their favored proposals.

Alternative Specification: Policy Networks, Influence, Beliefs, Proposed Solutions, and Lobbying Tactics

Central to the understanding of the alternative specification process is knowledge about the composition and influence structure of the policy community from which policy ideas and proposals were generated. Such knowledge will help us to understand who wields power and influence and whose views are represented in a democracy, which are the two fundamental issues underlying policymaking and politics (Mawhinney, 2001). Our study of the state reading policy domain revealed that the reading policy communities in all nine states were characterized by both proliferation and diversity. With an average size of 27 actors, the state reading policy communities included not only government agencies and a few traditional educational interests, but also a wide variety of groups and individuals mobilized and committed to shaping reading policy.

Actors in the state reading policy communities were not acting alone, but were interacting with one another as members of reading policy networks. Employing network analytic methods, we found that the reading policy networks in the eight states where network data were available were all well connected, with extensive open channels of communication that allowed timely exchange of information and resources among member of the networks. We also found that all the eight state reading policy networks demonstrated a core-periphery structure, which stood in sharp contrast with the hollow-core structure in some of the national policy domains (Heinz, Laumann, Nelson, & Salisbury, 1993), and reflected the differentiation in network involvement and hence policy influence among the state reading policy actors. Although both the core and the periphery of the networks contained a mix of government and nongovernment actors, the mix was by no means thorough or random. All the networks demonstrated positional differentiations between different types of actors. In particular, government actors tended to concentrate in particular regions of the policy networks, so did single-issue nongovernment actors, which suggests that both types of actors tended to interact with actors similar to themselves.

In addition to the structural properties and interactional patterns of the state reading policy networks, our network analyses also shed light on the influence system of the state reading policy domain. We found that government actors, particularly state departments of education, occupied significantly more central and prestigious network positions than nongovernment actors in all eight states, which is consistent with findings on perceived influence measured with the reputational approach. With regard to the influence of nongovernment actors, a major finding from our study was that teacher organizations were not as influential as suggested by previous research, which, according to many respondents, was largely due to their lack of focus on the issue of reading. As for policy entrepreneurs, the activists within the policy communities, we found that those who worked for particularly government agencies or interest groups often played pivotal roles as policy advocates for the organizations that they represented and contributed significantly to the visibility and influence of these organizations. Individual policy actors acting on their own, on the other hand, were generally of limited policy influence.

In short, the state reading policy networks were heterogeneous in both composition and actor influence. In this pluralistic policy arena, power was certainly not distributed evenly across the plurality of actors, but largely concentrated within state governments spearheaded by policy entrepreneurs. Nevertheless, the center of influence was not entirely dominated by government actors; certain nongovernment actors (e.g., Alabama's A+ Education Foundation and the University of Maine) could also be highly influential and share the central stage with government actors. In other words, the center of power was not a closed circle of insiders, but permeable to outside groups with blurred boundaries.

Variations in policy actor influence existed not only within states but also between states. Such variations are not surprising given the complex, dynamic, and fluid nature of influence, which is affected by a multitude of factors, including each state's unique social and political cultures, and the resources, knowledge, reputation, and political skills of the policy actors, to name just a few (e.g., Marshall & Gerstl-Pepin, 2005; Thomas & Hrebenar, 1990, 1992).

While state reading policy actors possess varying levels of influence, they tended to agree on key policy issues. They all agreed that reading achievement levels were unacceptably low, but were optimistic that things were improving. Debates about reading pedagogy were far less rancorous than before, and consensus was emerging around a balanced approach that was perhaps somewhat tilted towards phonics. State reading policy actors were also overwhelmingly supportive of state reading standards, but somewhat more divided about state reading tests.

Another important component of state reading policy actors' belief systems is their perceptions about the causes of the reading problem. These actors offered a variety of explanations for low reading achievement, most of which portrayed the problem as an unintended consequence of certain sociocultural factors (e.g., demographic shifts and media influence) or purposeful human actions (e.g., flawed pedagogy, inadequate teacher preparation, and lack of parental involvement). Rarely was low reading achievement seen as an intended consequence of purposeful human actions. Causal stories about complex systems or institutions/historical causes were also relatively rare. In a sense, the causal stories told by state reading policy actors seem to suggest that everyone is to blame for the reading problem and we all share the responsibility for addressing the problem.

Consistent with the diversified nature of state reading policy actors' causal stories, a variety of policy solutions had been adopted by the states, which employed different types of policy instruments (i.e., mandates, inducements, capacity-building, system-changing, and hortatory polices) and often aimed to tackle the problem from multiple angles, particularly curriculum and instruction. In general, these policy solutions were largely congruent with the causal stories circulating among the state reading policy communities, and clear linkages were evident between proposed solutions and perceived problem causes.

We not only explored what state reading policy actors believed and proposed, but also what they did to promote their beliefs and favored policy proposals. In particular, we examined interest groups' use of lobbying tactics, or influence strategies, which have been studied extensively by political scientists, but received scant attention from education researchers. We found that interest groups' use of lobbying tactics varied substantially across states, across different types of tactics, and across different types of groups. Variations were also evident in the relationships between tactic use and actor influence across states, tactics, group types, and alternative measures of influence. Nevertheless, the correlations between tactic use and influence were overwhelmingly positive, and were quite strong in many cases, suggesting that the intensive use of a variety of influence tactics might indeed help to raise the visibility of policy actors and contribute to their influence on the outcomes of the alternative specification process.

IMPLICATIONS FOR POLICY RESEARCH IN EDUCATION

Theory-Guided Educational Policy Research

As Valencia and Wixson (2000) lament, our knowledge about policy development in reading, an essential area of schooling, is unfortunately insufficient. Malen (2001) also observes that our understanding of the critical roles interest groups play in shaping educational policies is inadequate, and calls for placing analyses of interest groups to the center of politics of education research agenda. Not only is policy research in education lacking, most existing research has been focusing on what happens after polices are made, that is, the implementation and impacts of existing policies. There has been very little effort to study how educational policies emerge from the interactions among a constellation of policy actors vying for influence under a given policy context. One obvious reason for this imbalance is the increasingly heavy emphasis on accountability and outcomes in the field of education. Another reason is policymakers' tendency to focus on change as an indicator for improvement. A less obvious reason is that research on the nebulous policy development process appears far more challenging than research on what happens with concrete existing policies. As Sabatier (1999a) states,

> Understanding the policy process requires a knowledge of the goals and perceptions of hundreds of actors throughout the country involving possibly very technical scientific and legal issues over periods of a decade or more when most of those actors are actively seeking to propagate their specific "spin" on events. (p. 4)

Given the "staggering complexity" of the policy process, Sabatier (1999a) argues, the analyst "*must* [emphasis original] find some way of simplifying the situation in order to have any chance of understanding it" (p. 4), and "simplifying theories are an absolute necessity" (Sabatier, 1999b, p. 261). Ripley (1985) similarly observes that conceptual models render "what is incredibly complex and idiosyncratic in any individual case into a set of relationships that are both simpler and more recurrent" (p. 31). We could not agree more. The entire process of our study—from research design to the interpretation of findings—has been grounded in several theoretical frameworks, particularly Kingdon's (1995) multiple streams framework of policymaking and the social network perspective. Stone's (2002) theory of causal stories and McDonnell and Elmore's (1987) framework of alternative policy instruments also facilitated our understanding about important aspects of the state reading policy systems. Guidance from these theoretical frameworks contributed to a productive research endeavor that generated a wealth of knowledge about the development of state reading policy.

Our investigation of the state reading policy processes was greatly informed by Kingdon's (1995) multiple streams framework of policymaking. Rated as one of the seven "more promising theoretical frameworks of the policy process" by Sabatier (1999a) and one of the three classic public policy theories since the 1980s by John (2003),[1] Kingdon's (1995) multiple streams framework served as a "simplifying theory," in Sabatier's (1999a) terms, that guided our research. It brought a certain degree of order to a complex process that often appears muddled and irrational, and provided a roadmap guiding our venture into the highly dynamic and intricate terrain. The multiple streams framework helped us to identify areas to explore, research questions to ask, data to collect, and what to look for in the data gathered. It allowed us to understand both happenings within the problem, political, and policy streams, and see the general flow of the streams and how they converged at open policy windows.

Our research was also guided by the social network perspective. Although not a fully elaborated theory on policymaking, the social network perspective has much to offer for studies of policy domains. With its unique focus on actor relationships, the social network perspective recognizes the embedded nature of policy actors and activities, and is ideally suited for policy studies. It allows researchers to discover—from a structural perspective—underlying patterns and regularities that would not have been revealed through alternative theoretical lenses and traditional social science research methods.

The social network perspective not only helps us to understand social systems conceptually, but also offers a set of finely designed methodological tools for examining social systems empirically. It enables researchers to explore in a systematic way the structural context of a given policy domain and its implications for both actors embedded in the domain and the overall domain itself. Although social network analysis is not new to the field of education, studies employing network analytic methods have been scarce and focused overwhelmingly on affective relationships in school settings (e.g., Cause, 1986; Cohen, 1977; and Ray, Cohen, & Secrist, 1995), with a handful addressing substantial issues in education (e.g., Minden, Henry, Tolan, & Gorman-Smith, 2000; Oetting & Beauvais, 1986). Virtually none of the studies dealing with policy issues other than a recent dissertation study by McDaniel (2001) and the dissertations of both authors based on the research presented in this book (Song, 2003; Young, 2005). The study reported here provides one concrete illustration of how the social network perspective can be fruitfully employed in policy research in education.

The combination of the multiple streams framework of policymaking and the social network perspective generated far richer insights into the state reading policy processes than what would have been obtained with either approach alone. Indeed, as Cook (1977) claims, "No single theoretical perspective will enable us to explain everything about organizational interaction" (p. 77). Peters (1999) similarly argues, "Some eclecticism of approach is likely to pay greater intellectual dividends ... than is a strict adherence of a single approach" (p. 2). Thus, whenever possible, multiple theoretical perspectives should be employed to guide social science inquiries, so that richer and less biased findings could be obtained. Further, the use of this multiple-lens strategy, according to Sabatier (1999a), would help to clarify the conditions under which one perspective is superior to another. Knowledge as such would enable researchers to identify and apply appropriate theoretical perspectives to their investigations in a more productive way.

Limitations of the Study and Directions for Future Research

As the most significant research endeavor on state reading policy development in the United States to date, our cross-state study has greatly expanded our knowledge base in reading policy development. While it shed light on many important policy-relevant questions, it also left many questions unanswered. Given its cross-sectional design, for instance, our study was unable to examine the evolution of policy networks over time, which would be a promising direction for future research. As Heclo (1978) points out, policy networks are not static, but fluid and dynamic, with actors moving in and out constantly, which makes a longitudinal design for network analyses particularly appropriate. Although a longitudinal design poses a higher demand on data collection than a cross-sectional design, the findings would be much more illuminating: we may understand not only the structural properties of the policy networks and their impacts on the actors at a given point in time, but also factors that lead to changes in network configurations and properties as well as the effects of structural changes on both actors and the overall networks.

Another limitation of the design of our study has to do with the measurement of actor relationships for social network analyses. In this study, the relationships of interest were defined rather broadly as any interactions or collaborations regarding reading-related issues between two state reading policy actors. The relationships could be anything from casual exchanges of opinions to formal interorganizational collaborations. It is likely that the specific nature of the relationships—other than the quantity and strength of the relationships—would also have effects on the actors involved. Future research, therefore, may consider using in-depth qualitative data to supplement the quantitative relational data to examine the nature of the relationships as well as its implications. Such qualitative data can be elicited by using specific probing questions during interviews, and may also be collected in the form of journal entries or logs written by study participants and field notes taken by researchers employing ethnographic methods.

A major function of the measurement of actor relationships in our study was to assess the relative levels of influence of diverse policy actors. It should be noted, however, our focus on structural determinants of policy influence is not meant to deny the importance of individual attributes and institutional settings, which are best viewed as complementary sources of policy influence. Moreover, these different types of factors are probably not totally independent of each other, but are collectively shaping policy development. Individual attributes and institutional settings, for example, might affect the ways actor relationships are established as well as the nature of the relationships. Conversely, relationship patterns might also influence individuals' behavior and well-being and institutional settings. A challenging agenda for future research on policy influence, an enduring topic in research on education policy and politics, is to recognize the values of different theoretical perspectives and research traditions, explore the connections among them, and develop ways to integrate them into a coherent and comprehensive model of policy influence that could be tested and continuously refined.

Obviously that the research agendas outlined above are not subject-specific, but apply to subject areas and policy issues beyond those covered in the research reported here. Given the paucity of policy research in education, there are still many blank pages in this literature waiting to be filled. Using network analytic methods, for example, future researchers may study a wide range of issues both in reading and in education in general. In addition to actor centrality and prestige, network density and positional differentiation, researchers may examine other structural properties of education policy networks, such as cohesion and structural equivalence, track the evolution of the fluid policy networks, investigate the diffusion of policy ideas across networks, and explore the linkage between the relational context and policy actors' beliefs and behaviors as well as policy outcomes.

Policy researchers in education will not only benefit from additional methodological tools such as social network analysis, but, more importantly, benefit from knowledge about theoretical frameworks that might inform their research. Given the paucity of policy research in education, it comes as no surprise that general theories of policymaking in education are lacking.[2] Thus, it is advisable that educational policy researchers be familiar with theories developed in other social science fields, such as public policy and political science, and be able to critically apply relevant theories to their research. As a matter of fact, many policy theories are generalizable beyond the fields from which they were originally developed. Kingdon's (1995) multiple streams framework is one such example (Zahariadis, 1999), and the advocacy coalition framework developed by Sabatier and Jenkins-Smith (1988, 1993) is another powerful theoretical lens that has the potential to be fruitfully employed in diverse social science fields.[3] Sabatier (1999c) provides an excellent introduction to seven major contemporary policy theories. A more comprehensive review of public policy theories can be found in Parsons (1995).

EMPOWERMENT OF EDUCATIONAL PROFESSIONALS AND PRACTITIONERS

Having reached the end of this book, many readers are probably wondering about the "so what" question—what is the practical value of the findings from this study for educators and practitioners? The most significant contribution of policy research such as the one presented in this book, we believe, lies in its potential for empowering educational professionals and practitioners and consequently leading to better informed education policies and improved policy outcomes.

The lack of influence of nongovernment actors such as educational professionals and practitioners has been a consistent finding in our study on state reading policy and in prior educational policy research (Marshall, Mitchell, & Wirt, 1989; Mazzoni, 1993). While government actors are often labeled "insiders" and "power centers," nongovernment actors are often associated with "outsiders," "peripheral actors," or even "forgotten players" (Marshall et al., 1989, p. 221). Indeed, despite their professional expertise and real-world knowledge about teaching and learning in schools, educators and practitioners are often marginalized in the policy arena. As Marshall and Gerstl-Pepin (2005) note, the most frequent refrain in educators' lounges is, "Those politicians make policy, but they just don't know what it's like in real schools" (p. 31). The frustration and sense of powerlessness are particularly acute among educators as states have been strengthening their control over education policymaking during the past decade (Song, forthcoming). Concerned about the loss of local control, two Texas reading researchers (Patterson & Gerla, 1997) lament:

> We no longer assume that the primary decision makers are reading researchers and educators, that we can close our classroom doors and ignore statewide initiatives.... We no longer see top-down mandates as impotent, particularly when they are linked to competitive grant monies and high-stakes testing. (para. 23)

For educational professionals to become powerful policy advocates with a strong voice on education decision making, expertise and knowledge about teaching and learning are not enough. It is essential that they also both possess knowledge about the policy system and are equipped with effective strategies for political actions. Although focusing on the area of reading, the study that we have presented has much to offer for educational professionals seeking to have a stronger presence in the policymaking process in the field of education in general. The findings from our study will not only help them to understand how the policy system works, but also provide them with concrete strategies for effective political participation in the policy arena.

Empowerment With Knowledge about the Policy System

As the maxim goes, knowledge is power. Applied to the education policy domain, it could be interpreted as meaning that to become powerful players in the decision-making process, one needs to have a clear understanding about the policy system. As the president of a professional association noted during an interview on national reading policy, some groups were more effective at influencing reading policy because of "being knowledgeable about how the system works or doesn't work.... And knowing what action is going to work" (Song, 2001, p. 26). Similarly, a policymaker observed that some organizations were able to make an impact because "they understand the political process and they understand how to work within that process very well in terms of leveraging support and what are the right moments when things are aligned to get movement" (p. 26).

Our investigation of reading policy development in nine states has generated a wealth of knowledge about this policy arena. Findings from our study have revealed who are the key players and who are not, what their values and beliefs are about policy problems and solutions, what they do to acquire and exert power, how the influence hierarchy is structured, and how diverse actors interact with one another and collectively shape reading policy development in the states. Knowledge as such will help policy actors to develop strategic plans for advancing their political agendas, and make wise judgments in choosing policy allies and building coalitions for effective political actions.

Importantly, knowledge about the larger political context reduces the environmental uncertainty that hinders effective decision making. According to the open systems perspective, organizations are influenced by and dependent upon their external environments; and environmental uncertainty due to inadequate information poses a fundamental problem for decision makers (Hoy & Miskel, 2007; Thompson, 1967). Such environmental uncertainty could be lessened at least partially with knowledge generated from our study or similar policy research, which illuminates the complex, dynamic, and often unpredictable policy arena. Policy actors with such knowledge, therefore, will be at an advantage in engaging in effective decision making than actors who lack such knowledge and therefore have to make decisions in the face of greater uncertainty about their political environment.

Networking as a Means for Acquiring and Exercising Influence

Policy actors may reduce environmental uncertainty not only through being informed by findings from policy research, but also through acquiring policy-relevant information first-hand from their network connections. Exchanges of policy-relevant information between network contacts, according to Laumann and Knoke (1987), are "the main way in which organizations cope with a highly uncertain environment in which many actors engage in the competitive and cooperative processes of collective decision making" (p. 207). Indeed, network connections provide actors with access to valuable and timely information about opportunities and constraints, among other things, in the policy environment; and are an important means for reducing environmental uncertainty. There is, however, more to it than that.

Like individual attributes such as money, social status, knowledge, and expertise (Clark, 1968; Laumann & Knoke, 1987; Rosenthal, 1998), network involvement is also an important determinant of policy actor influence. Network connections provide policy actors with direct access to useful information and alternative resources as well as control over other actors. Moreover, network connections may compensate for relatively weak resources or to make less valuable resources more potent (Brass & Burkhardt, 1993; Molm, 1990). In support, our study show that actors engaged in extensive relationships generally occupied more central and prestigious network positions and exerted stronger influence on state reading policy compared with actors with sparse connections. Mintrom and Vergari's (1998) study on innovation diffusion likewise suggests that policy entrepreneurs with greater involvement in policy networks could better tap network resources, and were hence more likely to attain their policy goals. Laumann and Knoke (1987) also emphasize the importance of establishing network relationships for influence acquisition, claiming:

> If organizations are to have any impact upon the outcomes of collective decisions that affect their interests, they must maintain ready access to potential allies, opponents, and targets of influence efforts. It is no exaggeration to say: no information, no influence. (p. 207)

The importance of making contact was also noted by some of the participants in our study. In response to the question who was particularly influential on state reading policy, for example, an education association representative in Michigan answered:

> People that lobby. People that work in the lobby front and work with all these people on this list are the people that are going to help shape the way it's done. And that tends to be your lobby presences.

Similarly, a Texas senator commented, "The most important [influence strategy] is contacting legislators and the commissioner and combining that with presenting research findings. If you have good research and you make contact, you probably are 80% of the way down the road." One implication of the senator's comment is that what is important is not just making contact, but also whom to contact. Given the stronger influence of government actors compared with nongovernment actors, the senator's suggestion seems to be a wise one.

Indeed, contacting policymakers and speaking up may be an effective means to make a difference. In most instances, as Elmore and Fuhrman (1994) point out, policymakers are sufficiently aware of their own limitations and are willing to listen to professional advice when it is well formed and articulated. However, policymakers seldom refrain from making policy in the absence of sound professional advice, particularly when they are under strong pressures to act. It follows that keeping communication channels open between education professionals and policymakers is crucial for making well-informed policy decisions. Further, in order to maximize their impact, education professionals should not just rely on a few formal channels to policymakers, but need to forge informal points of access to the state legislature, the governor's office, and the state education agency.

While it is important for education professionals to reach out to policy-makers, it is also important for them to build network connections among themselves. As Elmore and Fuhrman (1990) note, education policies depend increasingly on institutional interdependencies and on people with boundary-spanning skills, and professional networks will become increasingly influential in determining both the content of education policy and its implementation. Using standards as an example, they argue that:

> In the presence of a well-organized professional network, standards become, in effect, what professionals say they are. In other areas, where professional interests are less well organized and less focused in the application of their expertise, policy will probably be influenced more by diffuse political interests. (p. 214)

CLOSING REMARKS

Indeed, networking—both contacting policymakers and cultivating professional networks—and acquiring policy-relevant knowledge can be powerful means to gain and exercise power. Although education professionals generally lack policy influence, they do have the potential for making a difference. It is essential that they are aware of and able to realize such potential so that education policies could be well informed by their professional expertise, facilitate rather than hinder effective teaching and learning, and produce a positive impact on the lives of schoolchildren.

From the perspective of policymakers, the empowerment of educators should not be seen as posing a threat to their authority, but as creating a win-win situation. Including educators at the decision-making table will help bridge the gap between politicians and educators, and enable policy products to be more attuned to the realities in and around schools. Further, a truly collaborative decision-making style is also necessary to ensure faithful policy implementation. Although educators' control over policy development may be weak, their power over policy implementation is not to be overlooked. As McLaughlin (1987) reminds us, "Change is ultimately the problem of the smallest unit ... and what actually is delivered or provided under the aegis of a policy depends upon the individual at the end of the line" (p. 175). Marshall and Gerstl-Pepin (2005) similarly observe that policy outcomes are often shaped by the so-called "lowerar-chy." Only when educators and practitioners are part of the policymaking process will they have a sense of ownership over the policy product, will it be possible that the policy be faithfully implemented and bring about desired impact.

While it is essential that both policymakers and education professionals be integral participants of policymaking, the optimal power allocation among those inside and outside of government is not easy to define, as it is likely contingent on a multitude of factors (e.g., policy content, and state social and political culture). Nevertheless, it is an important consideration for all actors engaging in political actions. The optimal power allocation cannot be achieved through power struggles or turf battles, but it could be achieved when the boundaries between insiders and outsiders become permeable, and when all actors share a common focus on students and embrace a common commitment to educational excellence and equity.

NOTES

1. The seven "more promising theoretical frameworks" identified by Sabatier (1999c) are: the stages heuristic, institutional rational choice, multiple-streams framework, punctuated-equilibrium framework, advocacy coalition framework, policy diffusion framework, and the funnel of causality and other frameworks in large-N comparative studies. The three classic public policy theories identified by John (2003) include: multiple-streams framework, punctuated-equilibrium framework, and advocacy coalition framework.

2. One exception is Mazzoni's (1991) arena model of political initiation of policy innovation in the state education policy domain. Policy innovations, according to the model, take place in four arenas or decision sites—subsystem arena, macro arena, commission arena, and leadership arena—and often involve shifts between arenas.

3. The advocacy coalition framework focuses on the interaction between advocacy coalitions within a policy subsystem, with each coalition composed of actors from various organizations who share a set of normative and causal policy beliefs. Policy change, according to the framework, is a function of both competition within the subsystem and events outside the subsystem.

APPENDIX A

DESIGN OF THE STATE READING POLICY STUDY

Sampling Design

The State Reading Policy Study was a nine-state study carried out by a research team, including both authors of the book, at the University of Michigan. The study started under the auspices of a field-initiated study grant from the U.S. Department of Education's Office of Educational Research and Improvement (OERI) (currently The Institute of Education Sciences), which provided support for our investigation of reading policy in five states: California, Connecticut, Michigan, North Carolina, and Texas. These five states were selected using the following criteria: (1) different National Assessment of Educational Progress (NAEP) trends in reading, (2) evidence of recent or proposed reading policy initiatives, and (3) geographic diversity.

With the passage of the Reading Excellence Act (REA) in 1999, our research team became interested in how state reading policymaking among REA recipients might differ from REA nonrecipients. With additional funding from the Spencer Foundation, we were able to expand our original sample to include four additional states—Alabama, Indiana, Maine, and Utah, so that the final sample included four REA states and five non-REA states. However, by the end of the study, all of the states in the sample with the exception of Michigan had received REA grants, thus comparisons between REA and non-REA states would no longer be possible. Nevertheless, the expanded state sample allowed for more comprehensive comparisons of the states in a variety of aspects, such as the composition and structure of the reading policy networks, and the policymaking processes and outcomes.

Although there was sufficient diversity among the nine states in our study to offer useful insights into state reading policymaking in general, the nine states were not a nationally representative sample randomly selected from all 50 states. Therefore findings from this study may not generalize to all states.

The second sampling stage involved the identification of policy actors from each of the nine states, with policy actors defined as government agencies, interest groups, and individuals not representing any organizations or groups that had a substantive interest in shaping state reading policy. We started the identification process with extensive systematic archival searches. We examined documents related to state reading initiatives in all our sampled states, state and interest group web cites, major state newspapers, press releases, journal articles, and bibliographies to identify policy actors involved in state reading policy. From this archival search, we generated a list of preliminary policy actors to be interviewed. We then asked one or two consultants that we knew to be knowledgeable and active in the state's reading policy arena (based either on our document review or personal contacts) to add or subtract actors from our preliminary list.

Further, to ensure that we identified all relevant policy actors in each state, we expanded the initial sample of actors by means of the snowball (Goodman, 1961; Kingdon, 1995) or sequential sampling (Heinz, Laumann, Nelson, & Salisbury, 1993) technique. That is, during the interviews, we asked study participants to identify other key individuals or groups actively involved in state reading policy. Policy actors receiving multiple nominations were subsequently added to the initial sample, if they were not already in it. The above sampling procedures yielded a comprehensive list of state reading policy actors, and allowed us to obtain an adequate coverage of the state reading policy domain and gather observations and insights from informants across a wide range of perspectives, beliefs, experiences, and interests both inside and outside of the government.

We sought to interview at least one individual from each organization or group in the sample of policy actors, with the most likely candidate being the head of the organization, a high-ranking elected or appointed official, the director of government relations, or the policy liaison. For organizations that were particularly active or had extensive responsibilities with respect to state reading policy development, more than one individual might have been interviewed. Examples include state departments of education and state legislatures. Overall, an effort was made to locate potential respondents informed enough to provide information about their groups' perspectives concerning reading policy, to describe their individual or organization's interactions with other reading policy actors, and to comment on the reading policy environment in general.

There were a few instances, primarily in California, when respondents represented more than one organization during the time period studied, as horizontal movement or revolving doors between the public and private spheres is a common occurrence in politics (e.g., Heclo, 1988; Hula, 1999; Salisbury, Johnson, Heinz, Laumann, & Nelson, 1989; Schlozman & Tierney, 1986). Bill Honig, for example, was both the State Superintendent for Public Instruction for California and the founder of Consortium on Reading Excellence during the period studied. For these respondents, we asked them to participate as a spokesperson for their primary organizational affiliation, which was determined by their time in the position and their level of reading policy activities. If a respondent wished to represent another organization, his or her interview would be recognized as such. In total, we identified 433 potential individual respondents, of whom 366 individuals representing 243 policy actors participated in our study, with an overall response rate of 85% across the nine states. Table A.1 lists the number of each type of respondents as well as the response rates by state.

Data Collection and Management

Our primary data collection instruments included a set of standard open-ended structured interview schedules developed specifically for

Table A.1. Number of Respondents and Response Rate by State

State	Government Agency Representatives	Interest Group Representatives	Individual Policy Actors	Response Rate
Alabama	5 (15)	21 (26)	0 (0)	63%
California	13 (14)	33 (38)	6 (6)	90%
Connecticut	15 (15)	24 (25)	3 (3)	98%
Indiana	14 (16)	25 (30)	0 (0)	85%
Maine	16 (19)	19 (23)	0 (0)	83%
Michigan	26 (26)	30 (31)	0 (0)	98%
North Carolina	13 (17)	21 (25)	1 (1)	83%
Texas	15 (19)	31 (44)	0 (0)	71%
Utah	15 (17)	19 (22)	1 (1)	88%
Total	132 (158)	223 (254)	11 (11)	85%

Note: Numbers in parentheses are numbers of individuals that we contacted.

policymakers, representatives of non-media interest groups, and members of the media (see Appendix B for the full interview schedules). Prior to the interview, each participant was asked to sign an informed consent statement that both served as a formal agreement for study participation and provided guarantee of anonymity for the participant. The guarantee for anonymity reduced the potential risks for the respondents associated with their study participation and increased the likelihood that they would speak candidly and provide accurate information.

In addition to the interview schedules, we also prepared a collaboration table for each state for eliciting network data. Each collaboration table has three columns. The first column lists the key policy groups and individual actors that we identified during the sampling stage. The other two columns have the headings "You Initiated" and "They Initiated" respectively, which were intended to capture the direction of the relationships between the respondent and other policy actors. The use of the collaboration tables facilitated respondents' capacity to accurately recall and report their network connections and were thus likely to enhance the reliability of the network data elicited (Marsden, 1990).

Approximately half of the respondents were interviewed in person and half over the telephone. There were also two participants who provided their responses to the interview questions via e-mail. Most of interviews were conducted during 2000-2001, with a few conducted in 2002. The interviews ranged from approximately 20 minutes to 2 hours, averaging about 30 to 45 minutes. Except for the e-mail responses, all interviews were tape-recorded and transcribed. To ensure anonymity, participants' names and organizational affiliations were removed from the transcripts and replaced with randomly assigned numerical codes before being stored in Atlas.ti, a qualitative data analysis software program (Scientific Software Development, 2001).

Code Development and Coding Process

We employed thematic analysis proposed by Boyatzis (1998) to capture the qualitative richness of the interview data. To do so, a scheme of thematic codes was developed to map onto the major concepts involved in the research questions. Code development for this study was primarily theory-driven. To minimize researcher projection bias and to discover "what the data may be saying" (Boyatzis, 1998, p. 35), the theory-driven code development was also complemented and hence enhanced by modification in light of the actual data collected. The creation of the codes followed the steps outlined by Boyatzis (1998). Specifically, each theme was labeled and carefully defined. For each theme, indicators for the occurrence of the theme, or the "coding moment," were listed; qualifications and exclusions were described where appropriate; and prototypical examples were selected from the actual data to illustrate the relevance and application of the code (see Miskel, Coggshall, DeYoung, Osguthorpe, Song, & Young, 2003, for detailed coding scheme).

After the coding categories were developed, two members of the research team independently read each transcript and identified and marked information related to specific themes using the ATLAS.ti software program. The two independently coded transcripts were then merged into a single document in ATLAS.ti for "consensus coding," during which the two researchers compared their codings and resolved any discrepancies identified, with the help of other team members if necessary.

The consensus coding process ensured the reliability and accuracy of data coding and also assisted in calculating the reliability estimates for themes related to policy actors' beliefs about reading achievement levels and trends, reading pedagogy, state standards, and state tests. For these themes, we calculated both intracoder and intercoder reliabilities using the formula suggested by Miles and Huberman (1994): Coder reliability = number of agreements / (total number of agreements + disagreements). In addition, we computed Pearson's correlation coefficients as an alternative measure of coder reliabilities. The intracoder reliability estimates ranged from .86 to 1.00. The intercoder reliabilities ranged from .70 to 1.00 across the five themes based on the Miles-Huberman formula. Results based on Pearson's correlations were similar.

APPENDIX B

INTERVIEW SCHEDULES FOR
THE STATE READING POLICY STUDY

B.1. Interview Schedule for Policymakers

Before we start our discussion of reading policy, I would like to confirm some information with you.

—Purpose of the study.
—Review the informed consent statement.
—Verify name, position and organization.
—Does your organization publish newsletters or produce other documents that detail your organization's stance on reading issues? If so, would you provide us copies, or indicate how we can get them?

Recent debates about reading policy or initiatives in [STATE NAME] include issues relating to reading performance, pedagogy, standards and assessments.

1. How have you been involved in state reading policy, programs, or initiatives?
2. During the past 10 years or so, what significant issues in reading have you and others been addressing?
3. The NAEP percentage of [STATE NAME] fourth grade students achieving below basic inreading is XX%. Do you think that this percentage accurately depict your students' reading level?
4. Changing to possible solutions over the past 5 years or so, what new approaches or programs in reading have been proposed in the state?
5. Do you support state standards for reading? Explain.
6. Do you support state tests for reading? Explain.
7. Should reading instruction be based primarily on phonics, whole language, balanced approach, integrated approach, or some other approach? Explain why you prefer this approach.
8. Overall, what key components should form the state's policy for reading? Many groups and individuals have been identified with

trying to influence state reading policy or initiatives. Examples include K-12 and higher education associations and unions, parents and citizens, think tanks, government agencies, media, business, and foundations.

9. Which of the following individuals or groups have contacted you or your office with regard to reading policy, proposed legislation, rules and so forth?

10. What groups and individuals, including government agencies are active in state reading policy?

11. What groups or individuals have worked against you and your efforts with regard to state reading policy?

12. Using the following activities, circle those activities that characterize these individuals and organizations:

1. Testifying at legislative or agency hearings.
2. Contacting legislators or other government officials.
3. Organizing letter-writing and telephone campaigns.
4. Presenting research findings.
5. Monitoring officials for new policy developments.
6. Drafting legislation and regulations.
7. Serving on commissions.
8. Engaging the mass media in reading policy.
9. Endorsing policy allies for elective office.
10. Forming coalitions with other groups and individuals.
11. Raising funds to promote policy issues.
12. Advertising for new members based on policy issues.
13. Other

13. Which groups or individuals do you believe to be particularly influential?

14. What groups or individuals are least influential?

15. Any other observations that you think might be of interest to me?

Thank you for your time and assistance!

B.2. Interview Schedule for Non-Media Interest Group Members

Before we start our discussion of reading policy, I would like to confirm some information with you.

—Purpose of the study.
—Review the informed consent statement.
—Verify name, position and organization.
—Does your organization publish newsletters or produce other documents that detail your organization's stance on reading issues? If so, would you provide us copies, or indicate how we can get them?

Under which of the following categories would you place your organization?

_____Citizen group: open-membership organization that mobilizes members, donors, or activists around interests other than their vocation or profession

_____Educational association: organization that represents the interests and concerns of professionals in a particular field within education (e.g., Iowa Education Association and Maine Principals Association)

_____Educational institution—K-12 school system

_____Educational institution—higher education institution

_____Government agency

_____Labor union

_____Media: electronic or print media

_____Noneducation association: organization that represents the interests and concerns of professionals, businesses, or other types of organizations outside education

_____Philanthropic foundation: organizations that funds educational projects in the public interest

_____Private/For-profit firm

_____Think tank or policy institute: organization that engages in research on public policy questions and possibly advocacy for particular ideas

_____Other (specify)

Recent debates about reading policy or initiatives in [STATE NAME] include issues relating to reading performance, pedagogy, standards and assessments.

1. We have read of your involvement in reading policy through your work with _____. How have you been involved in state reading policy, programs, or initiatives?

2. During the past 10 years or so, what significant issues in reading have you and others been addressing?

3. The NAEP percentage of [STATE NAME] fourth grade students achieving below basic in reading is XX%. Do you think that this percentage accurately depicts your students' reading level?

4. Changing to possible solutions over the past 5 years or so, what new approaches or programs in reading have been proposed in the state?

5. Do you support state standards for reading? Explain.

6. Do you support state tests for reading? Explain.

7. Should reading instruction be based primarily on phonics, whole language, balanced approach, integrated approach, or some other approach? Explain why you prefer this approach.

8. Overall, what key components should form the state's policy for reading? Many groups and individuals have been identified with trying to influence state reading policy or initiatives. Examples include K-12 and higher education associations and unions, parents and citizens, think tanks, government agencies, media, business and foundations.

9. With which of the following groups and individuals have you collaborated with regard to state reading policy? Can you tell me whether you initiated the joint efforts of whether the other organization did so?

10. What groups and individuals, including government agencies are particularly active in state reading policy?

11. What groups or individuals have worked against you and your efforts with regard to state reading policy?

12. Organizations use a variety of strategies or tactics to try to influence government or public policy. For each of the following strategies, I would like to know how often you or your organization uses it to influence reading policy within the past year: (Ask for examples to positive replies.)

	Never	*Occasionally*	*Sometimes*	*Frequently*
Testifying at legislative or agency hearings.	____	____	____	____
Contacting legislators or other government officials.	____	____	____	____
Organizing letter-writing and telephone campaigns.	____	____	____	____
Presenting research findings.	____	____	____	____
Monitoring officials for new policy developments.	____	____	____	____
Drafting legislation and regulations.	____	____	____	____
Serving on commissions.	____	____	____	____
Engaging the mass media in reading policy.	____	____	____	____
Endorsing policy allies for elective office.	____	____	____	____
Forming coalitions with other groups and individuals.	____	____	____	____
Raising funds to promote policy issues.	____	____	____	____
Advertising for new members based on policy issues.	____	____	____	____
Other, please specify.	____	____	____	____

13. Which groups or individuals do you believe to be particularly influential?
14. What groups or individuals are least influential?
15. Any other observations that you think might be of interest to me?

Thank you for your time and assistance!

B.3. Interview Schedule for Members of the Media

Before we start our discussion of reading policy, I would like to confirm some information with you.

—Purpose of the study.
—Review the informed consent statement.
—Verify name, position, and organization.

Recent debates about reading policy or initiatives in your state include issues regarding reading performance, pedagogy, standards and assessments.

1. What significant issues in reading have you observed during the past 10 years?
2. When writing about reading, on what sources do you rely or consult for reporting the level of student reading achievement?
3. What new approaches or programs in reading have you seen proposed in the past 5 years?
4. Are there any observations you can offer on the topic of state standards for reading?
5. Are there any observations you can offer on the topic of state tests for reading?
6. Are there any observations you can offer on the phonics vs. whole language debate?
7. During the 1990s, have there been political events or new ideas that have brought reading closer to the top of the state's policy agenda? Many groups have been identified with trying to influence reading policy. Examples include K-12 and higher education associations and unions, parents and citizens, think tanks, government agencies, the media, business and foundations.
8. What groups or individuals are most active in trying to influence state reading policy?
9. Are there any factors that help to explain the effectiveness of these groups?
10. If preparing a report on reading policy, are there particular policymakers, researchers, or groups you would contact for information?
11. Are there any other observations that you think might be of interest to me?

Thank you for your time and assistance!

APPENDIX C

**VALUES AND CORRELATIONS OF CENTRALITY,
PRESTIGE, AND PERCEIVED INFLUENCE OF ACTORS IN
EIGHT STATE READING POLICY NETWORKS**

**Table C.1.   Values and Correlations of Centrality, Prestige, and
Perceived Influence of Actors in
the Alabama Reading Policy Network (N = 18)**

Policy Actor	Centrality (Rank)	Prestige (Rank)	Perceived Influence (Rank)
A+ Education Foundation (A+EF)	.94 (1)	.82 (3)	.53 (2)
Alabama House Education Committee (AHEC)	.94 (1)	.71 (6)	.06 (7)
Alabama Office of the Governor (AOG)	.88 (3)	.88 (1)	.24 (4)
Alabama Education Association (AEA)	.88 (3)	.88 (1)	.00 (9)
Alabama State Department of Education (ASDE)	.88 (3)	.76 (4)	.71 (1)
Alabama State Board of Education (ASBE)	.88 (3)	.71 (6)	.29 (3)
Auburn University (AU)	.82 (7)	.76 (4)	.00 (9)
University of Alabama (UA)	.76 (8)	.65 (9)	.00 (9)
Alabama Senate Education Committee (ASEC)	.71 (9)	.71 (6)	.06 (7)
Alabama Reading Association (ARA)	.71 (9)	.47 (11)	.12 (5)
Council for Leaders in Alabama School (CLAS)	.71 (9)	.41 (13)	.00 (9)
Alabama Eagle Forum (AEF)	.71 (9)	.35 (16)	.12 (5)
Public Affairs Research Council—Alabama (PARCA)	.65 (13)	.59 (10)	.00 (9)
Alabama Association of School Boards (AASB)	.65 (13)	.47 (11)	.00 (9)
Alabama Parent Teacher Association (APTA)	.65 (13)	.41 (13)	.00 (9)
Samford University (SU)	.47 (16)	.41 (13)	.00 (9)
University of North Alabama (UNA)	.29 (17)	.29 (17)	.00 (9)
Central Alabama Laubach Literacy Center (CALLC)	.29 (17)	.18 (18)	.00 (9)

	Spearman Rho Correlations		
	Centrality	Prestige	Perceived Influence
Centrality	1.00		
Prestige	.85**	1.00	
Perceived Influence	.65**	.46~	1.00

Note: Centrality, prestige, and perceived influence are all standardized indices.
~ p < .10, ** p < .01 (2-tailed).

Table C.2. Values and Correlations of Centrality, Prestige, and Perceived Influence of Actors in the California Reading Policy Network (N = 38)

Policy Actor	Centrality (Rank)	Prestige (Rank)	Perceived Influence (Rank)
California State Department of Education (CSDE)	.95 (1)	.84 (1)	.38 (3)
California State Board of Education (CSBE)	.86 (2)	.84 (1)	.97 (1)
LA Times (LAT)	.86 (2)	.54 (13)	.14 (9)
California Reading and Literature Project (CRLP)	.81 (4)	.73 (3)	.08 (15)
Sacramento County Office of Education (SCOE)	.81 (4)	.73 (3)	.30 (4)
California Assembly Education Committee (CAEC)	.76 (6)	.68 (5)	.30 (4)
California Office of Governor/Secretary for Education (COGSE)	.76 (6)	.65 (6)	.65 (2)
California Reading Association (CRA)	.76 (6)	.59 (8)	.11 (11)
California County Superintendents Education Services Association. (CCSESA)	.70 (9)	.62 (7)	.03 (21)
California Committee On Teacher Credentialing (CCTC)	.68 (10)	.54 (13)	.08 (15)
California Schools Boards Association (CSBA)	.68 (10)	.59 (8)	.11 (11)
Association of California School Administrators (ACSA)	.65 (12)	.57 (11)	.05 (19)
Sacramento Bee and New Times (SBNTR)	.65 (12)	.30 (26)	.00 (27)
California Senate Education Committee (CSEC)	.62 (14)	.57 (11)	.27 (6)
California Teachers Association (CTA)	.62 (14)	.59 (8)	.11 (11)
American Publishers Association (APA)	.59 (16)	.54 (13)	.00 (27)
Consortium of Reading Excellence (CORE)	.59 (16)	.54 (13)	.19 (7)
California Federation of Teachers (CFT)	.57 (18)	.54 (13)	.14 (9)
California State Parent and Teachers Assoc. (CSPTA)	.57 (18)	.51 (18)	.03 (21)
Institute for Education Reform, CASU (IERCSU)	.54 (20)	.49 (19)	.03 (21)
Individual Policy Actor (Academic)–Shefelbine	.46 (21)	.46 (20)	.05 (19)
David and Lucile Packard Found. (DLPF)	.43 (22)	.41 (21)	.08 (15)
National Center to Improve the Tools of Education (NCITE)	.43 (22)	.38 (22)	.09 (7)
William D. Lynch Found. for Children (WLFC)	.43 (22)	.35 (23)	.00 (27)
California Association of Bilingual Educators (CABE)	.41 (25)	.35 (23)	.00 (27)
Individual Policy Actor (Lobbyist)—Birdsall	.38 (26)	.32 (25)	.00 (27)
California Reads Roundtable (CRR)	.32 (27)	.24 (29)	.00 (27)
Individual Policy Actor (Academic)–Krashen	.32 (27)	.30 (26)	.08 (15)
Pacific Research Institute (PRI)	.32 (27)	.14 (33)	.00 (27)
Individual Policy Actor (Academic)– McQuillan	.30 (30)	.22 (30)	.00 (27)
California Assoc of Teachers of English (CATE)	.27 (31)	.11 (37)	.03 (21)

Tabel continues on next page.

Table C.2.   Values and Correlations of Centrality, Prestige, and Perceived Influence of Actors in the California Reading Policy Network (N = 38) Continued

Policy Actor	Centrality (Rank)	Prestige (Rank)	Perceived Influence (Rank)
Individual Policy Actor (Academic)–Moats	.27 (31)	.27 (28)	.11 (11)
Individual Policy Actor (Academic)–Moustafa	.27 (31)	.14 (33)	.00 (27)
PACE Institute (PACEI)	.24 (34)	.19 (31)	.00 (27)
Whole Language Umbrella (WLU)	.22 (35)	.11 (37)	.00 (27)
Sacramento City USD (SCUSD)	.19 (36)	.19 (31)	.03 (21)
California Association. for Education of Young Child (CAEYC)	.14 (37)	.14 (33)	.03 (21)
West Ed (WE)	.14 (37)	.14 (33)	.00 (27)

Spearman Rho Correlations

	Centrality	Prestige	Perceived Influence
Centrality	1.00		
Prestige	.93**	1.00	
Perceived Influence	.66**	.73**	1.00

Note: Centrality, prestige, and perceived influence are all standardized indices.
** $p < .01$ (2-tailed).

Table C.3.   Values and Correlations of Centrality, Prestige, and Perceived Influence of Actors in the Connecticut Reading Policy Network (N = 26)

Policy Actor	Centrality (Rank)	Prestige (Rank	Perceived Influence (Rank)
Connecticut State Department of Education (CSDE)	.96 (1)	.96 (1)	.84 (1)
Connecticut General Assembly's Education Committee (CGAEC)	.72 (2)	.72 (2)	.48 (2)
Connecticut Education Association (CEA)	.68 (3)	.60 (3)	.12 (7)
University of Connecticut–Reading-Language Arts Center (UC)	.60 (4)	.56 (4)	.12 (7)
Connecticut Association of Boards of Education (CABE)	.52 (5)	.44 (7)	.04 (12)
Connecticut Assoc of Public School Superintendents (CAPSS)	.52 (5)	.52 (5)	.04 (12)
Individual Policy Actor–Rep. Moira Lyons	.52 (5)	.48 (6)	.12 (9)
Connecticut General Assembly's Commission on Children (CGACC)	.48 (8)	.44 (7)	.44 (3)
Connecticut Reading Association (CRA)	.48 (8)	.28 (16)	.12 (7)
Individual Policy Actor–Sen. Judith Freedman	.48 (8)	.36 (10)	.12 (7)
Hartford Courant (HC)	.48 (8)	.24 (18)	.04 (12)

Table continues on next page.

Policy Actor			
Connecticut General Assembly's Office of Fiscal Analysis (CGAOFA)	.44 (12)	.40 (9)	.00 (19)
Connecticut Federation of Education & Professional Employees (CFEPE)	.40 (13)	.28 (16)	.04 (12)
Haskins Laboratories (HL)	.40 (13)	.36 (10)	.16 (5)
Connecticut Association for Reading Research (CARR)	.36 (15)	.36 (10)	.20 (4)
Connecticut Association of Schools (CAS)	.36 (15)	.36 (10)	.00 (19)
Capitol Region Education Council (CREC)	.36 (15)	.32 (14)	.04 (12)
Connecticut Office of the Governor (COG)	.32 (18)	.32 (14)	.16 (5)
Connecticut Business and Industry Association (CBIA)	.24 (19)	.20 (19)	.04 (12)
Connecticut Parent Teacher Association (CPTA)	.20 (20)	.20 (19)	.00 (19)
Individual Policy Actor–Spear-Swerling	.20 (20)	.20 (19)	.00 (19)
Connecticut Association of Urban Superintendents (CAUS)	.16 (22)	.12 (22)	.00 (19)
Connecticut Council of Teachers of English (CCTE)	.16 (22)	.12 (22)	.00 (19)
Reading and Lang Arts Think Tank (CCSU)	.12 (24)	.08 (24)	.04 (12)
Connecticut Association of Independent Schools (CAIS)	.08 (25)	.08 (24)	.00 (19)
Yankee Institute for Public Policy (YIPP)	.08 (25)	.00 (26)	.00 (19)

Spearman Rho Correlations

	Centrality	Prestige	Perceived Influence
Centrality	1.00		
Prestige	.93**	1.00	
Perceived Influence	.67**	.67**	1.00

Note: Centrality, prestige, and perceived influence are all standardized indices.
** $p < .01$ (2-tailed).

Table C.4. Values and Correlations of Centrality, Prestige, and Perceived Influence of Actors in the Indiana Policy Network ($N = 28$)

Policy Actor	Centrality (Rank)	Prestige (Rank)	Perceived Influence (Rank)
Indiana House Education Committee (IHEC)	.89 (1)	.89 (1)	.15 (5)
Indiana State Department of Education (IDOE)	.89 (1)	.89 (1)	.48 (1)
Indiana Senate Education Committee (ISEC)	.81 (3)	.81 (3)	.04 (13)
Indiana Office of the Governor (IOG)	.74 (4)	.74 (4)	.37 (2)
Indiana State Board of Education (ISBE)	.74 (4)	.70 (5)	.04 (13)
Indiana State Teachers Association (ISTA)	.74 (4)	.63 (6)	.30 (3)
Indiana Association of School Principals (IASP)	.63 (7)	.33 (18)	.07 (9)

Table continues on next page.

Table C.4.   Values and Correlations of Centrality, Prestige, and Perceived Influence of Actors in the Indiana Policy Network (N = 28) Continued

Policy Actor	Centrality (Rank)	Prestige (Rank)	Perceived Influence (Rank)
Indiana School Boards Association (ISBA)	.63 (7)	.59 (7)	.04 (13)
Indiana Reading Association (IRA)	.59 (9)	.56 (8)	.22 (4)
Middle Grades Reading Network (MGRN)	.59 (9)	.41 (14)	.15 (5)
Indiana Association for Education of Young Child (IAEYC)	.56 (11)	.52 (10)	.00 (18)
Indiana University, Bloomington (IU)	.56 (11)	.56 (8)	.07 (9)
Parent's Coalition for Literacy (PCFL)	.56 (11)	.52 (10)	.04 (13)
Indiana Association of Public School Superintendents (IAPSS)	.52 (14)	.44 (13)	.07 (9)
Indiana Chamber of Commerce (ICC)	.52 (14)	.41 (14)	.11 (8)
Indiana Professional Standards Board (IPSB)	.48 (16)	.48 (12)	.04 (13)
Indiana Education Policy Center (IEPC)	.41 (17)	.41 (14)	.00 (18)
Indiana Federation of Teachers (IFT)	.41 (17)	.37 (17)	.00 (18)
Indiana Parent Teacher Association (IPTA)	.41 (17)	.33 (18)	.00 (18)
Association of Indiana Intermediate Media Educators (AIIME)	.33 (20)	.11 (25)	.00 (18)
Lilly Endowment (LE)	.33 (20)	.33 (18)	.00 (18)
Reading Recovery Center, Purdue University (RRC)	.33 (20)	.26 (21)	.15 (5)
Indiana Association of Supervision and Curriculum Development (IASCD)	.30 (23)	.19 (22)	.00 (18)
Indiana Council of Teachers of English (ICTE)	.26 (24)	.15 (23)	.00 (18)
Indiana Right to Read Foundation (IRRF)	.19 (25)	.15 (23)	.07 (9)
The Indianapolis Star (IS)	.19 (25)	.01 (25)	.00 (18)
Milton and Rose Friedman Foundation (MRFF)	.11(27)	.07 (27)	.00 (18)
Indiana Eagle Forum (IEF)	.07 (28)	.04 (28)	.00 (18)

	Spearman Rho Correlations		
	Centrality	Prestige	Perceived Influence
Centrality	1.00		
Prestige	.93**	1.00	
Perceived Influence	.67**	.62**	1.00

Note: Centrality, prestige, and perceived influence are all standardized indices.
** $p < .01$ (2-tailed).

Table C.5.   Values and Correlations of Centrality, Prestige, and Perceived Influence of Actors in the Maine Reading Policy Network (*N* = 19)

Policy Actor	Centrality (Rank)	Prestige (Rank)	Perceived Influence (Rank)
Maine State Department of Education (MSDE)	1.00 (1)	.94 (1)	.50 (1)
University of Maine -Orono (UMO)	.83 (2)	.72 (2)	.39 (2)
University of Southern Maine (USM)	.67 (3)	.61 (3)	.22 (6)
Maine Joint Standing Committee on Education and Cultural Service (MJSCECS)	.61 (4)	.61 (3)	.39 (2)
Maine State Board of Education (MSBE)	.50 (5)	.44 (5)	.17 (8)
Maine Humanities Council (MHC)	.39 (6)	.28 (7)	.00 (17)
Maine Office of the Governor (MEOG)	.39 (6)	.33 (6)	.33 (4)
Maine Christian Coalition (MCC)	.33 (8)	.11 (17)	.06 (15)
Maine Council for English Language Arts (MCELA)	.33 (8)	.22 (9)	.00 (17)
Maine Education Association (MEA)	.33 (8)	.22 (9)	.22 (6)
Maine Office of the First Lady (MOFL)	.33 (8)	.28 (7)	.33 (4)
Maine School Boards Association (MSBA)	.33 (8)	.22 (9)	.11 (10)
Maine Reading Association (MRA)	.28 (13)	.22 (9)	.11 (10)
Maine School Superintendents Association (MSSA)	.22 (14)	.22 (9)	.17 (8)
Maine Coalition for Excellence in Education (MCEE)	.17 (15)	.17 (14)	.11 (10)
Maine Leadership Consortium (MLC)	.17 (15)	.17 (14)	.06 (14)
Maine Principal's Association (MPA)	.17 (15)	.17 (14)	.11 (10)
Maine Public Radio (MPR)	.17 (15)	.00 (19)	.00 (17)
Maine Parent Teacher Assoc (MPTA)	.11 (19)	.11 (17)	.06 (14)

Spearman Rho Correlations

	Centrality	Prestige	Perceived Influence
Centrality	1.00		
Prestige	.91**	1.00	
Perceived Influence	.64**	.77**	1.00

Note: Centrality, prestige, and perceived influence are all standardized indices.
** $p < .01$ (2-tailed)

Table C.6.   Values and Correlations of Centrality, Prestige, and Perceived Influence of Actors in the Michigan Reading Policy Network (*N* = 29)

Policy Actor	Centrality (Rank)	Prestige (Rank)	Perceived Influence (Rank)
Michigan State Department of Education (MSDE)	1.00 (1)	1.00 (1)	.50 (3)
Michigan Office of the Governor (MIOG)	.86 (2)	.82 (2)	.64 (1)
Michigan State Board of Education (MSBE)	.79 (3)	.75 (3)	.21 (8)
Michigan Reading Association (MRA)	.75 (4)	.71 (4)	.36 (4)
Michigan Association of School Boards (MASB)	.71 (5)	.68 (5)	.29 (6)
Michigan Education Association (MEA)	.71 (5)	.57 (10)	.57 (2)
Michigan Business Leaders for Education Excellence (MBLEE)	.64 (7)	.61 (6)	.11 (10)
Michigan Senate Education Committee (MSEC)	.64 (7)	.61 (6)	.36 (4)
Michigan Association of School Administrators (MASA)	.61 (9)	.57 (10)	.18 (9)
Michigan House Education Committee (MHEC)	.61 (9)	.57 (10)	.25 (7)
Michigan State University (MSU)	.61 (9)	.61 (6)	.07 (12)
Reading Plan for Michigan Advisory Council (RPMAC)	.61 (9)	.61 (6)	.07 (12)
Michigan Federation of Teachers (MFT)	.54 (13)	.50 (13)	.11 (10)
Middle Cities Education Association (MCEA)	.50 (14)	.50 (13)	.04 (14)
Booth Newspapers (BN)	.46 (15)	.00 (28)	.00 (15)
Michigan Association of Secondary School Principals (MASSP)	.43 (16)	.36 (15)	.00 (15)
Michigan School Business Officials (MSBO)	.36 (17)	.32 (16)	.00 (15)
Western Michigan University (WMU)	.36 (17)	.25 (17)	.00 (15)
University of M Michigan I (UM)	.32 (19)	.25 (17)	.00 (15)
Michigan Elementary and Middle School Principals Association (MEMSPA)	.29 (20)	.25 (17)	.00 (15)
Public Sector Consultants (PSC)	.29 (20)	.25 (17)	.00 (15)
Michigan Foundation for Education Leadership (MFEL)	.25 (22)	.25 (17)	.00 (15)
Michigan Library Association (MLA)	.25 (22)	.07 (23)	.00 (15)
Michigan Dyslexia Institute (MDI)	.21 (24)	.07 (23)	.00 (15)
Michigan Council for Teachers of English (MCTE)	.18 (25)	.04 (26)	.00 (15)
Eastern Michigan University (EMU)	.11 (26)	.07 (23)	.00 (15)
Michigan For Public Education (MPE)	.11 (26)	.04 (26)	.00 (15)

Table continues on next page.

Whole Language Umbrella—NCTE (WLU)	.11 (26)	.11 (22)	.00 (15)
Detroit News (DN)	.07 (29)	.00 (28)	.00 (15)

	Spearman Rho Correlations		
	Centrality	*Prestige*	*Perceived Influence*
Centrality	1.00		
Prestige	.93**	1.00	
Perceived Influence	.91**	.88**	1.00

Note: Centrality, prestige, and perceived influence are all standardized indices.
** $p < .01$ (2-tailed).

Table C.7. Perceived Influence of Actors in the North Carolina Reading Policy Network (*N* = 24)

Policy Actor	Perceived Influence	Rank
North Carolina State Board of Education (NSBE)	.30	1
North Carolina Association of Educators (NAE)	.26	2
North Carolina State Department of Public Instruction (NSDPI)	.26	2
North Carolina Right to Read Foundation (NRRF)	.22	4
North Carolina General Assembly (NGA)	.17	5
Charlotte-Mecklenburg PTA (CMPTA)	.13	6
North Carolina Office of the Governor (NOG)	.09	7
North Carolina Reading Association (NRA)	.09	7
North Carolina School Administrators Association (NSAA)	.09	7
North Carolina Association of College Professors of Reading (NACPR)	.04	10
North Carolina Principals/Assistant Principals Association (NPA)	.04	10
North Carolina School Boards Association (NSBA)	.04	10
North Carolina Teacher Academy (NTA)	.04	10
Individual Policy Actor–Johnson (Johnson)	.00	14
International Dyslexia Association (IDA)	.00	14
John Locke Foundation (JLF)	.00	14
Learning Disabilities Association of NC (LDANC)	.00	14
North Carolina Eagle Forum (NEF)	.00	14
North Carolina Literacy Resource Center (NLRC)	.00	14
North Carolina Partnership for Children (Smart Start) (NPC)	.00	14
North Carolina Professional Teaching Standards Commission (NPTSC)	.00	14
Professional Educators of North Carolina (PENC)	.00	14
University of North Carolina –Chapel Hill (UNCCH)	.00	14
University of North Carolina –Wilmington (UNCW)	.00	14

**Table C.8.   Values and Correlations of Centrality, Prestige, and
Perceived Influence of Actors in
the Utah Reading Policy Network (N = 21)**

Policy Actor	Centrality (Rank)	Prestige (Rank)	Perceived Influence (Rank)
Utah State Office of Education (USOE)	.90 (1)	.85 (1)	.60 (1)
Utah Office of the Governor (UOG)	.85 (2)	.70 (2)	.40 (3)
Utah Parent Teacher Association (UPTA)	.70 (3)	.70 (2)	.35 (4)
Utah State Board of Education (USBE)	.70 (3)	.65 (4)	.35 (4)
Utah Senate Education Committee (USEC)	.70 (3)	.65 (4)	.35 (4)
Utah Educational Association (UEA)	.65 (6)	.60 (6)	.10 (10)
Individual Policy Actor–Rep Allen	.60 (7)	.55 (7)	.00 (12)
University of Utah Reading Center (UURC)	.60 (7)	.55 (7)	.15 (9)
Utah School Boards Association (USBA)	.55 (9)	.55 (7)	.20 (8)
Utah Eagle Forum (UEF)	.50 (10)	.10 (18)	.25 (7)
Utah House Education Committee (UHEC)	.50 (10)	.40 (10)	.45 (2)
AFT/ Utah (AFTU)	.45 (12)	.30 (12)	.00 (12)
Utah Partners in Education (UPE)	.45 (12)	.40 (10)	. 00 (12)
Utah School Superintendents Association (USSA)	.45 (12)	.30 (12)	.10 (10)
Brigham Young University (BYU)	.30 (15)	.30 (12)	.10 (10)
SLC Chamber of Commerce (SLCCC)	.30 (15)	.10 (18)	.10 (10)
Utah Association of Elementary School Principals (UAESP)	.30 (15)	.25 (15)	.10 (10)
Granite School District (GSD)	.25 (18)	.10 (18)	.10 (10)
Utah State Board of Regents (USBR)	.25 (18)	.20 (17)	.10 (10)
Utah State University (USU)	.25 (18)	.25 (15)	.10 (10)
Utah Council of Teachers of English/Language Arts (UCTELA)	.05 (21)	.05 (21)	.10 (10)

	Spearman Rho Correlations		
	Centrality	Prestige	Perceived Influence
Centrality	1.00		
Prestige	.92**	1.00	
Perceived Influence	.82**	.71**	1.00

Note: Centrality, prestige, and perceived influence are all standardized indices.
** $p < .01$ (2-tailed).

APPENDIX D

SUMMARY OF READING-RELATED POLICIES IN NINE STATES (1995-2001)

Table D. Summary of Reading-Related Policies in Nine States (1995-2001)

State Policy (Year)	Instrument Type	Originating State Government Agency	Focus
Alabama			
Act 95-313 (State Code 16-6B-1): Education Accountability Act (1995)	M/SC	State Legislature	Accountability; standards; assessment
The Alabama Reading Initiative (1996)	I/CB	State Board of Education and State Department of Education	Literacy demonstration sites; professional development
California[a]			
*AB 170: Content of Basic Instructional Materials for Reading and Math (1995)	M/I	Governor and State Assembly	Instructional materials; pedagogy
*AB 1504: Adoption of Basic Instructional Materials (1995)	M/I	Governor and State Assembly	Instructional materials
*AB 3482: K-3 Teacher Reading Instruction (1996)	M/I/CB	Governor and State Assembly	Professional development; instructional materials
*SB 1777: Class Size Reduction (1996)	I	Governor and State Senate	Class size

Table continues on next page.

**Table D.   Summary of Reading-Related Policies in
Nine States (1995-2001) Continued**

State Policy (Year)	Instrument Type	Originating State Government Agency	Focus
*SB 1789 Class Size Reduction Facilities Funding (1996)	I	Governor and State Senate	Class size
*SB 1414: Class Size Reduction (1996)	I	Governor and State Senate	Class size
*AB 3075: Teacher Credentialing Requirements (1996)	M	Governor and State Assembly	Teacher licensure; pedagogy
*AB 1178: Teacher Credentialing Reassessment Instruction Skill Assessment (1996)	M	Governor and State Assembly	Teacher licensure
*SB 1924: Teacher Credentialing Standards for Reading Certificate (1996)	M	Governor and State Senate	Teacher licensure
*SB 1568: Teacher Credentialing Standards for Reading Specialist Certificate (1996)	M	Governor and State Senate	Teacher licensure
SB 316: Student Academic Partnership Program (1997)	CB/I	State Senate	Preservice training
AB 1086: Teacher Training for Reading Instruction (1997)	M/I/CB	State Assembly	Professional development; pedagogy
SB 376: Standardized Testing and Reporting (STAR) Program (1997)	M	State Senate	Assessment
AB 2041: State Instructional Materials Fund (1998)	I	State Assembly	Instructional materials
AB 2519: Instructional Materials: Adoption Criteria (1998)	M/I	State Assembly	Instructional materials
AB 1656: Budget Bill (1998)	M/I/CB	State Assembly	Professional Development; low-performing schools
AB 862: California Public School Library Act (1998)	I	Legislature	School libraries
English-Language Arts Content Standards for California Public Schools: Kindergarten Through Grade Twelve (1997)	M	State Board of Education	Standards

Table continues on next page.

Reading/Language Arts Curriculum Framework for California Public Schools (1999)	M	State Board of Education	Alignment of standards with curriculum and instruction
AB 2X: Pupil Reading and Reading Staff Development Programs (1999)	I/CB/H	Governor and Legislature	Professional development; teacher preparation; reading campaign "READ California;" classroom libraries
SB 1X: Public Schools Accountability Act (1999)	M/SC	Governor and State Senate	Accountability
AB 466: Mathematics and Reading Professional Development Program (2001)	M/I/CB	State Assembly	Professional development; instructional materials
AB 961: High Priority Schools Grant Program for Low Performing Schools (2001)	I	State Assembly	Low-performing schools
AB 75: The Principal Training Program (2001)	I/CB	State Assembly	Professional development for instructional leaders
Connecticut			
PA 98-243: An Act Concerning Early Reading Success (1998)	M/I/CB	General Assembly	State grants to needy districts and schools; early reading programs; early reading assessment; summer reading programs; promotion; class size reduction; teacher training; school construction
PA 98-168: Supplement to PA 98-243 (1998)	I/CB	General Assembly	Special grants to 12 "transitional" districts
PA 99-227: An Act Concerning a Statewide Early Reading Success Institute (1999)	M/CB	General Assembly	Convening expert panel to review research; district needs assessment; professional development
HB No. 6764: An Act Concerning School Accountability (1999)	M	House of Representatives	Accountability; elimination of social promotion
HB No. 6876: An Act Concerning the School Readiness and Early Reading Success Grant Programs (2001)	M	House of Representatives	Preliteracy standards; school-readiness plans; curriculum and instruction;
The Connecticut Framework: K-12 Curricular Goals and Standards (1998)	M	State Department of Education	Standards

Table continues on next page.

**Table D.   Summary of Reading-Related Policies in
Nine States (1995-2001) Continued**

State Policy (Year)	Instrument Type	Originating State Government Agency	Focus
Standards of Reading Competency for Students in Grades K-3 (1998)	M	State Department of Education	Standards
Governor's Summer Reading Challenge (1996)	I/H	Governor	Reading awareness campaign
Indiana			
Reading and Literacy Initiative for a Better Indiana (1997)	I/CB	State Department of Education	Early literacy grants; school libraries; adult education
Reading and Literacy Initiative for a Better Indiana (1997)	I/CB	State Department of Education	Early literacy grants; school libraries; adult education
PL 146 (1999)	M	General Assembly	Standards
PL 221: Public School Accountability (1999)	M/SC	Governor, State Superintendent of Public Instruction and General Assembly	Accountability
Senate Enrolled Act 352: Teacher Instruction in the Teaching of Reading (2000)	M	Senate	Teacher licensure
Maine			
Learning Results Standards (1997)	M	Legislature	Standards and assessment
Read with ME (2000)	I/CB/H	Office of the First Lady	Reading campaign
Michigan			
Reading Plan for Michigan (1998)	M/I/CB/H	Governor	Reading campaign-READY kits; early literacy assessment; professional development; summer reading programs
HB 4378: Reading Credits (2000)	M	House of Representatives	Teacher licensure
HB 5802 (PA 230): School Code (2000)	M	House of Representatives	Assessment; summer reading programs

Table continues on next page.

North Carolina

SB 1139: The School-Based Management and Accountability Program (ABCs of Public Education) (1996)	M/I/SC/CB	Senate	Accountability; standards; pedagogy; professional development

Texas

SB 1: Texas Education Code (1995)	M	Senate	Standards; assessment; accountability
Texas Reading Initiative (1997)	M/I/CB	Governor and House of representatives	Diagnostic assessment; research-based instruction; reading academies; family literacy; professional development; teacher certification; state tests
SB 4: School Finance and Property Tax Relief (1999)	M/I/CB	Senate	Assessment; social promotion; remedial reading programs; professional development; research-based instruction
SB 955: Ready to Read Initiative (1999)	I	Office of The First Lady and Senate	Early literacy
HB 2307: Master Reading Teacher Grant Program (1999)	M/I/CB	Office of the Lieutenant Governor and House of representatives	Teacher certification; professional development

Utah

HB 67: Children's Reading Skills (1997)	M/I	Legislature	Assessment; pedagogy; remediation
HB 8: Child Literacy Programs (1999)	M	House of representatives	Tiered literacy programs; research-based instruction; family support for literacy
Utah's Promise /Utah Reads (1999)	H	Office of the Lieutenant Governor	School-community based literacy programs
Read to Me (1999)	H	Office of The First Lady	Reading readiness campaign
HB 312: State Literacy Program (1999)	M/I	House of representatives	School literacy plan; personalized instruction plans; remediation
HB 63: Reading Skills Development Center (1999)	CB	House of representatives	Reading center; professional development
HB 75: Incentive for Elementary Reading Performance Improvement (1999)	I	House of representatives	Reading improvement awards program

Table continues on next page.

**Table D.   Summary of Reading-Related Policies in
Nine States (1995-2001) Continued**

State Policy (Year)	Instrument Type	Originating State Government Agency	Focus
HB 109: Educator Licensing and Professional Practices Act (1999)	M/SC	House of representatives	Teacher licensure
HB 177: Assessing, Reporting and Evaluating Student Performance (2000)	M/SC	House of representatives	Assessment

Note: M = mandates; I = inducements; CB = capacity-building; SC = system-changing;
and H = hortatory.
[a] The set of legislations marked with a "*" have been collectively referred to as the
California Reading Initiative of 1996.

APPENDIX E

**CORRELATIONS BETWEEN FREQUENCY OF TACTIC USE
AND ACTOR PRESTIGE/PERCEIVED INFLUENCE**

Table E.1. Correlations Between Frequency of Tactic Use and Actor Prestige by State

Lobbying Tactics	AL (N=13)	CA (N=25)	CT (N=17)	IN (N=21)	ME (N=14)	MI (N=21)	TX (N=21)	UT (N=14)	Total (N=146)
Inside Lobbying	.65*	.39~	.59*	.53*	.40	.27	25	.56*	.42***
Serving on commissions	.61*	.24	-.07	.42~	.43	.36	.38~	.69*	.37***
Testifying at legislative or agency hearings	.10	.32	.55*	.55*	.16	.41~	.21	.56*	.34***
Drafting legislation and regulations	.36	.30	.54*	.55*	.04	.25	.01	.40	.29**
Presenting research findings	.71*	.12	.69**	.31	.52	-.23	.30	.09	.25**
Contacting government officials	.52~	.35	.51*	.10	.26	.09	-.11	.13	.23**
Outside Lobbying	.67*	.36	.52*	.37	.40	.06	-.05	.28	.28***
Engaging the mass media	.17	.46*	.58*	.38~	.69*	-.14	-.03	.65*	.31***
Endorsing policy allies for elective office	.79**	.34	.33	.22	.24	.12	.05	-.17	.17*
Organizing letter-writing and telephone campaigns	.24	-.06	.38	.26	.13	.15	-.12	.21	.12
Organizational Maintenance	.30	.39~	.59*	.32	.10	.21	.14	.25	.27***
Monitoring officials for policy developments	.56~	.08	.52~	.49*	.25	.29	.37	-.02	.30***
Forming coalitions	.19	.48*	.51~	.13	.04	.22	.03	.39	.25**
Advertising for new members	-.09	.23	.44~	.31	.16	.03	-.09	.31	.13
Raising funds to promote policy issues	.13	.19	.32	-.04	-.21	.10	.17	.14	.12
Total Number of Different Types of Tactics Used	.62~	.40~	.65*	.32	.68*	.39~	.23	.46	.45***

Note: Frequency of tactic use was measured on a scale from 0 to 3: 0 = never; 1 = occasionally; 2 = sometimes; 3 = frequently.
~ $p < .10$, * $p < .05$, ** $p < .01$, *** $p < .001$.

Table E.2. Correlations Between Frequency of Tactic Use and Perceived Influence by State

Lobbying Tactics	AL (N=13)	CA (N=25)	CT (N=17)	IN (N=21)	ME (N=14)	MI (N=21)	NC (N=18)	TX (N=21)	UT (N=14)	Total (N=164)
Inside Lobbying	.34	-.15	.29	.46~	.42	.28	.18	.05	.68*	.21*
Testifying at legislative or agency hearings	.16	-.18	.33	.33	.34	.37	.20	.17	.64*	.22**
Serving on commissions	.24	.10	-.17	.49*	.24	.39~	.27	.10	.31	.20*
Presenting research findings	.32	-.07	.50*	-.03	.44	-.06	-.11	.22	.43	.19
Contacting government officials	.28	-.28	.35	.36~	.28	.16	-.05	.04	.40	.12
Drafting legislation and regulations	.21	-.13	.18	.47*	.29	.06	.26	-.27	.57*	.09
Outside Lobbying	.24	-.12	.30	.60**	.57~	.14	.23	-.15	.54~	.18*
Engaging the mass media	.27	.09	.23	.39~	.61~	-.13	.11	.23	.60*	.17*
Endorsing policy allies for elective office	.11	-.00	.39	.51*	.32	.23	.27	-.22	.08	.16~
Organizing letter-writing and telephone campaigns	.06	-.26	.48~	.54*	.50	.20	.15	-.32	.56*	.10
Organizational Maintenance	.54~	-.17	.32	.39~	.19	.20	-.11	.09	.65*	.20*
Forming coalitions	.29	.03	-.01	.43~	.03	.22	.14	.14	.70**	.20*
Monitoring officials for policy developments	.31	-.38~	.22	.34	.25	.29	.39	.16	.31	.15~
Raising funds to promote policy issues	.51~	-.09	-.02	.08	-.16	.07	-.23	.21	.47	.12
Advertising for new members	.43	.02	.09	.24	.41	.04	-.42	-.22	.61*	.09
Total Number of Different Types of Tactics Used	.38	-.01	.49~	.40~	.53	.40*	.02	.05	.62*	.26**

Note: Frequency of tactic use was measured on a scale from 0 to 3: 0 = never; 1 = occasionally; 2 = sometimes; 3 = frequently.
~ $p < .10$, * $p < .05$, ** $p < .01$, *** $p < .001$.

Table E.3. Correlations Between Frequency of Tactic Use and Actor Prestige by Group Type

Lobbying Tactics	Citizens Groups (N=16)	Education Associations (N=75)	Higher Education Institutions (N=20)	Business/ Foundations/ Firms (N=16)	Research Organizations (N=19)	Total (N=146)
Inside Lobbying	.48~	.43***	.46~	.37	.58*	.42***
Testifying at legislative or agency hearings	.24	.43***	.49*	.24	.34	.34***
Contacting government officials	.33	.35**	.13	-.17	.26	.37***
Presenting research findings	.49~	.06	.46~	.48~	.42~	.23**
Drafting legislation and regulations	.42	.30*	.33	.31	.45~	.29**
Serving on commissions	.37	.36**	.05	.50~	.51*	.25**
Outside Lobbying	.20	.28*	.37	.16	.43~	.28***
Engaging the mass media	.48~	.34**	.40	.07	.32	.31***
Organizing letter-writing and telephone campaigns	.13	.09	.27	.11	.26	.17*
Endorsing policy allies for elective office	-.13	.18	.15	.18	.43	.12
Organizational Maintenance	.43~	.48***	.07	.18	.15	.27***
Monitoring officials for policy developments	.45~	.38**	.08	.24	.45~	.30***
Forming coalitions	.32	.42**	-.04	.41	.24	.25**
Raising funds to promote policy issues	.28	.28*	.12	.11	-.16	.13
Advertising for new members	.27	.32**	-.02	-.17	-.17	.12
Total Number of Different Types of Tactics Used	.50~	.46***	.40	.35	.53*	.45***

Note: Frequency of tactic use was measured on a scale from 0 to 3: 0 = never; 1 = occasionally; 2 = sometimes; 3 = frequently.
~ *p* < .10, * *p* < .05, ** *p* < .01, *** *p* < .001.

Table E.4. Correlations Between Frequency of Tactic Use and Perceived Influence by Group Type

Lobbying Tactics	Citizens Groups (N=21)	Education Associations (N=85)	Higher Education Institutions (N=22)	Business/ Foundations/ Firms (N=16)	Research Organizations (N=20)	Total (N=164)
Inside Lobbying	.18	.16	.25	.41	-.00	.21*
Testifying at legislative or agency hearings	.05	.16	.40~	.43	.19	.22**
Contacting government officials	.10	.09	.17	.15	-.11	.20*
Presenting research findings	.20	.06	.27	.59*	-.32	.12
Drafting legislation and regulations	.20	.06	-.14	-.02	.22	.09
Serving on commissions	.18	.19	-.06	.44	.06	.19
Outside Lobbying	.15	.14	.24	.14	.32	.18*
Engaging the mass media	.30	.11	.26	.31	-.01	.17*
Organizing letter-writing and telephone campaigns	.01	.04	.23	-.10	.57**	.16~
Endorsing policy allies for elective office	.09	.19	.06	.06	.44~	.10
Organizational Maintenance	.30	.17	.00	.40	-.09	.20*
Monitoring officials for policy developments	.28	.13	-.01	.30	-.10	.15~
Forming coalitions	.18	.22	.06	.48~	-.04	.20*
Raising funds to promote policy issues	.28	.00	-.09	.39	.04	.09
Advertising for new members	.17	.10	.05	.14	-.16	.12
Total Number of Different Types of Tactics Used	.23	.24*	.22	.34	.07	.26**

Note: Frequency of tactic use was measured on a scale from 0 to 3: 0 = never; 1 = occasionally; 2 = sometimes; 3 = frequently.
~ $p < .10$, * $p < .05$, ** $p < .01$, *** $p < .001$.

REFERENCES

Alabama Association of School Boards. (2005, October 1). *U.S. Secretary of Education lauds the Alabama Reading Initiative*. Retrieved February 1, 2007, from http://www.theaasb.org/asb.cfm?DocID=1673

Alabama Department of Education. (1998a). *Knowledge and skills teachers need to deliver effective reading instruction*. Retrieved April 25, 2006, from ftp:// ftp.alsde.edu/documents/90/Appendix_B_-_Knowledge_and_Skills.doc

Alabama Department of Education. (1998b). *Report on Review of Research*. Retrieved April 25, 2006, from ftp://ftp.alsde.edu/documents/90/ Appendix_A_-Report_Review_of_Research.doc

Baumgartner, F. R., & Leech, B. L. (1998). *Basic interests: The importance of groups in politics and in political science*. Princeton, NJ: Princeton University Press.

Berliner, D. C., & Biddle, B. J. (1995). *The manufactured crisis*. Reading, MA: Addison Wesley.

Berry, J. M. (1977). *Lobbying for the people: The political behavior of public interest groups*. Princeton, NJ: Princeton University Press.

Berry, J. (1997). *The interest group society* (3rd ed.). New York: Longman.

Boje, D. M., & Whetten, D. A. (1981). Effects of organizational strategies and constraints on centrality and attributions of influence in interorganizational networks. *Administrative Science Quarterly, 26*, 378-395.

Bolland, J. M. (1988). Sorting out centrality: An analysis of the performance of four centrality models in real and simulated networks. *Social Networks, 10*, 233-253.

Borgatti, S. P. (2002). *NetDraw* (Version 0.60). Natick: Analytic Technologies.

Borgatti, S. P., Everett, M. G., & Freeman., L. C. (1999). *UCINET 5.0* (Version 1.00). Natick: Analytic Technologies.

Boyatzis, R. E. (1998). *Transforming qualitative information*. Thousand Oaks, CA: Sage.

217

Brandes, U., Kenis, P., Raab, J., Schneider, V., & Wagner, D. (1999). Explorations into the visualization of policy networks. *Journal of Theoretical Politics, 11*(1), 75-106.

Brass, D. J. (1984). Being in the right place: A structural analysis of individual influences in an organization. *Administrative Science Quarterly, 29,* 518-539.

Brass, D. J. (1985). Men's and women's networks: A study of interaction patterns and influence in an organization. *Academy of Management Journal, 28,* 327-343.

Brass, D. J., & Burkhardt, M. E. (1993). Potential power and power use: An investigation of structure and behavior. *Administrative Science Quarterly, 29,* 518-539.

Browne, W. P. (1998). *Groups, interests, and U.S. public policy.* Washington, DC: GeorgetownUniversity Press.

Burkhardt, M. E., & Brass, D. J. (1990). Changing patterns or patterns of change: The effect of achange in technology on social network structure and power. *Administrative Science Quarterly, 35,* 104-127.

California Department of Education. (1995). *Every child a reader: The report of the CaliforniaReading Task Force.* Sacramento: California Department of Education.

California Department of Education. (1996). *Teaching reading: A balanced, comprehensive approach to teaching reading in pre-kindergarten through grade three.* Sacramento: California Department of Education.

Campbell, R. F., & Mazzoni, T. L., Jr. (1976). *State policy making for the public schools.* Berkeley, CA: McCutcheon.

Cause, A. M. (1986). Social networks and social competence: Exploring the effects of early adolescent friendships. *American Journal of Community Psychology, 14,* 607-628.

Chall, J. S. (1996). *Learning to read: The great debate* (3rd ed.). Fort Worth, TX: Harcourt Brace.

Chrispeels, J. H. (1997). Educational policy implementation in a shifting political climate: The California experience. *The American Educational Research Journal, 34*(3), 453–481.

Chubb, J. E. (1983) *Interest groups and the bureaucracy: The politics of energy.* Stanford, CA: Stanford University Press.

Cibulka, J. G. (2001). The changing role of interest groups in education: Nationalization and the new politics of education productivity. *Education Policy, 15*(1), 12-40.

Clark, T. N. (1968). *Community structure and decision-making.* San Francisco: Chandler.

Cobb, R. W., & Elder, C. D. (1983). *Participation in American politics* (2nd ed.). Baltimore, MD: John Hopkins University.

Coggshall, J. G. (2002). *Alabama reading policy: Problems, processes, and participants.* Ann Arbor, MI: University of Michigan, Center for the Improvement of Early Reading Achievement.

Coggshall, J. G., & Osguthorpe, R. D. (2002). *Maine reading policy: Problems, processes, and participants.* Ann Arbor, MI: University of Michigan, Center for the Improvement of Early Reading Achievement.

Cohen, J. M. (1977). Sources of peer group homogeneity. *Sociology of Education,* *50,* 227-241.

Coleman, J. (1961). *The adolescent society.* New York: Free Press.

Connecticut State Department of Education. (2000) *Connecticut's blueprint for reading achievement: The report of the Early Reading Success Panel.* Hartford, CT: Connecticut Department of Education.

Cook, K. S. (1977). Exchange and power in networks of interorganizational relations. *The Sociological Quarterly, 18,* 62-82.

Council of Chief State School Officers. (2000). *Key state education policies on K-12 education: Time and attendance, graduation requirements, content standards, teacher Licensure, school leader licensure, student Assessment: 2000.* Washington, DC: Author.

Daft, R., & Becker, S. (1978). *Innovations in organizations.* New York: Elsevier North-Holland.

DeYoung, D. A. (2002). *Indiana reading policy: Problems, processes, and participants.* Ann Arbor, MI: University of Michigan, Center for the Improvement of Early Reading Achievement.

DeYoung, D.A. (2004). *Of problems, policies, and politics: Using multiple streams to describe and explain state reading policy development.* Unpublished doctoral dissertation, University of Michigan.

DeYoung, D. A., & Athan, R. G. (2002). *North Carolina reading policy: Problems, processes, and participants.* Ann Arbor: University of Michigan, Center for the Improvement of Early Reading Achievement.

Education Commission of the States. (2007). *Recent State Policies/Activities: Reading/ Literacy.* Retrieved April 24, 2007, from http://www.ecs.org/ecs/ecscat.nsf/ WebTopicView?OpenView&count=300&RestrictToCategory=Reading/ Literacy

Education Week. (2000). Quality Counts 2000: Who should teach? The states decide. *Editorial Projects in Education, 19*(18), 8-9. Retrieved May 9, 2007, from http://counts.edweek.org/sreports/qc00/templates/article.cfm? slug=execsum.htm

Eisenhart, M., & Towne, L. (2003). Contestation and change in national policy on "scientifically based" education research. *Educational Researcher, 32*(7), 31-38.

Elmore, R. F., & Fuhrman, S. H. (1994). Education professionals and curriculum governance. In R. F. Elmore & S. H. Fuhrman (Eds.), *The governance of curriculum: 1994 yearbook of the Association for Supervision and Curriculum Development* (pp. 210-215). Alexandria, VA: Association for Supervision and Curriculum Development.

Etzioni, A. (1964). *Modern organizations.* Englewood Cliffs, NJ: Prentice-Hall.

Fowler, L. L. & Shaiko, R. G. (1987). The grass roots connection: Environmental activistsn and Senate roll calls. *American Journal of Political Science, 31,* 484-510.

Freeman, L. C. (1979). Centrality in social networks: I. Conceptual clarification. *Social Networks, 1,* 215-239.

Freeman, L. C. (2000). Visualizing social networks. *Journal of Social Structure, 1*(1). Retrieved September 25, 2004, from http://moreno.ss.uci .edu/freeman.pdf.

French, J. R. P., & Raven, B. (1959). The bases of social power. In D. Cartwright (Ed.), *Studies in social power* (pp. 150-167). Ann Arbor: University of Michigan Institute for Social Research.

Fuhrman, S. H. (1987). Educational policy: A new context for governance. *Publius: The Journal of Federalism, 17*(3), 131-143.

Fuhrman, S. H. (1994). Legislatures and education policy. In R. F. Elmore & S. H. Fuhrman (Eds.), *The governance of curriculum: 1994 yearbook of the Association for Supervision and Curriculum Development* (pp. 30-55). Alexandria, VA: Association for Supervision and Curriculum Development.

Galaskiewicz, J. (1979). *Exchange networks and community politics*. Beverly Hills, CA: Sage.

Galaskiewicz, J., & Wasserman, S. (1994). Introduction: Advances in the social and behavioral sciences from social network analysis. In S. Wasserman & J. Galaskiewicz (Eds.), *Advances in social network analysis: Research in the social and behavioral sciences* (pp. xi-xvii). Thousand Oaks, CA: Sage.

Goodman, L. A. (1961). Snowball sampling. *Annals of Mathematical Statistics. 32,* 148-170.

Granovetter, M. (1985). Economic action and social structure: The problem of embeddedness. *American Journal of Sociology, 91,* 481-510.

Gray, V., & Lowery, D. (1993). Stability and change in state interest group systems: 1975 to 1990. *State and Local Government Review, 25,* 87-96.

Greenwald, C. S. (1977). *Group power: Lobbying and public policy.* New York: Praeger.

Hallinan, M. T. (1979). Structural effects of children's friendships and cliques. *Social Psychology Quarterly, 42,* 3-54.

Heclo, H. (1978). Issue networks and the executive establishment. In A. King (Ed.), *The New American Political System* (pp. 87-124). Washington, DC: American Enterprise Institute.

Heclo, H. (1988). The in-and-outer system: A critical assessment. *Political Science Quarterly, 103*(1), 37-56.

Heinz, J. P., Laumann, E. O., Nelson, R. L., & Salisbury, R. H. (1993). *The hollow core: Private interests in national policy making.* Cambridge, MA: Harvard University Press.

Hoy, W. K., & Miskel, C. G. (2007). *Educational administration: Theory, research and practice* (8th ed.). New York: McGraw-Hill.

Hrebenar, R. J. (1997). *Interest group politics in America* (3rd ed.). Armonk, NY: M. E. Sharpe.

Hula, K. W. (1999). *Lobbying together: Interest group coalitions in legislative politics.* Washington, DC: Georgetown University Press.

Indiana Department of Education. (2000a). *Phonics tool kit.* Indianapolis: Author.

Indiana Department of Education (2000b). *Phonics online.* Indianapolis: Author.

James, T. (1991). State authority and the politics of educational change. In G. Grant (Ed.), *Review of research in education* (pp. 169-224). Washington, DC: American Educational Research Association.

John, P. (2003). Is there life after policy streams, advocacy coalitions, and punctuations: Using evolutionary theory to explain policy change? *Policy Studies Journal, 31*(4), 481-498.

Jones, W., Jr., & Keiser, K. R. (1987). Issue visibility and the effects of PAC money. *Social Sciences Quarterly, 68*(1), 170-176.

Karper, J. H., & Boyd, W. L. (1988). Interest groups and the changing environment of state educational policymaking: Developments in Pennsylvania. *Educational Administration Quarterly, 24*(1), 21-54.

Kingdon, J. W. (1995). *Agendas, alternatives, and public polices* (2nd ed.). New York: Harper Collins.

Knoke, D. (1986). Associations and interest groups. *Annual Review of Sociology, 12*, 1-21.

Knoke, D. (1990a). *Organizing for collective action: The political economies of Associations*. New York: Walter de Gruyter.

Knoke, D. (1990b). *Political networks: The structural perspective*. New York: Cambridge University Press.

Knoke, D., & Burt, R. S. (1983). Prominence. In R. S. Burt & M. J. Minor (Eds.), *Applied network analysis* (pp. 195-222). Newbury Park, CA: Sage.

Knoke, D., & Kuklinski, J. H. (1982). *Network analysis*. Newbury Park, CA: Sage.

Knoke, D., & Laumann, E. O. (1982). The social organization of national policy domains. In N. Lin & P. V. Marsden (Eds.), *Social structure and network analysis* (pp. 255-270). Beverly Hills, CA: Sage.

Kollman, K. (1998). *Outside lobbying: Public opinion and interest group strategies*. Princeton, NJ: Princeton University Press.

Krackhardt, D. (1990). Assessing the political landscape: Structure, cognition, and power in organizations. *Administrative Science Quarterly, 35*, 342-369.

Kruskal, J. B., & Wish, M. (1978). *Multidimensional scaling*. Beverly Hills, CA: Sage.

Laumann, E. O. (1979). Network analysis in large social systems: Some theoretical and methodological problems. In P. W. Holland & S. Leinhardt (Eds.), *Perspectives on social network analysis* (pp. 379-402). New York: Academic Press.

Laumann, E. O., & Knoke, D. (1987). *The organizational state: Social choice in national policy domains*. Madison: University of Wisconsin Press.

Laumann, E. O., & Pappi, F. U. (1973). New directions in the study of community elites. *American Sociological Review, 38*, 212-230.

Laumann, E. O., & Pappi, F. U. (1976). *Networks of collective action: A perspective on community influence systems*. New York: Academic Press.

Lewis, D. A., & Maruna, S. (1999). The politics of education. In V. Gray, R. Hanson, & H. Jacob (Eds.), *Politics in the American states: A comparative analysis* (7th ed., pp. 393-433). Washington, DC: Congressional Quarterly Press.

Lusi, S. F. (1994). Systemic school reform: The challenges faced by state departments of education. In R. F. Elmore & S. H. Fuhrman (Eds.), *The governance of curriculum* (pp. 109-130). Alexandria, VA: Association of Supervision and Curriculum Development.

Maine Department of Education. (2000). *A solid foundation: Supportive contexts for early literacy programs in Maine schools*. Augusta, ME: Author.

Malen, B. (2001). Generating interest in interest groups. *Educational Policy, 15*(1), 168-186.

Manzo, K. K. (2002). Federal Program Will Test States' Reading Policies. *Edweek, 21*(41), 1, 16-17. Retrieved April 20, 2006, from http://www.edweek.org/ew/newstory.cfm?slug=41read.h21

Marsden, P. V. (1990). Network data and measurement. In W. R. Scott (Ed.), *Annual review of sociology* (pp. 435-463). Palo Alto, CA: Annual Reviews.

Marsden, P. V., & Laumann, E. O. (1977). Collective action in a community elite: Exchange, influence processes, and issue resolution. In R. J. Liebert & A. Imershein (Eds.), *Power, paradigms, and community research* (pp. 199-250). London: Sage.

Marshall, C., & Gerstl-Pepin, C. (2005). *Re-framing educational politics for social justice*. Boston: Allyn & Bacon.

Marshall, C., Mitchell, D., & Wirt, F. (1986). The context of state level policy formulation. *Educational Evaluation and Policy Analysis, 8*(4), 347-378.

Marshall, C., Mitchell, D., & Wirt, F. (1989). *Culture and education policy in the American states*. New York: The Falmer Press.

Mawhinney, H. B. (2001). Theoretical approaches to understanding interest groups. *Educational Policy, 15*(1), 187-214.

Mazzoni, T. L. (1991). Analyzing state school policymaking: An arena model. *Educational Evaluation and Policy Analysis, 13*(2), 115-138.

Mazzoni, T. L. (1993). The changing politics of state education policy making: A 20-year Minnesota perspective. *Educational Evaluation and Policy Analysis, 15,* 357-379.

Mazzoni, T. L. (1995). State policy-making and school reform: Influences and influentials. In J. D. Scribner & D. H. Layton (Eds.), *The study of educational politics* (pp. 53-73). Washington, DC: Falmer Press.

McDaniel, J. E. (2001). *The shaping of national reading policy: Using the structural approach to examine the politics of reading.* Unpublished dissertation, The University of Michigan, Ann Arbor.

McDaniel, J. E., Sims, C. H., & Miskel, C. G. (2001). The national reading policy arena: Policy actors and perceived influence. *Education Policy, 15*(1), 92-114.

McDonnell, L. M. & Elmore, R. F. (1987). Getting the job done: Alternative policy instruments. *Educational Evaluation and Policy Analysis, 9,* 133- 152.

McFarland, A. S. (1992). Interest groups and the policymaking process: Sources of countervailing power in America. In M. P. Petracca (Ed.), *The politics of interests* (pp. 58-79). Boulder, CO: Westview Press.

McLaughlin, M. W. (1987). Learning from experience: Lessons from policy implementation. *Educational Evaluation and Policy Analysis, 9*(2), 171-178.

Minden, J., Henry, D. B., Tolan, P. H., & Gorman-Smith, D. (2000). Urban boys' social networks and school violence. *Professional School Counseling, 4*(2), 95-104.

Mintrom, M., & Vergari, S. (1998). Policy networks and innovation diffusion: The case of state education reforms. *Journal of Politics, 60*(1), 126-148.

Mintzberg, H. (1983). *Power in and around organizations*. Englewood Cliffs: NJ: Prentice-Hall.

Miskel, C. G., & Athan, R. (2001, December). *National reading policy in transition: The policy and program initiatives of the Bush Administration.* Paper presented at the annual meeting of the National Reading Conference, San Antonio, Texas.

Miskel, C. G., Coggshall, J. G., DeYoung, D. A., Osguthorpe, R. D., Song, M., Young, T. V. (2003, August). *Reading Policy in the States: Interests and Processes. Final Report for the Field Initiated Studies Grant PR/Award No. R305T990369,*

Office of Educational Research and Improvement, U.S. Department of Education and the Spencer Foundation Major Research Grants Program Award # 200000269. Ann Arbor: University of Michigan.

Miskel, C. G., & Song, M. (2002, May). *Elite policy actors and Reading First: Network structure, involvement and beliefs.* Paper presented at the annual convention of the International Reading Association, San Francisco.

Miskel, C. G., & Song, M. (2004). Passing Reading First: Prominence and processes in an elite policy network. *Educational Evaluation and Policy Analysis, 26*(2), 89-109.

Mitchell, R. K., Agle, B. R., & Wood, D. J. (1997). Toward a theory of stakeholder identification and salience: Defining the principle of who and what really counts. *Academy of Management Review, 22*(4), 853-896.

Molm, L. D. (1990). Structure, action, and outcomes: The dynamics of power in social exchange. *American Sociological Review, 55,* 427-447.

Moreno, J. L. (1932). *Application of the group method to classification.* New York: National Committee on Prisons and Prison Labor.

Moreno, J. L. (1934). *Who shall survive?* Washington, DC: Nervous and Mental Disease.

Murphy, J. T. (Ed.). (1980). *State leadership in education: On being a chief state school officer.* Washington, DC: George Washington University, Institute for Educational Leadership.

National Commission on Excellence in Education. (1983). *A Nation at risk: The imperative for educational reform.* Washington, DC: U.S. Department of Education.

National Education Goals Panel. (1999). Shining star. *The NEGP Monthly, 2*(11), 1–10.

National Reading Panel. (2000). *Teaching children to read: An evidence-based assessment of the scientific research literature on reading and its implications for reading instruction.* Washington, DC: National Institute of Child Health and Human Development.

Nownes, A. J., & Freeman, P. (1998). Interest group activity in the states. *The Journal of Politics, 60*(1), 86-112.

Oetting, E. E., & Beauvais, F. (1986). Peer cluster theory: Drugs and the adolescent. *Journal of Counseling and Development, 65,* 17-22.

Osguthorpe, R. D. (2002). *Utah reading policy: Problems, processes, and participants.* Ann Arbor: University of Michigan, Center for the Improvement of Early Reading Achievement.

Parsons, W. (1995). *Public policy: An introduction to the theory and practice of policy analysis.* Northampton, MA: Edward Elgar.

PBS. (2000, October 17). *Presidential debate: Vice President Al Gore v. Gov. George W. Bush.* Retrieved April 29, 2006, from http://www.pbs.org/newshour/bb/election/2000debates/3rdebate2.html

Peters, B. G. (1999). *Institutional theory in political science: The "new institutionalism."* New York: Continuum.

Petracca, M. P. (1992). The rediscovery of interest group politics. In M. P. Petracca (Ed.), *Politics of interests: Interest groups transformed* (pp. 3-31). Boulder, CO: Westview.

Pfeffer, J. (1981). *Power in Organizations*. Boston: Pitman.

Polsby, N. (1984). *Political innovation in America*. New Haven, CT: Yale University Press.

Porter, L. W., Allen, R. W., & Angle, H. L. (1981). The politics of upward influence in organizations. In L. L. Cummings & B. M. Staw (Eds.), *Research in organizational behavior* (Vol. 3, pp. 109-149). Greenwich, CT: JAI Press.

Putnam, J. (2002, August 19). Phonics finds favor in Michigan schools. *Booth Newspapers*. Retrieved April 28, 2006, from http://www.nrrf.org/article_putnam-8-19-02.htm

Ravitch, D. (2000). *Left back: A century of battles over school reform*. New York: Simon & Schuster.

Ray, G. E., Cohen, R., & Secrist, M. E. (1995). Best friend networks of children across settings. *Child Study Journal, 25*(3), 169-188.

Ripley, R. B. (1985). *Policy analysis in political science*. Chicago: Nelson-Hall.

Rosenthal, A. (1993). *The third house: Lobbyists and lobbying in the states*. Washington, DC: Congressional Quarterly Press.

Rosenthal, A. (1998). *The decline of representative democracy: Process, participation, and power in state legislatures*. Washington, DC: CQ Press.

Rosenthal, A., & Fuhrman, S. (1983). State legislatures and education policy. *The Education Digest, 48*, 22-25.

Rowley, T. J. (1997). Move beyond dyadic ties: A network theory of stakeholder influences. *Academy of Management Review, 22*(4), 887-910.

Sabatier, P. A. (1988). An advocacy coalition framework of policy change and the role of policy-oriented learning therein. *Policy Sciences, 21*(2-3), 129-168.

Sabatier, P. A. (1999a). The need for better theories. In P. A. Sabatier (Ed.), *Theories of the policy process* (pp. 3-17). Boulder, CO: Westview Press.

Sabatier, P. A. (1999b). Fostering the development of policy theory. In P. A. Sabatier (Ed.), *Theories of the policy process* (pp. 261-275). Boulder, CO: Westview Press.

Sabatier, P. A. (Ed.). (1999c). *Theories of the policy process*. Boulder, CO: Westview Press.

Sabatier, P. A., & Jenkins-Smith, H. C. (1988). (Symposium Issue) Policy Change and Policy Oriented Learning: Exploring an Advocacy coalition framework. *Policy Sciences, 21*, 123-272.

Sabatier, P. A., & Jenkins-Smith, H. C. (Eds.). (1993). *Policy change and learning: An advocacy coalition approach*. Boulder, CO: Westview Press.

Salisbury, R. (1990). The paradox of interest groups in Washington: More groups, less clout. In A. King (Ed.), *The new American political system* (2nd ed., pp. 203-229). Washington, DC: AEI Press.

Salisbury, R. H. (1991). *Putting interests back into interest groups*. In A. J. Cigler & B. A. Loomis (Eds.), *Interest group politics* (3rd ed., pp. 371-384). Washington, DC: Congressional Quarterly.

Salisbury, R. H., Johnson, P., Heinz, J. P., Laumann, E. O., & Nelson, R. L. (1989). Who you know versus what you know: The uses of governmental experience for Washington lobbyists. *American Journal of Political Science, 33*(1), 175-195.

Schlozman, K., & Tierney, J. (1986). *Organized interests and American democracy*. New York: Harper & Row.

Schneider, A., & lngram, H. (1990) Behavioral assumptions of policy tools. *Journal of Politics, 52*(2): 510-29.

Scientific Software Development. 2001. *ATLAS.TI: The knowledge workbench Version WIN 4.2 (Build 059).* Berlin: Scientific Software Development.

Scott, J. (2000). *Social network analysis: A handbook* (2nd ed.). London: Sage.

Schattschneider, E. E. (1960). *The semi-sovereign people.* New York: Holt, Rinehart and Winston.

Shepley, T. V. (2002a). *Michigan reading policy: Problems, processes, and participants.* Ann Arbor: University of Michigan, Center for the Improvement of Early Reading Achievement.

Shepley, T. V. (2002b). *Texas reading policy: Problems, processes, and participants.* Ann Arbor: University of Michigan, Center for the Improvement of Early Reading Achievement.

Shrum, W., Cheek, N. H., & Hunter, S. M. (1988). Friendship in school: Gender and racial homophily. *Sociology of Education, 61,* 227-239.

Sipple, J. W., Miskel, C. G., Matheney, T. M., & Kearney, C. P. (1997). The creation and development of an interest group: Life at the intersection of big business and educationreform. *Educational Administration Quarterly, 33*(4), 440-473.

Smith, H. (1986). *The power game.* New York: Ballantine Books.

Smith, M. S., & O'Day, J. (1991). Systemic school reform. In S. H. Fuhrman & B. Malen (Eds.), *The politics of curriculum and testing, 1990 yearbook of the Politics of Education Association* (pp. 233-267). London and Washington, DC: Falmer Press.

Snell, R. K., Eckl, C., & Williams, G. (2003). *State spending in the 1990s.* National Conference of State Legislatures.

Snow, C. E., Burns, S., & Griffin, P. (Eds.). (1998). *Preventing reading difficulties in young children.* Washington, DC: National Academy Press.

Song, M. (2001). *Interest groups in national reading policy: Perceived influence and beliefs on reading instructional approach.* Unpublished dissertation, Ann Arbor, The University of Michigan.

Song, M. (2002). *Connecticut reading policy: Problems, processes, and participants.* Ann Arbor, University of Michigan, Center for the Improvement of Early Reading Achievement.

Song, M. (2003). *Influence in the reading policy domain: A cross-state social network analysis.* Unpublished dissertation, The University of Michigan, Ann Arbor.

Song, M. (Forthcoming). Reading from the top: State impact on reading curriculum and instruction. In B. Cooper, L. Fusarelli, & B. Fusarelli (Eds.), *The rising power of the state in education.* New York: State University of New York Press.

Song, M., & Miskel, C. G. (2002). Interest groups in national reading policy: Perceived influence and beliefs on teaching reading. *Theory and Research in Educational Administration, 1,* 77-96.

Song, M., & Miskel, C. G. (2005). Who are the influentials: A cross-state social network analysis. *Educational Administration Quarterly, 41*(1), 7-48.

Song, M., Miskel, C. G., Young, T. V., & McDaniel, J. E. (2000, November). *Perceived influence of interest groups in national reading policy.* Paper presented at the University Council of Educational Administration, Albuquerque, New Mexico.

Song, M., Miskel, C. G., Young, T. V., Osguthorpe, R., & Shepley, T. (2001, April). *Interest groups in national reading policy: Perceived influence and beliefs on reading instructional approach.* Paper presented at the annual meeting of American Educational Research Association, Seattle, Washington.

Stevens, F. (n.d.). *Reading First: Making reading first for Michigan and the Michigan Literacy Progress Profile* (MLPP). Retrieved April 28, 2006, from   http://www.mireadingfirst.org/downloads/mlppvsrf.pdf#search ='Michigan%20Literacy%20Progress%20Profile%20Reading%20First'

Stone, D. (2002). *Policy paradox: The art of political decision making.* New York: W. W. Nortion.

Sroufe, G. (1970). State school board members and education policy. *Administrator's Notebook, 19*(2), 1-4.

Texas Education Agency. (1997a). *Good Practice: Implications for Reading Instruction- A Consensus Document of Texas Literacy Professional Organizations.* Austin, TX: Author.

Texas Education Agency. (1997b). *Beginning reading instruction: Components and features of a research-based reading program.* Austin, TX: Author.

Texas Education Agency. (2002). *Beginning reading instruction: Components and features of a research-based reading program, Revised edition.* Austin, TX: Author.

The Connecticut Alliance for Great Schools. (n.d.) *The achievement gap.* Retrieved February 1, 2007, from http://www.ctags.org/gap.php

Thomas, C., & Hrebenar, R. (1999). Interest groups in the states. In V. Gray, R. Hanson, & H. Jacob (Eds.), *Politics in the American states: A comparative analysis* (7th ed., pp. 113-143). Washington, DC: Congressional Quarterly Press.

Thomas, C. S., & Hrebenar, R. J. (1991). Nationalization of interest groups and lobbying in thestates. In A. J. Cigler & B. A. Loomis (Eds.), *Interest group politics* (3rd ed.,) Washington, DC: Congressional Quarterly Press.

Thomas, C. S., & Hrebenar, R. J. (1992). Changing patterns of interest group activity: A regional perspective. In M. P. Petracca (Ed.), *The politics of interests: Interest groups transformed* (pp. 150-174). Boulder, CO: Westview Press.

Thomas, S. C., & Hrebenar, J. R. (1990). Interest groups in the states. In V. Gray, H. Jacob, & B. R. Albritton (Eds.), *Politics in the American states* (pp. 123-158). Glenview, IL: Scott, Foresman/Little, Brown.

Thompson, J. D. (1967). *Organizations in action.* New York: McGraw-Hill.

Valencia, S. W., & Wixson, K. K. (2000). Policy oriented research on literacy standards and assessments. In M. L. Kamil, P. B. Mosenthal, P. D. Pearson, & R. Barr (Eds.), *Handbook of reading research* (Vol. III, pp. 909-935). Mahwah, NJ: Erlbaum.

Walker, J. L. (1991). *Mobilizing interest groups in America.* Ann Arbor: University of Michigan Press.

Wasserman, S., & Faust, K. (1994). *Social network analysis: Methods and applications*: New York: Cambridge University Press.

Young, T. V. (2002). *California reading policy: Problems, processes, and participants.* Ann Arbor, University of Michigan, Center for the Improvement of Early Reading Achievement.

Young, T. V. (2005). *Understanding coalitions in state educational policy: The selection of alliance partners in reading policy issue networks.* Unpublished dissertation, The University of Michigan, Ann Arbor.

Young, T. V., Shepley, T. V., Miskel, C. G., & Song, M. (2002, December). *Reading from the top: The role of Governors in reading policy agenda setting.* Paper presented at the annual meeting of the National Reading Conference, Miami, Fl.

Young, T.V. & Miskel, C.G. (2006). Coalitions in State Reading Policy Issue Networks. In W. Hoy & C. Miskel (Eds.), *Research and Theory in Educational Administration* (pp. 1-25). Greenwich, CT: Information Age.

Zahariadis, N. (1999). Ambiguity, time, and multiple streams. In P. A. Sabatier (Ed.), *Theories of the policy processes* (pp. 73-93). Boulder: Westview Press.

Printed in the United States
96733LV00001B/25-39/A